Black, White, and Green

Black, White, and Green

FARMERS MARKETS, RACE,
AND THE GREEN ECONOMY

ALISON HOPE ALKON

THE UNIVERSITY OF GEORGIA PRESS
Athens & London

© 2012 by the University of Georgia Press
Athens, Georgia 30602
www.ugapress.org
All rights reserved
Designed by Walton Harris
Set in 10/13 Minion Pro

Printed digitally in the United States of America

Library of Congress Cataloging-in-Publication Data

Alkon, Alison Hope.
Black, white, and green : farmers markets, race, and the
green economy / Alison Hope Alkon.
        p.   cm. — (Geographies of justice and social
transformation ; 13)
Includes bibliographical references and index.
ISBN 978-0-8203-4389-1 (hbk. : alk. paper) — ISBN 0-8203-
4389-7 (hbk. : alk. paper) — ISBN 978-0-8203-4390-7 (pbk. :
alk. paper) — ISBN 0-8203-4390-0 (pbk. : alk. paper)
1. Farmers markets—Social aspects—United States.
2. Sustainable agriculture—Social aspects—United States.
3. Alternative agriculture—Social aspects—United States.
4. African American farmers—United States. 5. Food
supply—Social aspects—United States. 6. Community
development—United States. 7. Minorities—United States—
Economic conditions. 8. Social justice—United States.
I. Title.
HF5472.U6A45 2012
381'.41—dc23   2012009963

British Library Cataloging-in-Publication Data available

*For the managers, vendors, and customers at the
West Oakland and North Berkeley Farmers Markets,
and the many others working to create a more just
and sustainable food system.*

CONTENTS

ILLUSTRATIONS

PREFACE

This book has been almost a decade in the making. In 2005, I moved to Oakland to try to better understand how and to what end low-income communities of color were making use of local food systems. There, I met a group of people working to connect African American farmers and small business-people to residents of neighborhoods that lacked healthy food choices. The experiences of this group — which includes Jason Harvey, David Roach, Dana Harvey, Leroy Musgrave, Will Scott and the Scott family, Charlotte Coleman, Ted Dixon, Xan West, and Jada White — are at the core of this book. Their efforts, and their willingness to share them with me, had a profound effect on my thinking about race, food systems, and local economic (under)development, and I am incredibly grateful to them.

But in another way this project started long before I came to Oakland. I had begun to become involved in local food system work as an AmeriCorps volunteer in Atlanta. When it came time to choose a graduate program, Davis's vibrant alternative food scene had as much to do with my decision as the academics. I quickly connected with like-minded people through the Domes, a cooperative campus housing community that included gardens, chickens, fruit trees, and friends who would soon teach me how to live in such a place. These new friends, often well connected to the wider organic farming scene, helped me see our home as part of a larger movement for sustainable agriculture. And yet we couldn't help but notice that this movement was overwhelmingly white.

This book started out as an attempt to answer the question "Why are we all so white?" though I recognize now that this was the wrong question. There are growing numbers of people of color developing local food systems and challenging dominant ideas about food, agriculture, and the environment in exciting ways. I shifted my questions to explore how race intersected with thinking about local and organic food systems.

This shift in my questions guided me toward a comparative project. By also studying an affluent, predominantly white, progressive farmers market, I could follow the sociological dictate to "make the familiar strange" and treat this kind of local food system as something to analyze rather than take for granted. Here, I was fortunate to get to know the managers at the North Berkeley Farmers Market, particularly Rosalie Fanshel, Linda Bohara, Herman Yee, and Max

Cadji. I learned much from these individuals' impressive dedication to both sustainability and social justice, as well as from the Ecology Center's support for a just sustainability approach. I am also grateful to all the vendors and customers, too many to name, who shared their insights and their warmth.

Ethnographic work starts with data, and lots of it. The task then shifts to analyzing the data absent pre-established questions, figuring out what is most significant about a particular social world and what it has to say to both academics and laypeople. In this endeavor, I have been incredibly fortunate to be a part of multiple and intersecting communities of scholars. Tom Beamish shaped this work in a number of important ways, most fundamentally by suggesting that I think about farmers markets as places of economic exchange as well as social change.

Many aspects of this book were initially articulated and developed through related collaborative projects. Articles coauthored with Christie McCullen, Kari Norgaard, and Teresa Mares helped me gain a better understanding of why farmers markets and food movements are so culturally important. And the process of coediting *Cultivating Food Justice* (MIT Press 2011) with Julian Agyeman pushed me to sharpen my understanding of food justice as both a social movement and a body of academic work. I am also grateful to all our contributing authors, whose research has deepened this exciting and dynamic field.

During and beyond my graduate training, I have also benefited from the support of the UC Davis Environmental Justice Project (Julie Sze, Jonathan London, Marisol Cortez, Raoul Lievanos, and Tracy Perkins), the UC Multi-campus Research Group on Food and the Body (especially Julie Guthman, Melanie DuPuis, Kimberly Nettles-Barcelon, Carolyn de la Peña, and Laura-Anne Minkoff-Zern), colleagues and mentors in the UC Davis Sociology Department (Jim Cramer, Joan S. M. Meyers, Dina Biscotti, Julie Collins-Dogrul, Jen Gregson, Macky Yamaguchi, and Lori Freeman), and colleagues at the University of the Pacific (Marcia Hernandez, Ethel Nicdao, George Lewis, and Ken Albala). Thanks also to my friends, many of whom are incredibly passionate about issues of food justice and social change, especially Natalia Skolnik, Dana Perls, and my partner, Aaron Simon, as well as to my family, Penny, Michael, and Matty Alkon, for their love and good humor.

Lastly, a number of individuals at University of Georgia Press have helped me develop this manuscript into a book, and their work is strongly reflected in these pages. Particular thanks go to Nik Heynen, Derek Krissoff, and the anonymous reviewers, each of whom offered helpful suggestions. It goes without saying, however, that all errors are mine alone.

Black, White, and Green

CHAPTER ONE

Going Green, Growing Green

Green is how we describe a world of social justice, healthy
communities and ecological balance. Green is the color of hope.
> — Green America, nonprofit manager of the Green Business Network
> and publisher of the *National Green Pages* business directory

We must insist that the coming "green wave" lift ALL boats. Those
low-income communities that were locked out of the pollution-based
economy must be locked into the clean and green economy.
> — VAN JONES, "Forty Years Gone: MLK's Dream Today Would Be
> Colored Green"

If we wait for the magic of the market to solve inner-city food problems,
I fear we'll be left hungry for change.
> — TOM PHILPOTT, "Urban Farms Don't Make Money —
> So What?," *Grist*

It's Thursday afternoon, and the sun is shining. Customers stream into the
North Berkeley Farmers Market from all directions.[1] Some lock their bicycles
to parking meters behind the vendors' tents while others come on foot or have
parked nearby. Patrons stroll from one artfully decorated booth to the next,
sampling peaches in the summertime and apples in the fall. Approximately fifteen canopy-covered stalls fill a blocked-off city street, facing inward toward a
grassy, tree-lined median. Beneath the farmers' tents lies a cornucopia of fresh
food. The winter crops are mostly green — spinach, lettuce, cabbage, chard, and
kale — though carrots, oranges, and beets add splashes of color. Summertime
is a rainbow of tomatoes, summer squash, strawberries, melons, and peppers.

Patrons strolling through the market are surrounded by snippets of casual
conversation. Friends and neighbors greet one another, warmly inquiring about
families and common friends. Some seem to have run across each other unexpectedly while others have planned their meetings. Many visitors, especially

women and young children, sit on the grass and savor their purchases. At the various booths, customers animatedly share nutrition advice and food preparation techniques or probe farmers about their cultivation practices. Farmers seem to enjoy the social interaction. One farmer, for example, describes her pride in the compliments she receives. "People say the most incredibly generous things about your food," she says, "like, 'That was the best meal I've ever eaten,' or 'Thank you so much for doing this work.' Just the joy." She pauses for a moment before continuing. "I mean, around food is such a pure kind of wonderful joy! People are so supportive!" Other vendors, as well as managers and customers, often echo the sense of warmth and connection conveyed by this farmer, commonly describing the North Berkeley Farmers Market as sociable and relaxed, with a slower pace than other area markets and grocery stores.

Founded in 2003, North Berkeley is the most recent addition to the Berkeley Farmers Market landscape. Like its predecessors in south and downtown Berkeley, it is managed by the Ecology Center, one of the city's veteran environmental organizations. Since 1969, the Ecology Center has run a variety of urban sustainability initiatives, including Berkeley's curbside recycling program, the first in the country. While many farmers markets are associated with environmental themes, the Ecology Center ensures that such themes are the focal point. Its bylaws allow only organic produce from local growers, and all but one of its farmers come from within 150 miles of Berkeley.[2] Prepared foods must be at least 80 percent organic, use local ingredients whenever possible, and be served on compostable plates.

The North Berkeley Farmers Market is also extremely profitable for vendors. On the rare occasion that a space becomes available, potential applicants are evaluated on environmental considerations, including organic techniques and the miles the food will travel. Proponents of this farmers market tend to view the buying and selling of local organic produce as an environmental good because it decreases dependence on the fossil fuels necessary for transport, pest and disease management, and manufactured fertilizers. Vendor Antonio Magana, who sells vegan Mexican food, describes this sentiment when he declares, "Every time you come to my stand, you're part of the change." This linking of sustainable products and social change is important beyond food politics. It is the cornerstone of broad efforts to address environmental and social issues through ethical consumption.

Despite the presence of Latino/as, African Americans, and Asian Americans, the North Berkeley Farmers Market is largely affluent and white. It takes place in the so-called gourmet ghetto, a striking name given that its high-end boutiques and restaurants are the antithesis of the poverty the word

The North Berkeley
Farmers Market.

ghetto implies. Many of the surrounding restaurants share the farmers market's penchant for local and organic food—within a few blocks shoppers can find products such as biodynamic wine and organic pizza with seasonal toppings. The best-known neighborhood stalwart is Alice Waters's Chez Panisse, which was among the first restaurants to feature local and organic foods and to highlight farmers' contributions. Chez Panisse is widely thought of as the birthplace of "California cuisine," which fuses French-inspired techniques with fresh and seasonal ingredients and which is increasingly popular both within and beyond Berkeley. The farmers market's gourmet ghetto location imbues it with a sense of bohemian elegance that is simultaneously affluent and countercultural.

The affluent character of this farmers market is seemingly at odds with its dedication to social justice. And yet, the Ecology Center works to ensure that farmers market produce is widely available. "Sustainability is about the three E's—environment, economy, and equity," said executive director Martin Bourque.[3] "We need to ensure that equity remains a part of what we're working for." The Ecology Center's commitment to equity goes beyond its rhetoric. Proceeds from the farmers market support Farm Fresh Choice, a project designed to increase access to healthy food in low-income communities and communities of color. The program hires black and Latino/a youth from low-income parts of Berkeley to purchase produce from market farmers at bulk discounted rates and then resell it at stands in their neighborhoods. Market managers proudly refer to Farm Fresh Choice as the farmers market's "sister program." However, Farm Fresh Choice takes place outside the physical boundaries of the market, and not all customers are even aware of it. The North Berkeley Farmers Market's location in an affluent, predominantly white neighborhood feeds into the perception by some that local organic food is a luxury good.

Several miles to the south, another farmers market works directly to challenge the association between local organic food and cultural elitism. A far cry from the gourmet ghetto, the West Oakland Farmers Market takes place at the desolate end of a dead-end street, in a neighborhood colloquially known as the lower bottoms. The market sits beneath the elevated rail and freeway lines that segregate the lower bottoms from the rest of the city. Once a home to thriving

TABLE 1
Demographics of Farmers Market Neighborhoods

	ALAMEDA COUNTY	OAKLAND	WEST OAKLAND	BERKELEY	NORTH BERKELEY
Population	1,443,741	399,477	26,023	102,743	3,076
RACE					
Anglo	40.8%	23.4%	5.6%	62.7%	75.0%
Latino	19.0%	21.9%	17.3%	10.0%	5.6%
African American	14.4%	34.9%	65.7%	14.4%	2.8%
Asian/Pacific Islander	20.8%	15.6%	7.9%	17.4%	15.6%
INCOME					
Median household income	$55,946	$51,473	$26,432	$60,625	$86,222
Percent below the poverty rate	11.0%	19.4%	37.5%	20.0%	10.3%

Source: OnBoard LLC.

black-owned establishments including renowned jazz clubs, the area is now best known for its high crime rate and for a landscape rich in liquor stores and fast food establishments. This stark demographic contrast illustrates some of the raced and classed dimensions of food politics.

And yet on Saturdays, as farmer Leroy Musgrave describes it, the positive energy "bubbles up through the concrete into the air." Each weekend, Leroy drives the one hundred miles from his Central Valley farm to help create the West Oakland Farmers Market. Beneath cheerful orange tents, the market's largely African American vendors display brightly colored organic produce, homemade jams, and sweets. Two local nonprofit organizations, an urban farm and a school garden program, offer seedlings and food tastings. Market managers and regular shoppers take turns playing funk and soul music records. Stevie Wonder hits, the Jackson 5, and Gil Scott-Heron's classic "The Revolution Will Not Be Televised" are all on regular rotation. Occasionally, a customer or vendor launches into an impromptu dance performance. If the market is celebrating a special event, such as Black History Month, the turntables might be replaced by a live band.

As in Berkeley, deep ties among market participants make this farmers market feel more like a neighborhood gathering than a commercial venue. It is not uncommon for customers to join vendors behind their tables for extended conversations, though these exchanges are occasionally interrupted by the noise from a train passing overhead. The market's intimacy is also a product of its small size; it contains only four farmers' stalls and six to eight stalls selling prepared food and crafts. Farmers come from within 150 miles of the city, and other vendors are generally Oakland residents. The market's relaxed pace — significantly slower than in North Berkeley — allows plenty of time for customers and vendors to get to know one another, and many describe the market as an extended family.

The West Oakland Farmers Market seeks to create economic opportunities for black farmers to supply produce to residents of a neighborhood with few other options. "Being in California," said market founder David Roach, "you have the benefit of seeing farmers markets. But we did not see them in our communities." In 2003, he sought out Will Scott of Scott Family Farms, who was president of African American Farmers of California. "When David came to me, I dropped everything to come to West Oakland because he had a vision," remembers Scott, who, along with his wife and two adult children, makes the 150-mile trip from Fresno each Saturday. Influenced by Booker T. Washington's economically oriented Tuskegee model, which emphasized the need for community economics over political rights, David conceived the

The West Oakland Farmers Market. Photo by David Hanks.

market as a way to support black farmers while providing healthy food in West Oakland. As it grew, more farmers and vendors joined in, including Pots-to-Jars homemade canned goods, Dis_Scent natural skin-care products, and OBUGS school garden program.

The mix of products is intended to target black consumers. Leroy's table is always covered in greens — collards, mustard greens, and lamb's-quarters in addition to the kale and chard found at many other markets. Dis_Scent's skin care products are crafted from shea butter, derived from the nut of a tree native to Africa. However, despite this targeted marketing, nearly half the market's customers are white, and many are recent transplants to this rapidly gentrifying neighborhood. White customers are generally made to feel welcome, particularly when they adopt the farmers market's mission of supporting black farmers.

Market founder David Roach explains how this farmers market's goals are simultaneously economic, environmental, and social. "The market is about community, and it's about land, and it's about businesses in the community that provide basic needs," he explains. "Your economy can become more prosperous because of food. Food is connected to land, connected to health, and also connected to enterprises in the community." David and his allies view these concerns as deeply integrated and the West Oakland Farmers Market as a tool to address them simultaneously. Food becomes an organizing tool through which a community can build a strong, local, green economy, creating a healthy environment while providing economic opportunities. Market manager Jason Harvey describes this farmers market as "true grassroots, like the seeds I've been planting."

However, without the backing of an established organization like the Ecology Center or a neighborhood already oriented toward local and organic food, the West Oakland Farmers Market struggled to stay afloat. Dwindling sales led to discouragement and eventual disagreements among managers and vendors. A steady stream of the latter left the market, until it closed in the summer of 2009.

And yet this farmers market remains a cornerstone of food activism in West Oakland. A diverse assortment of food reform projects has sprouted in the past few years, nurtured by former farmers market managers and vendors. City Slicker Farms, which formerly sold seeds and starts at the farmers market, recently received a large grant to purchase land and establish an agricultural park in West Oakland. Jason Harvey went on to found and direct the Oakland Food Connection, a nonprofit dedicated to creating school gardens and providing nutrition education in low-income Oakland neighborhoods. Also in the summer of 2009, a worker-owned grocery store opened across the street from the market's former location. Its executive director, Dana Harvey, codirected the West Oakland Food Collaborative with David Roach and was a constant presence at the farmers market. Leroy Musgrave, now retired from farming, serves the cooperative as a nutrition educator. In addition, new ventures such as Phat Beets Produce and the Oakland Food Policy Council help create a more varied organizational scene. Although the West Oakland Farmers Market no longer exists, it was an early organization whose thinking about race, class, and local organic food shifted the landscape in which food justice projects continue to operate.

Bolstered by a popular literature developed by best-selling authors like Michael Pollan and Barbara Kingsolver, the North Berkeley and West Oakland Farmers Markets are two of a growing number of grassroots organizations and green businesses offering alternative ways to produce, distribute, and consume food. Food system reform, according to this discourse, is not only its own reward but a way to link our own sustenance to healthy environments, communities, and local economies. But efforts based in West Oakland and other places like it tell us that we cannot think about the food system without also thinking about social equity. Race and class have much to do with the ways that food systems operate, producing uneven access to food, health, and economic opportunities. Additionally, both farmers markets are a part of a growing green economy, which links the purchase of specific products to environmental, social, and economic goals. For this reason, it is important to understand how race and class shape the visions and practices associated with food and with the green economy more generally. If we are to transform our food system, and indeed our society, in meaningful ways, we will need to better comprehend and critically assess how differently located communities imagine and participate in green economic exchange.

FARMERS MARKETS AND THE GREEN ECONOMY

From fashion magazines to Fortune 500 companies, businesses are increasingly "going green." No longer confined to the countercultural fringe, "green" products, and advertisements for them, have become ubiquitous. Large corporations such as Wal-Mart and Safeway sell organic produce, Levi's features organic blue jeans, and General Electric invests in renewable energy. Nonprofit organizations such as Green America devote themselves to the promotion of green products, framing certain purchases as a way to "vote with your dollar" in favor of social and environmental goals. Indeed, Green America, which publishes the *National Green Pages* business directory and produces Green Festivals in cities across the country, describes its goal as the creation of market opportunities for green producers by encouraging individuals to purchase from them. Both the *Green Pages* and Green Festivals contain extensive sections devoted to food.

But green is not only the color of trees; it is also the color of money. The green economy promises economic as well as environmental benefits through the creation of new products, brands, and services. For this reason, going green might better be described as growing green. The green economy is often cast as a way to "do well by doing good," to quote a common refrain, and it is certainly doing the former. Green products represent a growing market valued at $228 billion and maintaining resilience in the midst of an economic recession (Rosenwald 2006; Chu 2009). Sales of organic foods have skyrocketed from a mere $1 billion in 1990 to an estimated $20 billion in 2007, and farmers markets are the fastest growing segment of the food economy (Organic Consumers Association 2007; USDA 2006).

Additionally, some activists believe that the growth of green might also be mobilized to address inequality. Van Jones, who is quoted in one of the epigraphs to this chapter, describes our current environmental conditions as "eco-apartheid." Affluent whites, he claims, live increasingly green lives while poor communities of color are left with the toxic consequences of environmental degradation (see, for example, United Church of Christ 1987, 2007). In response, Jones promotes a vision of "eco-equity," in which the growth of green provides well-paying jobs for communities that were economically devastated by the decline of the manufacturing sector (2008). He advocates for jobs in local and organic agriculture, particularly in low-income communities that often lack other sources of fresh food. Jones's vision coheres with what environmental social scientist Julian Agyeman (2005) has labeled "just sustainability," the integration of environmental concerns with those of social justice.

As promotion of a "green economy" has become more ubiquitous, the term itself has become more slippery. In the context of this study, the green economy is a set of relations and practices in which the production and consumption of goods becomes a strategy toward environmental and social change. Essentially, the growth of specific segments of the economy, such as organic food or clean energy, becomes the solution to social and environmental problems. While some activists seek government investment in the green economy, its core logic remains one in which individual consumer choice drives social change. In this way, it embodies the political-economic philosophy of neoliberalism, which asserts the primacy of the market in attending to human needs and well-being, and orients the state toward the facilitation of market mechanisms (Harvey 2005).

Although much has been written about the promise of the green economy, *Black, White, and Green* is the first book to examine it through the worldviews and lived experiences of its promoters, producers, and consumers. Through the lens of racial and economic inequalities, this book examines the possibilities for environmental protection and justice contained within the green economy. It also explores the narratives through which actors seeking social change align their goals with the profit imperative that characterizes market relations. At the same time, it makes visible those approaches to social change that remain incompatible with the green economy, highlighting the more radical discourses and strategies marginalized by this strategic shift. In sum, *Black White, and Green* examines how the green economy functions on the ground, the meanings that buyers and sellers of green products attribute to it, and the ways these meanings and practices are raced and classed.

Like members of social movements, proponents of the green economy envision its political potential through a variety of narratives, which influence who will and will not be drawn to participate (Polletta 2006). These narratives intersect with race and class in very different ways. With regard to race, narratives describing the benefits of the green economy generally purport to be color-blind, meaning that they do not believe that race affects green economic participation (Frankenberg 1993). For example, writing in the trade journal *LOHAS* (Lifestyles of Health and Sustainability), Brian Holland (2004) argues that the green market segment is influenced by values rather than demographic factors. And yet the most common narratives promoting the green economy are complicatedly entangled with white cultural histories and thus tend to draw in white adherents. In contrast, those seeking to promote green growth in places like West Oakland incorporate racially specific experiences and foodways — social and cultural practices surrounding food — through the celebration of products and producers from their communities. In progressive white communities such as Berkeley, venues dedicated to the green economy have also worked to include a racially diverse array of producers and consumers, though these attempts have been far more uneven.

These admirable efforts to counter color-blindness cannot, however, mitigate economic inequalities, in part because the green economy is not separate from the wider capitalist economy. Individuals participate in the green economy not as equal citizens, but as consumers with unequal access to wealth and products and as producers with unequal access to capital and markets. Those with greater economic resources have greater influence. Thus even individuals and communities dedicated to social change, such as those chronicled in this book, are constrained by the economic logics embodied by their green economic approaches. Those promoting the green economy do sometimes concede that accessibility is a problem but do not recognize how their promotion of the green economy, which is fundamentally a market-oriented approach to social change, has undercut some of their more radical visions.

In contrast to recent books celebrating the promise of the green economy, this ethnographic examination reveals a complex social world where deliberate strategies intersect with processes of identity formation and material inequalities, providing a host of intended and unintended consequences. The actors chronicled in this book are truly dedicated to pursuing both justice and sustainability and work diligently to develop approaches that address both goals. However, their admirable work is constrained by their adoption of market-based strategies, which divert attention away from more radical approaches to social and environmental change and exclude working-class and poor people from participation. Despite these important limitations, venues dedicated to promoting the green economy may still provide education on social and political issues as well as public spaces in which a more collective politics can be forged.

FARMERS MARKETS AS MOVEMENTS

Producers and consumers offer many reasons for buying and selling at farmers markets. The former often speak of increased returns while the latter emphasize the perceived health benefits of fresh, locally grown food (Szasz 2007; P. Allen 2004). But many farmers markets also profess a politics of everyday life, a set of practices that proponents believe can bring about social change outside of and despite unsupportive governments. In this way, farmers markets and other green economic venues represent a new strategy for social movements attempting to advance social and environmental goals.

The Food Movement

The worldview professed at the North Berkeley market coheres closely with what *New York Times* best-selling author Michael Pollan (2010) has begun to refer to as the food movement. Rooted in the environmental movement (Tovey 2002; Belasco 1993) and in a long history of dietary crusades (Biltekoff forthcoming), the food movement links the production and consumption of food to personal, planetary, and economic health. Fundamentally, the food movement is rooted in a critique of industrial agriculture as ecologically, socially, and economically destructive and advocates for the creation of sustainable and just alternatives.[4] Supporters argue that individuals who know "where their food comes from," a movement refrain indicating firsthand relationships with local producers and the places they cultivate, will be willing to pay a premium to secure healthy landscapes and farm livelihoods. Demand for local and organic food, advocates argue, will increase opportunities for small farmers, who will eventually outcompete the industrial model.

However, many efforts toward food system reform are largely missing from Pollan's singular characterization of the food movement. Migrant and other workers' rights movements are glaringly absent, as are indigenous sovereignty struggles and many efforts to prevent hunger. Understanding who is left out is important because Pollan's word choice, along with his popularity and prestige, creates a dominant image of what food activism looks like. This image influences whether and how activists working on various aspects of food system reform identify common interests and potential collaborations. Notably, many struggles that are excluded from Pollan's definition are led by, and disproportionately affect, people of color.[5] Some of these efforts have cohered around the banner of food justice.

Food Justice

Despite the stunning growth of organic food and farmers markets, many urban and rural areas remain without access to fresh produce. In response, activists based in these communities have articulated a desire for *food justice.*[6] According to those working in West Oakland and places like it, food justice includes not only providing equal access to healthy food but also addressing structural inequalities in the food system and in the wider distribution of environmental benefits. Proponents of food justice highlight discrimination against farmers of color and the absence of full-scale supermarkets in predominantly black and brown neighborhoods. They also champion local sustainable food systems by and for communities of color. Local food projects have sprouted in some of the nation's most disadvantaged cities and communities, including Detroit, Milwaukee, and Chicago's South Side. Food justice activists work to create green economic opportunities for low-income people of color to distribute local organic food in communities otherwise lacking access to it.

Food justice activism has roots in the environmental justice (EJ) movement, which has traditionally worked to prevent the disproportionate accumulation of locally unwanted land uses in communities of color and low-income communities (United Church of Christ 1987, 2007; Bullard 1990). EJ activists have historically favored strategies befitting their roots in the civil rights movement (Goldman 1996; Bryant and Mohai 1992), namely protests, political advocacy, and lawsuits. More recently, however, prominent EJ organizations have embraced the campaign for green jobs spearheaded by Van Jones (WE ACT 2010). In doing so, the movement has shifted to a strategy that pursues economic growth through the green economy. Through its emphasis on creating local, organic food systems, food justice activism coheres closely with this shift. Indeed, Jones's best seller *The Green Collar Economy* (2008) highlights West Oakland food justice activism as an example of the change he seeks to create.

Food justice activists' emphasis on race and racism is a challenge to the food movement's general blindness concerning racial inequalities and a challenge to its environmental privilege. Park and Pellow define environmental privilege as the various advantages that enable some groups "access to coveted environmental amenities such as . . . organic and pesticide-free foods, neighborhoods with healthier air quality, and energy and other products siphoned from the living environments of other peoples" (2011, 4). Although they highlight the environmental privileges enjoyed by many food movement adherents, food justice activists also define their scope in ways that illuminate some efforts while eliding others. Broadly, food justice activists tend to promote the creation of local organic food systems in low-income communities of color while minimizing issues of workers' rights and food policy reform. In other words, those who identify as food justice activists tend to emphasize green economic strategies rather than more collective efforts that are also aimed at making the food system more just.

FARMERS MARKETS AS MARKETS

Despite the fact that they attempt to enact a variety of social movement goals, farmers markets simultaneously remain economic spaces dedicated to fostering commerce. Indeed, it is in some ways ironic that activists pursuing just sustainability would choose economic exchange as their strategy for reform, given that previous generations of activists have named capitalism as the source of both environmental degradation and inequality (Marx 1992[1867]; O'Connor 1994). By encouraging customers to vote with their forks, the North Berkeley and West Oakland farmers markets attempt to tap into capitalism's resilience, embracing it in order to shift its reliance on the exploitation of nature and human labor. Through the purchase of locally grown organic food (and in West Oakland, food grown by black farmers), consumers are encouraged to create economic incentives for green production, small business, and meaningful social relationships through shifting market demand. This green economic strategy is a fundamental aspect of the logic of neoliberalism, as social change opportunities are removed from the public sphere and fostered through market behavior. It simultaneously embodies a "roll-back" of state responsibilities for public welfare and environmental protection and a complementary "roll-out" of market and civil society attempts to fill the state's responsibilities (Peck and Tickell 2002; see also Guthman 2008b and Harvey 2005).

This contradiction — between farmers markets' broad, radical aims and individually oriented economic strategies — lies at the heart of this study. After examining national and local contexts, this book explores how farmers markets seek to incorporate visions and practices of justice and sustainability, the ways these approaches intersect with race and class, and the narratives through which proponents come to embrace (and justify their embrace of) economic strategies. These questions reach beyond farmers markets and food politics, holding more general implications for the increasing adoption of green economic approaches by a variety of social movements.

For that reason, chapter 2 begins by tracing the emergence of the green economy as an approach to social change. Proponents of the green economy represent a stark departure from earlier generations of activists who argued for environmental and social limits to economic growth. The rise of sustainability as a dominant environmental discourse first shifted this position, convincing many activists that growth was not antithetical to environmental and equity goals. The idea of a green economy builds on this shift, depicting economic growth not only as compatible with, but as an essential pathway to, environmental protection and social justice.

It is not only ideas but places that provide the context in which farmers markets occur. Chapter 3 examines how the particular histories of North Berkeley and West Oakland shape each farmers market. The North Berkeley Farmers Market, and indeed the food movement more generally, can trace its beginnings to the bohemian counterculture of the 1960s, and Berkeley was a key site of its emergence. The West Oakland Farmers Market, on the other hand, has roots in the Black Panther Party, which emphasized community self-determination and self-sufficiency. The Black Panther Party's Free Breakfast for School Children program tied their political approach to issues of food and hunger. Both of these movements, however, differ from the present-day farmers markets they inspire because they were explicitly opposed to capitalism. Chapter 3 traces the farmers market's roots in these anticapitalist social movements in order to situate their embrace of the green economy. Taken together, chapters 2 and 3 reveal that the emergence of the green economy was not necessary or natural. Indeed, it is a striking reversal of a core tenet common to the social movements and local histories that inspire many farmers market proponents.

Chapters 4, 5, and 6 examine how the green economy functions in the North Berkeley and West Oakland farmers markets, and how it intersects with race and class. Each of these chapters probes one of the central promises offered by farmers markets: healthy environments, vibrant communities, and strong local economies. Chapter 4 explores how participants in each farmers market link their green economic practices to environmental goals and how these goals are integrated with social and environmental justice. It describes the kinds of environmental philosophies and practices that are incorporated into the green economy at farmers markets and analyzes how these practices affect racial and economic inequalities. This chapter approaches *just sustainability* as a site of struggle and contention and highlights how farmers market participants purposefully design strategies to pursue both environmental and social justice goals.

Proponents of farmers markets claim that such markets build vibrant local communities. Chapter 5 depicts how the North Berkeley and West Oakland farmers markets promote community through face-to-face interaction between neighbors and regional farmers, an approach that responds to long-standing concerns about the effects of urban society on social interaction. The market-based community becomes both the locus for and the beneficiary of each market's social change goals. The place-based notions of community asserted by each farmers market, however, implicitly and explicitly invoke race, class, and gender identities. Chapter 5 contains an intersectional analysis of each farmers market's definition of community and of the ways these definitions inspire and restrict participation in the green economy.

Environmental degradation and social injustice have historically been understood as consequences of a capitalist economic system in which the pursuit of profits necessitates the increasing exploitation of both workers and resources. Chapter 6 analyzes the narratives through which participants in farmers markets make their economic necessities compatible with their ethical goals. It is these narratives that make it possible to posit green economic growth as a strategy toward ecological protection, community development, and racial empowerment. Despite efforts to produce compatibility, unrecognized tensions do constrain the farmers markets' abilities to advocate for social and environmental change. These constraints are particularly problematic with regard to social justice goals, which cannot demand the premium prices accorded to commodities associated with environmental causes.

The green economy is an emergent phenomenon constantly created and re-created by its proponents and participants. It is popularly trumpeted as a way to achieve social and environmental ends through economic growth. *Black, White, and Green* seeks to understand how the green economy works in practice by focusing on emerging tensions between two farmers markets' environmental, social, and economic goals and by following the processes through which actors address them. It highlights the visions of justice and sustainability that farmers market participants pursue through green economic exchange, as well as the potential alternative visions eclipsed by this strategic choice. Throughout, the narrative maintains a focus on racial identity formation and racial and economic inequality, both of which color the promise and reality of the green economy.

CHAPTER TWO

Understanding the Green Economy

We can create new jobs, restore our environment, and promote social stability. The solutions are creative, practical, and profitable.
— PAUL HAWKEN, "Natural Capitalism"

Green economics cannot be a panacea for the ills of the current economy that actively displaces and marginalizes people of color, while requiring their cheap labor and participation as exploited consumers.
— RAQUEL RIVERA PINDERHUGHES, "Green Collar Jobs: Work Force Opportunities in the Growing Green Economy"

To delude ourselves into believing that growth is still possible and desirable if only we label it "sustainable" or color it "green," will just delay the inevitable transition and make it more painful.
— HERMAN DALY, "Sustainable Growth: An Impossibility Theorem"

In the past forty years, the environmental movement has shifted from emphasizing the ecological limits on economic growth to embracing green growth as a pathway to social change. Green entrepreneurship is promoted as a promising career path for environmentally minded individuals, and the number of green MBA programs is growing rapidly. Leading green entrepreneurs like Paul Hawken argue that economic growth is not inherently harmful to the environment and that ecological problems can present economic opportunities. Hawken's philosophy of natural capitalism asserts that when businesses value natural resources and human ingenuity, they become more efficient and hence more profitable (Hawken, Lovins, and Lovins 2008). This philosophy coheres with the logic of the green economy. Proponents of the green economy, such as advocates of farmers markets, argue not for decreased consumption, but for increased consumption of green goods.

Under the limits-to-growth approach that originated in the 1970s, economic growth was cast as a threat to environmental health, one that must be constrained in order to protect the planet. In the green economy, the opposite is seen to be true. Economic growth becomes a way to address environmental problems through the production and dissemination of goods that use fewer or renewable resources and, at least in some cases, involve more just labor relations. One step in the transition from a limits-to-growth approach to a green-growth approach was the rise of a sustainability paradigm in the 1980s. Rather than see economic growth, environmental protection, and social justice as in tension with one another, advocates of sustainability depicted them as an interdependent "triple bottom line." The view that economy, environment, and equity are mutually supporting paved the way for contemporary green thinking in which the logic of the market is marshaled in support of social change goals.

THE LIMITS TO GROWTH

In 1972, a groundbreaking study called *The Limits to Growth* modeled the effects of increases in population growth and resource consumption on ecological health. It concluded that if current trends continued, they would lead to "overshoot and collapse" in which human societies could no longer provide for themselves (Meadows, Randers, and Meadows 2004[1973]; see also Catton 1980). This influential report lent credence to two approaches to global development. One was the Malthusian argument against population growth, which had become popular among wealthy countries with already low growth rates. Emphasizing population without regard for consumption, however, places the burden of environmental problems entirely on the global South. Many activists

TABLE 2

The Economic Value of the Green Economy: Some Important Sectors in Billions of Dollars

	2006	2007	2008	2009	2010
CLEAN ENERGY	90	129	159	160	211
percent growth	57%	43%	23%	0.4%	32%
ORGANIC FOOD	17	20	24	25	27
percent growth	21%	19%	16%	5%	8%
ORGANIC NONFOOD	0.938	1.18	1.65	1.8	1.97
percent growth	4%	4%	4%	-1%	3%

Sources: Pew Charitable Trust (2009) and Organic Trade Association (2011).

seeking to preserve the natural world *and* increase social equity supported a second approach: zero economic growth or steady state economies. In contrast to macroeconomic policies commonly designed to produce growth, steady state systems aim for equilibrium, or for slight fluctuations, in both population and production. According to ecological economists like Herman Daly, whose words are among those introducing this chapter, a steady state economy does not excessively disrupt natural ecosystems and can protect natural resources (Daly and Townsend 1993).

The limits-to-growth argument was highly controversial. Among its most prominent critics was Columbia University economist Jagdish Bhagwati. In a widely read article in *Scientific American*, Bhagwati (1993) argued that economic growth would protect the environment, as profits garnered could be taxed and used for the abatement of pollution and for general remediation. To support this position, he pointed to the high numbers of environmental organizations in developed countries with high economic growth, arguing that growth is good for the environmental movement, and hence good for the environment itself. Extending his argument in 2009, Bhagwati accounts for social goods as well, arguing that "firms that make losses cannot finance corporate social responsibility policies" (38). Present-day proponents of the green economy similarly argue that economic growth leads to environmental protection.

The idea that there were environmental limits to economic growth greatly influenced the U.S. environmental movement in the 1970s, which departed from its preservationist predecessor to advocate state cleanup and control of pollution (Gottlieb 1993; Frank, Hironaka, and Schofer 2000). This is not to say that some environmentalists were not closely tied to, and even funded by, the business community, but it does indicate that the notion that growth could or should be limited held sway in some environmental circles (McCarthy and Prudham 2004). During the 1970s, environmentalists campaigned successfully for the passage of several laws through which the government claimed responsibility for the protection of humans and nonhuman nature from the excesses of industrial pollution. Polluting industries fought hard to protect their profits. For example, when ecologist Rachel Carson wrote *Silent Spring*, aiming her pen at the U.S. agribusiness corporations that manufactured DDT, the industry accused her of scientific bias and hysteria in an effort to prevent the profitable chemical from being banned. Similarly, the automobile industry opposed the passage of the Clean Air Act, claiming that building cleaner cars and adopting catalytic converters would threaten profits, and with them jobs. In each of these cases, however, under pressure from the environmental movement, the federal government passed legislation that would constrain profits, reflecting a popular belief that environmental and human health limits to economic growth were sometimes necessary.

At the same time, more radical environmentalists developed currents of environmental theory and practice that offered implicit and explicit critiques of industrial culture and sometimes of capitalism itself (Gottlieb 1993). Eco-socialists, eco-feminists, and social ecologists argued that domination of nature was a consequence of domination between people and had found its most "exacerbating development" under capitalism (Bookchin 2004 [1971], 24). Advocates of these positions called for collective ownership of the means of production and the restoration of the commons.[1] In addition, deep ecologists, who prioritize the intrinsic worth of nonhuman nature, emphasized its protection over economic growth. Their best-known strategy consists of direct action "tree sits" in which activists occupy land slated to be logged in order to protect it. Additionally, while a confrontation with capitalism was not always at the top of the agenda for the back-to-the-land movement, it attempted to escape the cultural and economic constraints of "mainstream" society through the creation of rural communes in which resources could be shared. These communes, as chapter 3 depicts, developed some of the early techniques that would enable organic farming and are an important predecessor for many of today's food movements and farmers markets. Participants in this kind of environmentalism advocated the creation of new, noncapitalist ways of being that they envisioned as close to and respectful of nonhuman nature. Despite their sometimes fiercely argued differences, these alternative voices (Brulle 2000) saw capitalism as something to escape from or confront if the environment and human society were to be sustained.

The popularity of environmental discourses arguing for limits on capitalism "came to represent a substantial and growing constraint on capitalist accumulation strategies [and thus was] ripe for neoliberal attacks" (McCarthy and Prudham 2004, 278). These attacks occurred in the wake of the late 1970s energy crisis, which made it difficult to argue against growth and helped propel the Reagan administration's pro-business and anti-environment agenda. In this context, the state abandoned its charge of protecting citizens from the excesses of capital, instead imagining its role as a creator of market conditions favorable to growth (Harvey 2005). In this reactionary political landscape, sustainability emerged as a discourse that could guide economic and cultural practices, fitting environmentalists' concerns into a pro-growth agenda. Environmental activists began to ignore the role of capitalism in environmental degradation, paving the way for a new sustainability paradigm in which economic growth and environmental protection were seen as interdependent. This set the stage for the kind of green capitalism that takes place at farmers markets.

SUSTAINABILITY

In recent decades, the word "sustainability" has become widely prominent; international governing bodies, state governments, businesses, and NGOs have all sought to incorporate this new terminology into their discourses and, to a lesser extent, their practices. "The concept of sustainability," as urban planner Scott Campbell (1996) presciently observed, "has won." It has become an unquestioned good nearly impossible to oppose. But sustainability is also characterized by the absence of a specific definition (Redclift 2006) and is often differently enacted based on the interests of those who pursue it. These differences lead to varying visions of the relationship between environment, equity, and economy.

Sustainable Development

The concept of sustainability was initially acclaimed in the context of global development, and its most common definition originated in that context. The World Commission on Environment and Development (also known as the Brundtland Commission) characterizes sustainability as "development that meets the needs of the present without compromising the ability of future generations to meet their own needs" (Brundtland Commission 1987). Through this definition, the Brundtland Commission attempts to mediate between classical economists like Bhagwati who advocate for economic growth and environmentalists and others who argue that growth has ecological limits. UN Division of Sustainable Development director Tariq Banuri describes sustainability as "a bridge [between] environment and development, North and South, government, business, and civil society, present and future, long term and short term, science and policy, and efficiency, equity, and participation" (2009, 4). This listing of opposites and interests in tension with one another suggests that sustainability is an attempt to create a discursive space in between. Essentially, its rhetoric advocates a middle path between continued economic growth in wealthy countries, the rights of nonindustrialized countries to develop, and the need for resource conservation. These three priorities are brought together in the so-called triple bottom line of economy, equity, and environment. However, in practice, the Brundtland Commission marginalized equity concerns. The key question became how can economic growth coexist with the protection of natural resources (Redclift 2006). In a classic example of sustainable development, so-called debt-for-nature swaps allowed governments and environmental organizations in the global north to forgive or buy a portion of a developing country's debt in exchange for conservation commitments. This seemingly win-win situation too often ignored the needs of indigenous populations who were dependent on now-protected areas and whose basic sustenance was often criminalized (Butler and Hinch 2007).

Environmental Sustainability

In the U.S. environmental movement, the relationship between economy, ecology, and equity has been similarly contested. The most common narrative history of the U.S. environmental movement traces its roots to the tradition of wilderness wanderings, and wilderness protection, embodied by John Muir's nineteenth- and early twentieth-century treks in the Sierra Nevada Mountains (but see Taylor 2009). Muir's activism helped create the system of national parks that protect extraordinary landscapes from development and degradation. For Muir and subsequent preservationists, wild lands were sites of spiritual uplift, "places to play in and pray in where nature may heal and cheer and give strength to the body and soul" (Muir and Cronon 1997; for similar contemporary writings see T. Butler 2002). This wilderness ideal motivates the preservationist work of many of the largest U.S. environmental organizations. Commonly known as the "Group of 10," these organizations include such household names as the Sierra Club, the Wilderness Society, and the Audubon Society (Brulle 2000). More radical environmental groups, such as Earth First!, also trace their reverence for the natural world to this position. Earth First! is among those environmental groups advocating for limits to economic growth in order to ensure environmental protection. However, in the 1980s, their adamant defense of old-growth forests in the Pacific Northwest was widely if erroneously characterized as responsible for the decline in logging jobs, earning the environmental movement the ire of many individuals employed in resource extractive industries. Against the context of this perception, environmental groups began to push not for preservation, but for sustainability.

The Wilderness and the City

The emergence of the sustainability paradigm required a spatial shift in environmental activism out of the wilderness and into cities and communities.

Intellectually, this shift came from environmental theorists working to reverse the false though deeply entrenched notion that human society is separate from nature (Cronon 1995; Heynen, Kaika, and Swyngedouw 2006). Industrial society, these authors argue, requires an exploitation of resources that must be justified through the mythological creation of a binary between the natural and the social. This perceived separation became "deepened, generalized and dramatically intensified" under capitalism (Heynen, Kaika, and Swyngedouw 2006; see also Smith 1984).

Some authors seeking to write across this society-nature divide turned their gaze to the wilderness. Against the assumption that wilderness is land free from human intervention, their writings revealed a diverse constellation of actions ranging from Native American land management to the selection of areas for protection (Cronon 1995; Freudenberg, Frickel, and Gramling 1995). Additional writings highlight the social nature of the meanings and practices commonly associated with nature, arguing that "nature is nothing if it is not social" (Smith 1984, 30; Braun and Castree 1998).

Other theorists work from the opposite side of the coin, illuminating the natural in urban territories assumed to be exclusively social. These authors follow David Harvey, who writes that it is "hard to see where 'society' begins and 'nature' ends" and that "in a fundamental sense, there is . . . nothing unnatural about New York City" (1996, 186). If human activity is part of the ecosystems we inhabit, then the products of human activity, whether skyscrapers, brownfields (abandoned industrial zones), or parks, must be as well. This tradition argues that all of nature is simultaneously natural *and* socially produced. As a political project, it urges humans to connect to and protect the landscapes we inhabit.

While popular recognition of the socialness of wilderness and the naturalness of cities has not been forthcoming, efforts both to protect wilderness and to sustain human habitats have abounded. National organizations have pushed the EPA to clean up and redevelop brownfields, to raise fuel efficiency standards for automobiles, and to provide incentives for green construction. At the local level, community-based groups have pressured cities and states to institute recycling programs, increase public transportation, and designate space for farmers markets. Others have sought to influence urban planning, moving it away from the separation of uses and low-density development that encourages urban sprawl and increased driving. In each case, the environment to be sustained is not some faraway place we might occasionally visit, but a habitat humans share with other species of plants and animals.

Toward a Just Sustainability

Despite a very different context, efforts to create sustainability in the U.S. environmental movement tend to use the previously described Brundtland Commission definition. This definition describes the need to preserve resources for future generations, but fails to mention how resources will be distributed within each generation. Many sustainability projects ignore or even marginalize low-income communities and communities of color. Efforts to brand places as sustainable, for example, have largely discounted working conditions and affordability. Portland and San Francisco are ranked as the two most sustainable cities in the United States but are among the worst in terms of affordable housing (SustainLane 2006). Measures of sustainability have addressed neither processes of uneven development (Marx 1992[1867]; Smith 1984) nor the racial and economic inequalities that affect who gets to live in what kind of places (Pulido 1996).

At the same time that the idea of sustainability was gaining currency, a separate but related movement was coalescing around the need for environmental justice (EJ). Against the well-established context of disproportionate siting of environmentally toxic land uses in communities of color (United Church of Christ 1987, 2007), activists define environmental justice as the right of all people to a safe, healthy, and clean environment, and their right to participate in environmental decision making (Alston 1990; Shrader-Frechette 2002). The EJ movement is best known for its successes at the local level, where communities have organized against numerous noxious land uses including the siting of incinerators (Cole and Foster 2001), sludge and sewage treatment facilities (Sze 2006), and toxic dumps (Bullard 1990). Activists have also worked at the national scale, notably achieving a 1994 Presidential Executive Order mandating that federal agencies address issues of disproportionate risk.

In addition, EJ activists have challenged the environmental movement to pay greater attention to issues of equity in a way that parallels food justice activists' challenge to the food movement (Taylor 2000). In 1990, leading EJ activists sent an open letter to this effect to the largest environmental organizations. This letter argued that many environmental campaigns and projects occurred in affluent communities and, by making these spaces off limits to polluters, actually increased the toxic burdens experienced by low-income people and people of color. Additionally, the letters claimed that people of color were too often absent from leadership positions in environmental organizations (Sandler and Pezzullo 2007). Even the environmental movement's literature speaks to its marginalization of people of color; in his writings, Muir regarded

Native Americans as "unclean animals that did not belong in the wilderness" (Merchant 2003). Additionally, the environmental movement's dominant historical narrative, which positions as its leaders white men such as Muir, Aldo Leopold, and Henry David Thoreau, disregards legacies of environmental activism among working-class people and people of color (Taylor 2009).

In response, many prominent environmental organizations have begun to acknowledge the need for both environmental protection and social justice and to work toward what Agyeman calls a *just sustainability* (2005; Montague 2002). In 1993, the Sierra Club's Board of Directors adopted a policy naming social justice and human rights as necessary components of its program. In 2001, the organization released its own set of environmental justice principles, adding the equitable distribution of risks and benefits and the inclusion of all people in environmental decision making to the organization's historical emphasis on preserving resources for future generations (Sierra Club n.d.). The Natural Resources Defense Council has partnered with community-based groups to work on Hurricane Katrina recovery in New Orleans, to clean up the Anacostia River in southeast Washington, D.C., and to improve air quality in predominantly Latino neighborhoods in Los Angeles (Natural Resources Defense Council n.d.). This shift is mirrored by organizations working at the local level. Oakland's Urban Ecology, for example, works toward healthy "human habitats" by engaging low-income urban neighborhoods in community design (Agyeman 2005), helping them assert their "right to the city" (Lefebvre 1992). Additionally, environmental publications such as *Orion* magazine and the online magazine *Grist* regularly feature articles devoted to race, poverty, and the environment. Although EJ issues represent only a small portion of the work of these organizations, their presence nonetheless reflects a greater emphasis on social justice than previously existed. Similarly, the Ecology Center's food justice program, which makes organic food available in low-income neighborhoods, is aligned with this broader shift toward incorporating social justice into the pursuit of sustainability.

While EJ activists were teaching environmentalists about the important links between environmental degradation and racial and economic inequality, they were also shifting toward a greater emphasis on environmental sustainability. Scholars have noted the potential for sustainability to advance the EJ movement beyond what David Harvey calls "militant particularism" (1996) to form broad coalitions with environmental and social justice organizations (Schlossberg 1999; Sze and London 2008). Some low-income communities of color invoke sustainability by drawing on ancestral traditions of ecological land management, often emphasizing the production of food in environmentally beneficial manners (Pulido 1996, 1998; Peña 1999, 2005). Additionally, some EJ organizations have undertaken sustainable development initiatives that seek to create small green businesses in communities of color (Lee 2005; Pinderhughes 2006). The West Oakland Farmers Market's work to support black farmers and to create economic opportunities for neighborhood residents brings these strategies together.

Additionally, collaborative efforts between EJ and environmental groups have campaigned for clean production, waste reduction, and increased access to local and organic food (Schlossberg 1999; Agyeman and Evans 2003). This cross-pollination of justice and sustainability activism represents a promising direction for both movements and sets the stage for activist-scholars like Raquel Pinderhughes, whose words introduce this chapter, to insist that the green economy provide economic opportunities for marginalized communities.

Sustainable Business

The ideal of sustainability has moved the environmental movement out of the wilderness and into the city, aligning it more closely with struggles for social and environmental justice. It has also transformed the movement's approach to economic growth, prompting a number of partnerships between business and environmental interests that encourage firms to integrate environmental priorities such as energy conservation into their bottom lines (Schmidheiny 1992; Murphy and Bendell 1997). Sustainability is sometimes described as a way for businesses to be "socially responsible" or "good corporate citizens." Other times it is depicted as "a global competitive advantage" and a "way to capture new market opportunities" (International Institute for Sustainable Development n.d.). The former description implies that a company's profits might be tempered by environmental or social concerns, while the latter reveals a belief that incorporating environmental and social concerns can lead to increased profits. Like sustainability itself, sustainable business is enacted differently depending on the interests at hand.

In practice, sustainable business tends to invoke some consideration of environmental and, less often, social factors in business decisions. Sometimes this consideration is minimal but plays a large role in a company's advertising. Critics argue that advertisements featuring environmental concerns can replace, rather than represent, practices that seek to ensure the well-being of the environment or workers. They refer to this practice as *greenwashing*. For example, despite the branding of oil giant BP as "beyond petroleum," in 2007, 93 percent of their investments went toward the extraction of fossil fuels (Barley

2009). This eco-branding, which was developed by renowned advertising agency Ogilvy and Mather, helped situate the company among environmental causes like the Rainforest Action Network's alternative energy campaign, whose slogan was "beyond oil" (Parr 2009, 16–17). Despite this branding, BP has been penalized by the Environmental Protection Agency for violations of the Clean Air Act and has lobbied against global warming legislation (24/7 Wall Street 2009). It seems likely, however, that the massive 2010 Gulf Coast Oil Spill will put an end to any credibility this greenwashing campaign might have once enjoyed.

However, not all eco-branding is greenwashing. Sometimes environmental concerns are integral to a sustainable business, as is true for many of the vendors featured in this book. Indeed, difficulty assessing the sustainability claims made by various businesses has led to the development of a number of third-party certification schemes, though the criteria through which businesses are evaluated sometimes remain oblique (Hatanaka, Bain, and Busch 2005). This labeling shifts the authority for regulating business practices from the state to civil society, a process of "roll-back neoliberalism" consistent with the green economy's emphasis on nonstate actors (Brown and Getz 2008).

Prominent environmentalists have often played advisory roles helping business become more sustainable. For example, corporate behemoth Wal-Mart employed high-profile environmental consultants (including former Sierra Club director Adam Werbach and *Natural Capitalism* coauthor Amory Lovins) to move the company toward bold goals such as zero waste production, reliance on only renewable energy, and showcasing of sustainable products. Its progress toward these goals, however, has been moderate (Fischman 2007). Additionally, these limited goals ignore the company's sprawling land use patterns, use of global supply chains, and poor working conditions (Parr 2009).

Other times, environmentalists themselves have founded sustainable businesses and watched them become incredibly profitable. Take, for instance, Burt's Bees cosmetics, which began as a way for homesteaders in northern Maine to supplement their back-to-the-land lifestyle and which features "effective natural ingredients for you, the environment and the greater good." The company was recently sold to Clorox for $913 million (Baysden 2008), though its website, which does not mention the sale, claims that "everything's pretty much the same here at Burt's Bees" (Quimby n.d.).

Within the business world, it is not surprising that issues of justice are marginalized, as those promoting social equity by organizing to improve worker pay and conditions have historically been cast as threats to capitalism (Brown and Getz 2008; Allen 2004). Burt's Bee's website makes vague references to social responsibility and a culture of caring but fails to mention worker pay or conditions. More egregiously, Wal-Mart may be reducing its ecological footprint, but the world's largest corporation continues to undermine employees' efforts to unionize and continues to face ongoing legal suits concerning race and gender discrimination. While sustainability as an approach has helped amplify social justice concerns in the environmental movement, such concerns are largely ignored in the business world. A notable exception would be some food importers who have attempted to highlight the importance of social equity by offering a fair price to cooperative producers in the global South. Such efforts certainly represent an attempt to promote social justice within sustainable business, but they also raise questions about whether export-oriented production in the global South can ever truly be sustainable (Lyon 2007).

Critics question whether these business models can be compatible with environmental protection and social justice. Deep ecologists, for example, argue that sustainable businesses value nature only to the extent that it can serve humans as a resource, rather than seeing its full worth. Other critiques come from proponents of the limits-to-growth approach, such as ecological economist Herman Daly, whose words introduce this chapter. Daly argues that economic growth cannot be sustained, no matter how green or sustainable it becomes. Although green industries and firms might theoretically supplant ecologically and socially destructive ones, providing economic development rather than aggregate growth, in practice that has not been the case. Sustainable business models work not to constrain old industries but to help existing firms shift in new, profitable directions or to build new industries alongside existing ones. Both proponents and critics have highlighted economic growth as the essence of sustainable development (Ekins 2000). In this way, sustainable development coheres with a capitalist resilience able to reappropriate critiques of growth as new engines for profit (Parr 2009).

Still other critics argue that sustainable business does not address the exploitative social and political conditions in which environmental degradation is rooted (Dryzek and Lester 1995). Social ecologists such as Murray Bookchin argue that sustainability is attainable only through what he calls confederal national politics — local direct democracies that would challenge corporate ownership of the means of production (Bookchin 2004 [1971], 1999). Further, Marxist theorists argue that capitalism is inherently at odds with environmental protection. Many environmental sociologists depict capitalism as a treadmill that requires ever-increasing economic production that will *always* lead to the exploitation of both workers and natural resources (Schnaiberg 1980; Schnaiberg and Gould 1994). O'Connor (1994) adds that capitalism undermines the reproduction of the physical environment, as well as labor, which he predicts will lead to crisis. Geographers add analyses of the contradictions inherent in attempts to manage nature via private property (Mansfield 2004; McCarthy and Prudham 2004), since private property can legitimate a social order of differential access. These theorists tend to advocate for an overhaul of the capitalist economy or, at a minimum, for the decommodification of land and labor and a more equitable distribution of wealth. Moreover, critics have argued that efforts to make a particular business, or even a locality, more sustainable do little to affect the logic of production that continues to inform the global economy. Some businesses like those featured in this study might limit or even eliminate their negative effects on the environment, and may even create more equitable working conditions, but the overwhelming majority of the global economy is neither sustainable nor just.

These critiques have been largely confined to thinkers in academia and activists on the radical fringe of the environmental movement. In the popular discourse, claims that business can and should become more sustainable are contrasted with those arguing that economic growth and technological innovation will solve environmental and social problems, or that environmental problems do not exist. In this context, the rise of a mainstream green discourse is quite extraordinary.

THE GROWTH OF GREEN

In contrast to the notion that there are environmental and social limits to economic growth, sustainability refers to the "triple bottom line" of economic growth, environmental protection, and social equity. But green thinking takes this logic one step further; not only is investment in sustainable business compatible with these goals, it becomes a key strategy to address them. This framework colors the approach to social change found at farmers markets.

Radical Resource Productivity

In their book *Natural Capitalism*, environmental entrepreneurs Paul Hawken and Hunter and Amory Lovins (2008) lay out the economic underpinnings of the green economy. They argue that the global economy is dependent on four types of capital. Human capital consists of labor, intelligence, and culture; financial capital is cash investments; manufactured capital refers to factories and infrastructure; and natural capital includes resources as well as the ecosystems on which all life depends. Industrial society uses the former three to turn the latter into commodities. However, when calculating the economic bottom line, there is no conventional way to factor in losses in or damage to natural capital. The authors claim that treating natural capital as if it were limitless has led to wastefulness, as has devaluing human capital. This wastefulness causes ecological and social harms. The authors argue that businesses must act as if human and natural capital had calculable values in order to create a more efficient economy. This "radical resource productivity" will reduce the use of natural capital and lessen the production of pollution while increasing the value of human ingenuity. This approach, according to the authors, is more efficient than models that waste human or natural capital, making it more profitable. Indeed, they predict that "companies that ignore the message of natural capitalism do so at their peril" (Hawken, Lovins, and Lovins 2008, [x]).

What makes *Natural Capitalism* an example of green discourse rather than a proposal for sustainable business is the authors' assumption that industry's adoption of natural capitalism will address environmental and social problems. As occurs in farmers markets, the locus of social change — traditionally the state — is now found in the marketplace. Radical resource productivity, according to these authors, will so reduce the need for resources such as energy that environmental crises will be averted. *Natural Capitalism* also claims to improve our daily lives by reducing waste and noise, which the authors claim are by-products of inefficiency, and by providing meaningful work. There is no role for government in this approach, save the elimination of subsidies to wasteful industries such as mining, coal, and agribusiness. And the only role for the public is to consume these inexpensive, efficient products. Natural capitalism assumes that markets are "natural" motivators of ecological and social change.[2] Industries that disregard natural capital need not be constrained; they will simply be outcompeted by newer, more efficient ones.

Green for All

Natural Capitalism proposes to improve quality of life and provide meaningful employment in developed countries and to enable countries in the global South to develop without depleting their resource base. Still, it is fundamentally an approach combining environmental protection and economic growth. Social justice issues are not wholly marginalized, as they are in models of sustainable business, but they receive less attention than other concerns. In contrast, activists wielding a critique rooted in an environmental justice framework have argued that the green economy is an opportunity to lift out of poverty those low-income communities and communities of color that have been so devastated by industrial capitalism. The most prominent individual associated with this critique is Van Jones, whose 2008 book *The Green Economy: How One Solution Can Fix Our Two Biggest Problems* was the first environmental best seller written by an African American author. In some ways, Jones's transition from a self-proclaimed communist in the early 1990s to a proponent of socially inclusive green economic growth parallels the path the U.S. environmental movement has traveled.

Jones argues that the environmental movement has existed in three phases, each of which has played out differently in white communities and communities of color. For whites, the first phase was the preservation of wilderness. Jones contrasts the white experience with the devastation of Native American communities living in these so-called virgin lands. Jones's second phase for whites is regulation, including the passage of the Clean Air and Water Acts and the creation of the Environmental Protection Agency. For people of color, the regulatory phase included the establishment and major campaigns of the environmental justice movement. Jones's third phase, which he calls investment, describes the rise of the green economy. The question he raises is the one described in chapter 1: Will society continue to create conditions of "eco-apartheid," in which the benefits derived from the green economy serve only wealthy and white communities, or will it move toward conditions of "eco-equity"?

Unlike natural capitalists, Jones sees strong roles for government and popular movements in the creation of market conditions that foster eco-equity. He envisions mass investment — public as well as private — as a driver of the green economy and has been at the forefront of popular efforts to persuade local, state, and even the federal government to fund and incentivize various green businesses. Jones and his colleagues have also organized at the grassroots level to pressure governments to create green job training programs in low-income communities of color. In the San Francisco Bay Area, adopted programs include Solar Richmond and Oakland's Ella Baker Center's Green Jobs Training Corps. Both train youth of color from neighborhoods that have long fought against environmental injustices for careers in green building and solar panel installation. Several Oakland food justice organizations adopt this logic by training youth for careers in agriculture.

Supporters of eco-equity and natural capitalists share the assumption that the creation of efficient, green industries and products is the key to addressing environmental degradation and inequality. Individuals are invited to contribute to social change through buying and selling. One becomes an environmentalist, for example, through the consumption of green products such as organic food rather than the more traditional means of voting, lobbying, or attending protests. While this strategy allows supporters to inscribe their social movement goals into their everyday life practices, it also creates individuals who infuse the logic of the market into both their ordinary behavior and their desires for social change (Larner and Craig 2005; Rose 1999). This is one way in which activist support for the green economy does ideological work.

In addition, this new way of pursuing social change redefines justice and sustainability in ways that are consistent with neoliberalism and economic growth. More radical notions such as those of eco-socialists and social ecologists, or even the limits-to-growth variant of environmentalism, are incompatible with green growth and thus made invisible by this increasingly dominant strategic choice. Both natural capitalists and supporters of the green-for-all approach adopt social change strategies that foster capitalist growth, and avoid those that challenge it. Activists encourage the purchase of green products, adding to overall economic growth, but do not work against the continued expansion of those doing social or environmental harm. Proponents of the green economy tend to justify their emphasis on the creation of alternatives through a belief that as increasing numbers of "enlightened consumers" choose green options, polluting industries will collapse for lack of sales (Danaher, Biggs, and Mark 2007; Hawken, Lovins, and Lovins 2008). Indeed, Green For All's campaigns to create state-funded green jobs training programs can be seen as a kind of roll-out neoliberalism, in which the state creates conditions to foster the primacy of the market (Peck and Tickell 2002; see also Guthman 2008b and Harvey 2005).

Commodities in the Green Economy

Proponents of green economic approaches to environmental and social problems argue that the creation of green industries will lead to a more just and sustainable society. But in order for such industries to grow, there must be demand for green products. Moreover, although natural capitalists argue that radical resource productivity will eventually make green products cheaper than their competitors, those products currently tend to be more expensive.

Businesses producing green products often appeal to their positive environmental and social effects in order to justify higher prices. For example, the food movement argues that the purchase of local organic food is a "vote with your fork" for environmental protection because it shifts market demand to farms eschewing chemical pesticides and lowering transport fuel costs. Farms aligned with food justice activism further promote their products as a way to help lift racially and economically marginalized communities out of poverty. In this way, the ideals of environmentalism and justice become commodified — they are part of what is for sale in the green economy.

The idea that collective social movements can become regarded as commodities for sale in the green economy is built on the notion of branding that has dominated marketing research, and social science analyses of it, for the past several decades. Branding is the linking of a social identity or lifestyle to a particular product in order to create a "*unique and compelling* customer experience" (LePla, Davis, and Parker 2003, emphasis in original). Consumers are urged to attain the lifestyle or identity through the purchase of the product (Klein 2000). So when a commercial for McDonalds depicts families enjoying one another's company, it attaches the lifestyle (leisure time, love, and belonging) to the commodity (fast food). Through branding, individuals begin to identify themselves as the kind of person associated with a particular product or line of products. Individuals identifying with one or another brand then organize themselves into "brand tribes" in which their sense of community is mediated by commodities and the identities they confer (ibid.). Green products confer the identity of environmentalist or supporter of social justice, and farmers markets and other green stores become key sites in which consumers create their brand tribes.

But the green economy allows environmentalism and justice to become more than just brand identities. When participants in farmers markets such as those depicted in this book bring their social movement goals to the market, they also bring the market's "rationalizing" force to their social movement goals (Castree 2008; Mansfield 2004). In order to promote justice and sustainability through the green economy, these ideals become regarded as commodities. In other words, by working through the green economy, food and food justice movements come to treat their social change goals as things to be bought and sold. For example, when buying an organic peach or a solar array, green consumers can reasonably believe themselves to be purchasing a contribution to environmental protection. Purchasing the same peach from an African American farmer, or hiring a solar panel installer from a low-income community of color, can similarly be seen as a small act that contributes to a more just and sustainable society. Economic sociologists have long argued that economic decisions are not the result of rational cost-benefit analyses, but constructed social worlds that can be infused with individual and collective identities and moral worldviews, including social movement goals (Zelizer 2007; Polanyi 2001[1944]). Within the green economy, social movement goals also become economic imperatives. This marketization of what have formerly been regarded as objects for collective struggle is a key component of the logic of the green economy.

Of course, an individual cannot really buy environmentalism or justice, as these social movement goals are not truly things like solar panels or peaches. They are fictitious commodities paralleling Polanyi's (2001[1944]) classic analysis of land and labor (as well as money). Fictitious commodities are those containing value that cannot be expressed in market terms, but whose buying and selling provides the foundation for modern economies. Environmentalism and justice are not foundational in the way that land and labor are, but they resemble Polanyi's fictitious commodities in that things that cannot really be bought are nonetheless for sale.

Polanyi argues that the commodification of land and labor requires that human beings and nature become subsumed by the market economy. That neither will be valued beyond their fictive economic worth ensures that both will be destroyed. This destruction is impeded, however, by what he calls a countermovement. Through countermovements, people will resist the destruction of nature and society by the market economy. Classic countermovements include the labor movement, which promotes government regulation to constrain the market economy's exploitation of human labor, or the limits-to-growth variant of environmentalism, which works to restrict the exploitation of nature. In the green economy, however, goals that were once the province of countermovements become a part of the market itself. Food and food justice activists do not work to constrain the supremacy of the market in this way.

Natural capitalists would argue that the commodification of land and labor within the economy is not, in and of itself, destructive, but that it is incomplete. Instead of arguing for the decommodification of land and labor, they argue that a full valuing of all human and ecosystem services on economic terms can prevent economic growth from destroying the natural and social systems on which it depends. The promise of the green economy is that the market can be made to value, and therefore to protect, humans and the environment. The following chapters trace the narratives and practices through which this promise is pursued, as well as some of its intended and unintended consequences.

THE DEVELOPMENT OF THE GREEN ECONOMY

The word *green* preceding *economy* connotes the belief that businesses can value human and natural capital and that the economic growth of industries that do so is sufficient to address environmental and social problems. Green approaches assume that industries that become more ecologically, socially, and economically efficient will eventually outcompete those that continue to exploit workers and destroy their resource base, leaving little to no role for government or popular movements.

Green is quite a departure from the limits-to-growth argument that dominated the environmental movement in the 1970s. Under attack from the right wing, the environmental movement shifted to a sustainability paradigm, in which environmental protection was conceptualized as compatible with economic growth as well as social equity. Sustainability provided an important context for the rise of the green economy.

The emergence of the green economy as a strategy for environmental protection and social justice is the intellectual context in which the North Berkley and West Oakland Farmers Markets pursue their goals. But it is essential to explore the local context as well. Both farmers markets trace their roots to the radically anticapitalist social movements that dominated Berkeley and Oakland in the 1960s. The next chapter describes the transformation from anticapitalist social movements to green economic development against the backdrop of Bay Area sociospatial histories.

CHAPTER THREE

The Taste of Place

[The Berkeley Farmers Markets have] a great sixties community
feel; after all, hippies started it all!
> — LUJRANNE DRAGER, Berkeley Farmers Market customer,
> quoted on http://www.localharvest.org

In the late 1960s [the Black Panthers] had this brilliant analysis
around the intersection of poverty, malnutrition and institutional
racism. They wanted to liberate Black communities, and they
knew that providing food for young people was key.
> — BRYANT TERRY, West Oakland food justice activist, chef,
> and author of *Grub: Ideas from an Urban Organic Kitchen*

On April 13, 1969, a group of student and community activists met at a collective house half a block from Berkeley's campus and proposed to create a "user developed community park" (Copeland 1969). Six days later, Stew Albert, who along with Abbie Hoffman and Jerry Rubin had founded the Yippies (Youth International Party), put out a call in the local *Berkeley Barb* for "one and all to bring building materials to the lot so they could build a community park" (Brenneman 2004). The next morning, between one hundred and two hundred volunteers arrived and removed the asphalt (ibid). Over the next four weeks, thousands of volunteers spent their days planting trees, vegetables, and flowers, listening to music, sharing food, and talking politics (Wittmeyer 2004). They named it People's Park in recognition of its populist roots.

Noted food historian Warren Belasco (1993) describes People's Park as an important site at which the activism and counterculture of the 1960s inspired new ways of thinking about the production and consumption of food, creating what he calls a *countercuisine*. The park's creation is one of several moments in Bay Area countercultural history cited by Berkeley farmers market supporters such as Lujranne Drager, whose words introduce this chapter, as important predecessors of their activities. Other predecessors include the San Francisco

Diggers, an anarchist, direct action street theater collective of the 1960s; the back-to-the-land movement of the 1970s; and Chez Panisse, founded in 1971. At the North Berkeley market, however, the populist roots of these events are tempered by the neighborhood's upscale bohemian atmosphere, which is reflected by Chez Panisse's development.

The predominantly white counterculture was not the only group linking food and politics in the 1960s. In January of 1969, four months prior to the founding of People's Park, eleven children received free breakfast at West Oakland's St. Augustine's Church. This simple act launched the Free Breakfast for School Children program of the Black Panther Party (BPP). Along with the BPP's other survival programs, the breakfast program aimed to meet basic needs while illuminating the failures of the state to do so. It was among the BPP's most popular initiatives. "We began with 11 youngsters the first day (a Monday) and by Friday we were serving 135 students," recalled St. Augustine Pastor Earl Neil (n.d.). By the end of its first year, the BPP had created similar programs in black neighborhoods throughout the country, and its members and volunteers were regularly feeding more than 10,000 children (Black Panther Party, n.d.). According to Neil, "this was the first nationally organized breakfast program in the United States, either in the public or private sector" (Neil n.d.). Indeed, former BPP minister of education Ericka Huggins claims that "the government was so embarrassed by our Free Breakfast Program that it started the national free breakfast program" (quoted in B. Jones 2007).

The counterculture that pervaded but was not exclusive to Berkeley in the 1960s gave rise to the desire for local and organic food so integral to farmers markets like North Berkeley (Belasco 1993). Similarly, we can see the roots of its West Oakland counterpart, and food justice activism more broadly, in the Free Breakfast for School Children program. Preventing child hunger may seem a far cry from the local organic produce that both farmers markets favor, but both link food provisioning to community empowerment and self-determination. The West Oakland Farmers Market also draws on the neighborhood's earlier history in which a thriving African American arts district was decimated by urban renewal and divestment.

Advocates of local cuisine, and of local economies more generally, often argue that their food and systems of exchange are shaped by the local biogeography and history of the places in which they exist. In short, they often argue that "place matters" (Kloppenburg, Hendrickson, and Stevenson 1996; Barlett 2005). Northern California's temperate climate and rich soils easily enable a twelve-month growing season, making it a much-sought-after site for conventional and alternative agriculture. In addition to ecological factors, participants

in the farmers markets analyzed in this book drew selectively from local social histories to shape the food systems they created. This chapter traces local
events that have shaped these farmers markets, first in Berkeley and then in
Oakland. In both cases, the farmers markets invoke and reflect aspects of their
neighborhoods' radical political histories. What is striking about these histories
is that although the events and movements most often cited by farmers market
participants are largely anticapitalist, they are invoked to animate support for
local green economic exchange.

RADICAL POLITICS AND THE COUNTERCUISINE

Former Berkeley student activist and historian Ruth Rosen described People's
Park as a "magical fusion" between the anarchist counterculture and socialist activists that comprised Berkeley's New Left social movements (quoted
in Kitchell 1990). For the activists, People's Park represented an opportunity
to move away from the center of campus, where police presence and police brutality had become pervasive.[1] According to Michael Delacour, "We
wanted a free speech area that wasn't really controlled like Sproul Plaza [in
the center of campus, the site of Mario Savio's famous arrest] was. It was
another place to organize, another place to have a rally" (Wittmeyer 2004).
Student activists were also reeling from the events of the 1968 Democratic
convention, during which ten thousand protesters attempted to pressure the
Democratic Party to take a stand against the United States' escalating involvement in Vietnam but were met with harsh violence by the Chicago Police
Department (Jennings and Brewster 1998). When a Wisconsin convention
delegate alerted the Democrats to the violence that surrounded them and
asked the party to support the demonstrations by adjourning the convention,
party leadership declared his comments out of order. This action led activists on campuses throughout the country to abandon any lingering hope of
having an impact on electoral politics. In the words of John Gage, an antiwar
organizer who worked on the 1968 McGovern campaign, "it seemed impossible that there could be any significant electoral path toward ending the war"
(Kitchell 1990).

Against this context, Berkeley activists took a more countercultural turn,
attempting to liberate a space where they could not only organize but develop
a utopian vision. Mario Savio, one of the free speech movement's most prominent leaders, emphasizes the Park's revolutionary purpose: "As I see it, the great
hope implicit in People's Park is that in our leisure time, so to speak, we will
make the social revolution. Property is not a thing to keep men apart and at

war, but rather a medium by which men can come together to play" (ibid). Seizing control of university land was a confrontational act that appealed to Berkeley's socialist activists. What they did with that land, however, embodied a countercultural ethic more closely associated with the hippies and Yippies. Former student activist Frank Bardacke, who would later spend decades organizing workers in the fields and canneries of Salinas, California, describes the vision of People's Park as both revolutionary and countercultural:

> In a down to earth way we were showing in our very activity the image of a new society. Our job is to form a counterculture. A more rural culture. A more decentralized culture that can develop counter values of cooperation, of production for use rather than production for profit. Develop that culture in the hope that it would be in revolutionary contradiction to bourgeois culture, and that we should view ourselves as revolutionaries but also as founding members of this counterculture. (ibid.)

In this remark, Bardacke demonstrates how the counterculture allowed activists to envision a decentralized alternative to the hierarchical, violent system they rebelled against.

In embracing the counterculture at People's Park, Berkeley activists tapped into a newly sprouted vision of using food for social change. Belasco (1993) traces the contemporary origin of this vision to the Diggers, a 1960s anarchist community action group based in San Francisco's Haight-Ashbury district. The Diggers took their name in part from an English group who, in the wake of the 1641 English civil war, sought to create small, egalitarian rural communities in order to reform the existing social order, igniting a brief radical period of British history. The 1960s Diggers, according to Belasco, "put food at the center of [their] program" (1993, p. 18). Radically anticapitalist and antihierarchical, they distributed food and literature during daily "feeds" in the panhandle of Golden Gate Park. Here, free food was often accompanied by the cry, "Food as medium!" or "It's free because it's yours!" (Metevsky 1966).

A local Berkeley newspaper described the spirit of the Diggers' feeds. "They talk about anything, smile about everything and do what they want to do with the food that they bring to each other" (Metevsky 1966). The Diggers were the first countercultural group to politicize the act of eating, an impulse that would soon spread. Later, beat poet Diane di Prima's *Revolutionary Letters* (1969) would also invoke the role of food in the counterculture, envisioning the "sustenance we give each other . . . the fact that we touch and share food . . . [as] a million earthworms tunneling under the structure till it falls." This poem presents a vision of a counterculture that can supplant the dominant one without direct confrontation, a kind of revolution by attrition that continues to be invoked by the food movement.

Food was an integral part of the creation of People's Park. Along with the more often remembered trees and children's playground, one of the first installations created was an organic garden. This action prompted Belasco (1993) to describe People's Park as a "seizure of public land for the purpose of producing free food." During the original gathering, those claiming the park were entertained by a band called "The Joy of Cooking." Food was cooked and shared daily.

In People's Park, food was a medium through which student activists embraced a more utopian strategy, creating a daily, personal practice from their political worldview. Additionally, People's Park radicalized the counterculture's approach to food by weaving an environmental ethic into the politics of the New Left. Indeed, it was People's Park that popularized the word *ecology*. In anticipation of a teach-in about ecology and politics that followed the establishment of People's Park, a local unit of the American Federation of Teachers wrote that the park's seizure spoke to environmental, land use, and quality of life issues. During the teach-in, Beat poet Gary Snyder likened trees to black people, Vietnamese people, and other oppressed groups, making the case for what Yippie Keith Lampe would call a "broader, ecologically-oriented radicalism" (quoted in ibid., 20–21). Belasco argues that this coming together of environmentalism and the New Left was a lasting contribution of People's Park.

At People's Park, the act of growing food linked environmentalism to the nonhierarchical, decentralized organizational forms favored by both the New Left activists and the counterculture. In organic gardens, some found a model for a new society. A spokesperson for one of Berkeley's People's Gardens told a local reporter that his collective used no pesticides or chemical fertilizers because their garden was "a harmony between as many lifeforms as possible." Later in the interview, he argued that gardens held a model for democratic decision making, creating a "self determined group" that might "lead in other cooperative directions" (quoted in ibid., 22).

As future chapters show, the most dedicated participants in the North Berkeley Farmers Market also seek cultural change in response to the perceived impossibility of electoral politics. The farmers market also embodies the counterculture's regard for rural life and decentralization. For some participants, the link between People's Park and the farmers market is material as well as ideological. Members of Food Not Bombs gather leftover produce from the farmers market and prepare and serve it to homeless people at People's Park.

When asked why they serve there rather than in Oakland, where poverty rates are much higher, one volunteer described an affinity for People's Park because of its role in the social movements of the 1960s.

Farmers markets such as North Berkeley link the production and consumption of food to environmental issues by stressing organic and local production. Indeed, as chapter 4 demonstrates, this farmers market's central theme is an environmental one. The North Berkeley Farmers Market also embodies the notion that our relationship with food contains the seeds to create a more decentralized, direct model of social organization.

The Country and the City

Embedded in the Diggers' radical street theater and objections to private property was an impulse to remove themselves from what they considered the physical and psychic heaviness of industrial life. Eventually, many of them left the city as part of the back-to-the-land movement. In 1967, the Diggers published "Sounds from the Seed-Power Sitar" in a local underground newspaper. Their column began with the following call:

> The return to the land is happening. Land is being made available at a time when many of us in the Haight-Ashbury and elsewhere are voicing our need to return to the soil, to straighten our heads in a natural environment, to straighten our bodies with healthier foods and [to do] Pan's work, toe to toe with the physical world, just doing what must be done. (quoted in Morgan 1991)

The column urged anyone with access to land, money to buy land, agricultural know-how, or the desire to learn to call the Diggers' shared phone number. Many of the Diggers moved first to Sonoma County's Morning Star and Wheeler Ranches, and from there, they joined and founded communes throughout northern California and the rest of the country (ibid.).

Jentri Anders was a Berkeley student activist who took the countercultural turn. She was among the first Bay Area dropouts to move to the Mateel community in Humboldt County. She later earned a PhD in anthropology studying the community she helped create. She describes the original Mateelians as sharing some central characteristics with the counterculture at large:

> A discontent with mainstream American society and a strong desire to avoid what society held for them. Their actions should be interpreted as efforts "counter" to those aspects of modern, industrialized American society they consider dehumanizing, ecologically unsound, and alienating. (Anders 1990, 7)

The back-to-the-land movement enabled the Diggers and other members of the counterculture to create an alternative to the society they criticized. The directive to grow their own food was essential to this vision, which was predicated on collective self-sufficiency. In this way, they became some of the region's first contemporary organic farmers. In place of chemical fertilizers and pesticides, which they refused to import, early countercultural farmers relied on composting, mulching, and other techniques that would become standards of organic production (Guthman 2004).

Nearly all of the North Berkeley market farmers of the appropriate age came to organic farming through participation in the counterculture. One farmer describes his journey in the following way:

> It was the 1960s and I was hitchhiking around and I got a ride with some folks who were on their way to California. . . . Well, they took me to this farm in Sonoma County and I got really into it. Before that, I never would have guessed that I'd spend my life farming there.

Even younger farmers often describe their attraction to organic farming in terms that evoke the counterculture. One young farm owner, for example, describes dropping out of Berkeley's School of Law to become a farmer.

> It was this kind of somatic, instinctual [impulse]. Like, what makes me feel less depressed? What makes me feel connected to something, like there's any kind of meaning? You know, anything that makes life feel better. And so that's how I got into gardening and then from there it was a matter of doing horticulture. [And I asked myself], "What would I want to grow most?" and then I said, "Well, actually, food."

In giving up a presumably lucrative career to seek personal fulfillment and spiritual connection, this young farmer embodies the spirit of the back-to-the-land movement. This and similar approaches to the cultivation and consumption of food evidence the farmers market's philosophical roots in Berkeley's countercultural history.

Although many members of the counterculture left the streets of San Francisco for the communes of northern California, some did not abandon the city completely. In "Sounds from the Seed-Power Sitar," the Diggers envisioned the formation of a cooperative food market in the Haight-Ashbury district supplied by back-to-the-land farmers. In his 1964 history of Haight-Ashbury, Charles Perry relayed the Diggers' prediction that "the Haight would remain a marketplace while the tribes dispersed into the bosom of nature."

Cooperatively owned grocery stores flourished not only in San Francisco but across the nation, and many were supplied by back-to-the-land farmers. Such farmers were also supported by "food conspiracies," networks of autonomous buying clubs that ordered produce as well as bulk dry goods. Food co-ops and buying clubs not only were instruments of food procurement but also served to "raise consciousness about the irrationality of the profit system" through cooperative ownership (Drew 1998, 323). The Berkeley Food Conspiracy was particularly politicized. It was founded amid the 1966 boycotts of Safeway in support of César Chávez and the United Farm Workers. Through the Berkeley Food Conspiracy, individuals supporting the strike could replace Safeway's scab grapes and lettuce with goods produced by northern California's organic farmers. One of the founding members of the food conspiracy is among the North Berkeley Farmers Market's most dedicated shoppers and serves on its community advisory committee. Additionally, Berkeley's co-op grocery sat just half a block from the farmers market's present location.

The Delicious Revolution

As popular as they are, the Berkeley farmers markets are not the best-known institution connecting urban dwellers to regional organic farmers. Instead, that honor belongs to a small restaurant located in a converted home just half a block south of the North Berkeley Farmers Market.

Chez Panisse is the life work of Alice Waters, one of the alternative foods movement's most beloved celebrity chefs. Waters had transferred to UC Berkeley at the height of the free speech movement and participated in some of its sit-ins and demonstrations. Her philosophy toward food was inspired by a semester abroad in France and especially by the fresh ingredients and simple preparations found in the countryside. Upon returning to Berkeley, Waters began to prepare meals for friends, imitating the food she had eaten abroad.

After graduation, Waters borrowed money from friends, acquaintances, and her parents to open Chez Panisse. Her original staff and clientele consisted largely of those Berkeley bohemians who had turned from political radicalism to the counterculture. Her original chef was a UC Berkeley philosophy graduate student whose only cooking experience was at home. Waiters and waitresses were artists and poets chosen for their personalities rather than skills.

From the beginning, Waters insisted on the freshest available ingredients, which at first came from some unusual places. Waters described her early food procuring strategies in her 1993 essay "The Farm Restaurant Connection":

The entrance to Chez Panisse Restaurant.

Not only did we prowl the supermarkets, the stores and stalls of Chinatown, and such specialty shops as Berkeley then possessed, but we also literally foraged. We gathered watercress from streams, picked nasturtiums and fennel from roadsides, and gathered blackberries from the Santa Fe tracks in Berkeley. We took herbs like oregano and thyme from the gardens of friends. One of these friends, Wendy Ruebman, asked if we'd like sorrel from her garden, setting in motion an informal but regular system of obtaining produce from her and other local gardeners. We also relied on friends with rural connections: Mary Isaak, the mother of one of our cooks, planted fraises des bois for us in Petaluma and Lindsey Shere, one of my partners and our head pastry cook to this day, got her father to grow fruit for us near his place in Healdsburg.

As the restaurant continued and grew, Waters employed "foragers" charged with finding the freshest ingredients at local farms. This practice would create a "moral community based on good food and goodwill [and] spawn a new generation of artisans and farmers" (ibid., 6–7). This ethic can also be seen at the North Berkeley Farmers Market, as customers are urged to develop personal relationships with those who grow their food. As is discussed in more detail in chapter 6, doing so is similarly framed as a moral imperative.

In the late 1980s, Waters began to define the quality of her ingredients not only by their taste but by their production. Inspired by the writings of Wendell Berry, the farmer and poet to whom Michael Pollan dedicates *The Omnivore's Dilemma*, she began to search for humanely treated meat and for produce grown without pesticides or chemical fertilizers (ibid., 236–239). This was the beginning of Chez Panisse's environmental sensibility and a key moment at which organic and local produce became associated with elite food practices.

Like the New Left activists growing vegetables in People's Park, Chez Panisse posits food as a way to promote ecological health. In her 2005 essay "The Delicious Revolution," Waters describes the relationship between food and environmental awareness: "If we don't care about food, then environmentalism will always be something outside of ourselves. And yet environmentalism can be something that actually affects you in the most intimate — and literally visceral — way. It can be something that actually gets inside you and gets digested." Waters helped create a philosophy that uses food to create an environmentalism of everyday practice. As we see in the following chapters, Waters's approaches to environment and community resemble the central themes of the North Berkeley Farmers Market.

Although Chez Panisse is just down the street, Waters herself is rarely sighted at the North Berkeley Farmers Market, perhaps for fear of being mobbed by adoring acolytes. Chez Panisse continues to buy much of its produce from market farms, and its employees are often among the farmers market's regular customers. Indeed, one Chez Panisse chef and farmers market customer remarked that her love for the farmers market was regarded positively in her performance evaluation. Waters herself is often on hand for market celebrations and special events, to the delight of many customers, managers, and vendors. For example, when describing the North Berkeley Farmers Market's opening event, manager Linda Bohara listed local celebrities who had attended: "Alice Waters came, the mayor came."

"Funny that Alice Waters is billed before the mayor," I responded.

"Around here, absolutely," she explained.

Waters was also one of the keynote speakers at the farmers markets' 2008 thirtieth anniversary celebration.

Despite her rare personal appearances, Waters and her restaurant color the spirit of the farmers market. Their influence can be seen not only in the market's regard for environmentalism and community, as described above, but also in its emphasis on excellent quality and high-end cuisine. Indeed, when the

North Shattuck Business Association attempted to brand their neighborhood by hanging a series of banners from the lampposts on busy Shattuck Avenue, they chose "gourmet" and "farmers market" as two of their themes. In addition, Waters is a key figure in the food movement's emphasis on creating a politics of pleasure. This concept refers not only to the movement's assertion that the bold flavors and infinite varieties offered at farmers markets contain stronger and more authentic tastes but also to the notion that the consumption of such foods can create a poetic and spiritually fulfilling sense of connection to local landscapes and communities (Gaytan 2004). Waters refers to the food movement as a "delicious revolution," a phrase that embodies the movement's desire to bridge personal pleasure with social change goals (2005).

High-quality food allows farmers market participants to justify its high prices. A speaker at a farmers market special event, for example, told the following parable:

> A man arrives at the farmers market in his Volvo. He looks around for a while before settling on some peaches. He asks the price, which is four dollars a pound.
>
> "Why are they so expensive?" he asks the farmer.
>
> "Why do you drive a Volvo instead of a Pinto?" the farmer questioned.
>
> "Because it's better," the man responded.
>
> "Well, my peach is better too," the farmer replied.

The moral of this story is that high-quality food can and should demand high prices. This only becomes possible because market produce is associated with the gourmet style of cooking Waters pioneered. Weekend dinner at Chez Panisse costs $95 for a three-course meal, not including wine and service charges. The association of local and organic foods with elite cuisine is perhaps Chez Panisse's strongest contribution to alternative food systems in Berkeley and beyond.

Although Chez Panisse is costly, Waters also works to increase the availability of and desire for local and organic food beyond her clientele. Most notably, she helped found and fund the Edible Schoolyard, a garden and cooking program at nearby King Middle School. Volunteers broke ground in 1995, when school gardens had all but disappeared. Although King is located in affluent North Berkeley, the Berkeley Unified School District buses students from all parts of the city. As in the restaurant, Waters uses food as a way to teach environmental ethics, but her audience has shifted from bohemian restaurant goers to students of all backgrounds. In a letter she sent to Bill and Hillary Clinton and Al Gore during Clinton's first presidency, Waters described the goal of the Edible Schoolyard as to "help us create a demand for sustainable agriculture,

North Berkeley's Edible Schoolyard.

for it is at the core of sustaining everyone's life" (McNamee 2007, 267). Waters was dismayed at their responses, each of which highlighted their own eating and gardening practices while failing to offer any political support.

Together, Chez Panisse and the Edible Schoolyard embody the Berkeley Farmers Markets' approach to issues of food access. The farmers market and restaurant emphasize high quality and tend to charge high prices (though the knowledgeable shopper can find bargains as well). Through programs such as the Edible Schoolyard and the Ecology Center's Farm Fresh Choice described in the introduction, low-income people are also encouraged to enjoy organic and local produce. Access to such food is promoted as creating a connection to the local environment and community among people who would otherwise be left out.

In sum, the North Berkeley Farmers Market invokes the countercultural ethics of Berkeley's radical past. North Berkeley is also a key site in which locally grown organic produce has come to embody a gourmet sensibility appropriate to the neighborhood's affluence. However, both the Ecology Center and Chez Panisse work to temper the elite connotations of their food politics by promoting access for low-income people and people of color. In contrast, West

Oakland's politics of food are fundamentally rooted in the neighborhood's history of radical resistance to racial and economic oppression.

SURVIVAL PENDING REVOLUTION

The central themes of the North Berkeley Farmers Market are connection to the natural world and the development of a community of like-minded individuals. The West Oakland Farmers Market, on the other hand, exists to increase access to healthy food among neighborhood residents and to provide green economic opportunities for black farmers and home-based businesspeople. And while the North Berkeley market can trace its philosophical heritage to the socialist New Left and anarchist counterculture of the 1960s as well as the eco-gastronomic aesthetic of Chez Panisse, the West Oakland Farmers Market is in many ways an intellectual descendent of the Black Panther Party (BPP).

Sensationalized by the media of its day and tarred by the FBI's counterintelligence program (COINTELPRO), mention of the Black Panther Party tends to evoke images of gun-toting young black men in black leather jackets.[2] Even their less glamorous everyday work, which combined self-defense and community empowerment, seems a far cry from the distribution of local organic produce. However, the West Oakland Farmers Market builds on the BPP's emphasis on empowering community members to provide for one another. This theme was particularly germane to the BPP's survival programs, which aimed to meet basic needs in the neighborhoods where the group was strongest. The survival program strategy began with Free Breakfast for School Children and posited basic nutrition as a precondition for the BPP's revolutionary goals.

Although he was too young to have been directly involved, market founder David Roach cites his older brothers' involvement in the Black Power movement as a source of inspiration. And when asked about his motivations, market manager Jason Harvey, who is in his late twenties, named the BPP's free breakfast program. Additionally, African American customers living in Oakland during the peak of the BPP's popularity identified as party members, attended meetings and rallies, and were fed as children by the free breakfast program.

The Black Panther Party for Self-Defense is an integral part of Oakland's history. It was founded by Huey Newton and Bobby Seale, who met while attending Oakland's Merritt Community College. The two participated in an organization called the Afro-American Association, which was headed by Berkeley law student Don Warden. They were dissatisfied, however, with the association's cultural nationalist politics, which they would later call "pork chop nationalism" (Hayes and Kiene 2000, 548). Newton and Seale's revolutionary black nationalism, on the other hand, was inspired by the radical political theory they read as participants in reading groups and street-corner rap sessions at both Merritt and Berkeley. Grounded in the works of Lenin, Mao, and Franz Fanon, their political philosophy "sought to blend Maoist socialism with cultural nationalism" (Self 2003, 224). The BPP's philosophy also shared commonalities with Berkeley's predominantly white student movements, namely their socialist opposition to capitalism.

However, unlike the Berkeley students, Newton and Seale fused their political philosophy with the everyday lived realities of what Newton called his "street brothers." These men included "the unemployed, the downtrodden, the brother who's robbing banks, who's not politically conscious" (Newton and Morrison 1999, 92). From Fanon, Newton had learned that if "you didn't relate to these cats, the power structure would organize these cats against you" (ibid.). Newton's regard for his street brothers was not merely strategic but deeply personal. He described his connection to them in his book *Revolutionary Suicide*:

> The street brothers were important to me, and I could not turn away from the life I shared with them. There was in them an intransigent hostility toward all sources of authority that had a dehumanizing effect on the community. . . . My comrades on the block continued to resist that authority, and I felt that I could not let college pull me away, no matter how attractive education was. These brothers had the sense of harmony and communication I needed to maintain that part of myself not totally crushed by the schools and other authorities. (Newton 1973, 73–74)

Engagement with underclass realities and class-based political theory differentiated the Black Panther Party from other black political programs of their day. It also inspired party leaders to link their community's basic needs to their political goals, a connection embodied by their "Ten Point Platform." The BPP's defining document includes demands for freedom and self-determination as well as material needs such as decent housing, free health care, and full employment. The tenth point summarizes the document, stating, "we want land, bread, housing, education, clothing, justice and peace" (Black Panther Party n.d.). Like the Black Panther Party, the West Oakland Farmers Market aims not merely to provide for the basic needs of West Oakland's most marginalized residents, but to empower members of the community to provide for one another.

From Guns to Grits

Before an October dawn in 1967, just six blocks west of the farmers market's current location, Huey Newton was pulled over by the Oakland police. The

Black Panther Party founder Bobby Seale surveys bags of groceries for the Free Breakfast for School Children Program. Photo by Howard Erker, March 31, 1972. Oakland Tribune Collection, the Oakland Museum of California, gift of ANG Newspapers.

ensuing shoot-out left the officer dead and Newton injured and under arrest. The "Free Huey" campaign would command the bulk of the BPP's time, press, and resources until his eventual release in 1970.

Exhausted by Newton's trial, and having narrowly escaped conviction for conspiracy to incite a riot at the 1968 Democratic National Convention, Bobby Seale sought an alternative to confronting the state. He began the BPP's survival programs during Newton's incarceration. Though seemingly mild in comparison to highly publicized arrests, these programs were among the party's most important political achievements. The BPP developed more than sixty such programs, including food distribution; shoe distribution; a free health-care clinic that offered, among other things, screenings for sickle-cell anemia; a school; and transportation for visitors to California prisons (Rhomberg 2004). Interestingly, according to then–chief of staff David Hilliard, the free breakfast program began with a series of regular food donations from the Diggers (Hilliard and Cole 1993; Patel 2011).

For BPP members, serving breakfast was not a departure from their political goals but a new way to engage them. In an unsigned article in their newsletter, party members describe the Free Breakfast for School Children program's political aims:

> For too long have our people gone hungry and without the proper health aids they need. But the Black Panther Party says that this type of thing must be halted, because we must survive this evil government and build a new one fit for the service of all the people. . . . The Black Panther Party will not let the malady of hunger keep our children down any longer. (Black Panther Party n.d.)

Additionally, in his memoir titled *Off the Pigs! The History and Literature of the Black Panther Party*, G. Louis Heath similarly describes the party's survival programs. "The new 'serve the people' theme [is] in harmony with Panther expectations to achieve 'power to the people'; in an eventual showdown with the 'racist power structure'" (1976, 82–83). Like other survival programs, the free breakfast program aimed to create black political empowerment and self-determination.

As recipients of free food, the schoolchildren could have been characterized as victims in need of charity. However, BPP leaders and volunteers used rhetoric to envision the children as subjects rather than subjugated objects. By referring to them as "little brothers," "little sisters," and "the only insurance we have of a new and different tomorrow," the Black Panther Party posited the children as entitled to, rather than merely in need of, free food (Hollis 2007). Years later, Elaine Brown, who eventually replaced Newton as party chairperson and later ran for Oakland City Council, would similarly portray the free breakfast program as an alternative to charity models of food provision.

> What I also believe today and what I see is important about this, is the right to eat. It's not just the question of, am I dealing with hunger, because I could set up a thousand charities that will feed a bunch of people. The question is, do I as a human being in this society, or in this life, have a right to eat. . . . The question is: are we prepared to make a commitment, at least, to our children that we will not put a price on their lives by denying them food unless their parents have the money to pay for it. (quoted in Heynen 2009)

Free Breakfast for School Children and other survival programs were intended not only to sustain the black community but to introduce them to the party's ideals, which included a right to food.

The free breakfast program also embodied the BPP's affirmation of black identity by emphasizing the foods commonly associated with African American cuisine. In her writings on the program's rhetoric, Dixon Charlotte Hollis argues that by serving particular foods, the BPP was able to call into being a black community united by their children's hunger: "Even in the first advertisements for the program, specific foods were to be served and donated, not just breakfast foods, but "'Soul food: grits, eggs, bread and meat,'" creating a Black identity through food that was familiar and labeled as specifically black, both within the community and by those outside the circle" (2007, 11–15). By demanding foods associated with black cuisine, and thus reproducing this association, party leaders emphasized both community empowerment and racial pride.

Managers, vendors, and customers in the West Oakland Farmers Market also use food to promote community self-reliance. This notion is key to their call to support black farmers and businesspeople. Indeed, one vendor offers copies of the newsletter for the Commemoration Committee for the Black Panther Party alongside his herb and vegetable starts. Vendors and managers emphasize foods commonly associated with black cuisine, such as collard greens and black-eyed peas. This association between food and black empowerment has roots in the free breakfast program. When asked how the two are similar, one regular customer and former party member responded, "At the Free Breakfast Program, Huey and the other [movement] builders just didn't want to see kids arrive at school hungry, and established that it was their right and their role in the community to champion that." Like the BPP, the West Oakland Farmers Market seeks not only to supply food but to create opportunities for African Americans to do, rather than be done for.

Moreover, as future chapters describe, the West Oakland Farmers Market links community empowerment to racial pride. Indeed, the theme that dominates this farmers market is a celebration of black identity. This theme is reflected in the vendors' offerings and market special events as well as in the casual conversations between managers, vendors, and customers. The farmers market draws connections between food, empowerment, and identity, connections firmly rooted in the legacy of the Black Panther Party. These links serve to construct a black community capable of agency despite their marginalization.

Inside the Red Line

In his analysis of race in postwar Oakland, historian Robert Self writes that the Black Panther Party's "theatric performance of radical Maoist nationalism" resonated strongly in West Oakland because "the black community was so thoroughly marginalized from the political life of the city" (2003, 226). West Oakland's political marginalization both is the result of and contributes to its physical marginalization. This marginalization is based not in physical geography — no hills or rivers separate this neighborhood from the rest of the city — but in a social history of segregation reinforced by urban renewal.

West Oakland sits adjacent to the Port of Oakland and was the original terminus for the transcontinental railroad. In the late 1800s, this transportation hub created opportunities for work, which were filled by white and black Americans as well as by Portuguese, Irish, Japanese, and Chinese immigrants. Additionally, the 1906 earthquake drove some San Francisco residents eastward in search of housing (Olmstead and Olmstead 1994).

Urban planners initially conceived of Oakland as a garden city. In contrast to the slums of the northeastern United States, where workers lived in close proximity to factories, Oakland's largely single-family homes offered quiet and tranquil living a short commute from the port and railroad lines. Indeed, early accounts of West Oakland life describe workers clocking out to raise vegetables, chickens, and even goats in their home yards (Self 2003).

During the New Deal years, many of Oakland's white residents took advantage of Federal Housing Authority (FHA) loans and moved to suburbs in the East Oakland hills. Such loans were restricted to new construction, and new suburbs were kept exclusively white via racial covenants. Remaining West Oakland residents were further denied public and private loans due to redlin-

Redlining map of Oakland and Berkeley. Courtesy of T-RACES: A Testbed for the Redlining Archives of California's Exclusionary Spaces, R. Marciano, D. Goldberg, and C. Hou.

ing, a process that categorized black neighborhoods as risky investments. Thus African Americans were largely confined to West Oakland even as their population grew sixfold. Existing housing was often subdivided, causing extensive overcrowding. The FHA did provide some housing for West Oakland's new and existing black residents through black-only housing projects (Johnson 1993).

As a result of racial exclusions, West Oakland changed from a racially heterogeneous neighborhood to a predominantly black one. Seventh Street, where the West Oakland Farmers Market stands today, was its commercial and cultural center. Long-term resident Tom Nash describes the business district:

> There was a lot going on. There were all kinds of businesses. As I said before, there were banks, cleaning, and pressing shops. You name it, and it was there. Whatever you needed, you didn't have to leave West Oakland to get it, see. So, consequently as a result of that, West Oakland was a city within a city. (quoted in Kinte Center n.d.)

Seventh Street was a place where residents could meet not only their needs but their desires. The Bay Area Blues Society refers to Seventh Street as the "home of Oakland Blues," and its website describes some of that history.

> Oakland's 7th Street was the entertainment center for the African American community and social center on any night of the week. The world famous Slim Jenkins Supper Club which included a restaurant, bar and show room was known as Oakland's high class blues & jazz club. 7th Street had something for everyone from high class Slim Jenkins to hole in the wall clubs. These clubs were lined up and down the street and were packed every Friday & Saturday night. . . . The music played and recorded on 7th Street produced some of today's most popular artists including B.B. King, Little Milton, Lowell Folsom, James Brown, Jimmy McCracklin, Stevie Ray Vaughn, Rod Stewart, the Rolling Stones, M.C. Hammer and even country star Allen Jackson. (Bay Area Blues Society n.d.)

Similarly, longtime West Oakland resident and occasional farmers market vendor Iyalode Kinney maintains memories of the neighborhood music scene.

> My mom used to bring me here because, along Seventh Street, that was the music place. You don't know about West Oakland? My God! That's where the jazz was . . . Ike and Tina Turner. All the greats used to come to the Barn and New Roofie's Inn . . . all those places. It was awesome! Lots of culture here.

What happened to this vibrant African American community mirrors the history of black neighborhoods across the country.[3] In the late 1950s and 1960s, urban redevelopment projects promised to replace so-called blighted

Slim Jenkins bar/restaurant, West Oakland, ca. 1950. Photo courtesy of the African American Museum and Library at Oakland.

areas and bring jobs and opportunities. Thousands were displaced from their homes. The elevated Grove-Shafter Freeway (Highway 980) separated West Oakland from the rest of the city, and the Cypress Freeway was constructed right through the neighborhood's center.[4] Seventh Street was demolished to make way for the construction of Oakland's main post office, as well as the Bay Area Rapid Transit (BART) system, which links the East Bay to San Francisco. While residents of wealthier neighborhoods successfully lobbied for more costly underground rails, the West Oakland station was built aboveground. Tom Nash describes the effect these programs had on his community:

> West Oakland was a beautiful place up until the city with the decree to clean out West Oakland came through, and through the process of eminent domain took over all of those homes — over five hundred homes down there — to put in the post office. It wiped out The Barn, one of the finest soul food restaurants that we

had. And they called it the Barn, because that's exactly what it was. A great big old empty barn and they brought — they put in a restaurant in there, and you could go in and there and get all kinds of soul food. Nevertheless, the city, through the process of eminent domain, took over all of that property down there and scattered the people. All of the Blacks, at that time it was almost one hundred percent Black in the West Oakland area. Scattered them. (Kinte Center n.d.)

Like residents of many African American neighborhoods, West Oaklanders built a community in the parts of the city to which they were confined. Then they watched as their neighborhood was decimated in the name of urban renewal. While there was certainly resistance to this destruction, led in part by the North and West Oakland Poverty Centers, where Huey Newton and Bobby Seale would later volunteer, it was ultimately unsuccessful (Bagwell 1982).

Today's West Oakland residents are greatly affected by this legacy of uneven urban development. Diesel emissions from trucks traversing the freeways contribute to the neighborhood's high rates of asthma (Ovetz 2008). Moreover, there's a sense among at least some West Oakland residents of being stuck here. "Do you know how many places there are to get off the freeway in West Oakland?" one West Oakland Farmers Market vendor asked me rhetorically. She pointed to a number of exits in several directions. "But there's nowhere to get *on* the freeway in West Oakland. It's like once you're here they don't want you to leave!"[5]

Despite the difficulty, West Oakland residents must leave the neighborhood to access most goods and services. Among the businesses that no longer exist in West Oakland are those that provided its residents with food. Nationwide, the 1960s and early 1970s witnessed the replacement of independent grocery stores with corporate retailers (Walker 2005). Following this trend, West Oakland contained 137 grocery stores in 1960 but only 22 in 1980. This was largely the result of increasing consolidation in the grocery industry, as a small number of large supermarkets replaced a larger number of smaller stores. This made supermarket location the key to food access (Fuller 2004). In the 1980s and 1990s, many supermarkets closed their urban locations in favor of suburban ones, citing high insurance costs, security problems, and low profits (Curtis and McClellan 1995). In his 2011 urban political ecology of West Oakland, geographer Nathan McClintock describes how this trend, combined with a local economy devastated by urban renewal, created obstacles to supermarket retention. By the 1990s, many of West Oakland's supermarkets had closed their doors. The neighborhood's last remaining grocery store closed in 2006. Following that, plans for British supermarket giant Tesco to open a West

Seventh and Mandela on a nonmarket day, taken from the BART station platform.

Oakland store fell through. As in many similar neighborhoods, West Oakland residents must leave to buy groceries, which they supplement with food from widely available liquor and fast food establishments (ibid.). For this reason, scholars and activists refer to it as a "food desert."

In their study "Designed for Disease," a group of researchers from UCLA's Center for Health Policy found that residents of food deserts are at significantly higher risk for diabetes and obesity (Babey et al. 2008). West Oakland's incidence rate for diabetes, for example, is 35 percent, 12 percent higher than for the county as a whole. Additionally, a report by the Bay Area Regional Health Inequities Initiative (2008) found that the average West Oakland resident lives ten years less than those living in the Berkeley hills and that food access is a significant factor in this disparity. Creating access to fresh food for West Oakland residents, and thus reducing such disparate health outcomes, is among the West Oakland Farmers Market's primary goals.

FROM ANTICAPITALISM TO GREEN CAPITALISM

In his 2001 book *Storied Land*, sociologist John Walton presents not only the history of a California city but also the collective process of creating a history. In this process, various groups compete for their interpretation of past events to be included in the historical record. And each group's account is itself a selective interpretation, not only telling what has happened but presenting a future-oriented narrative of who they are and where they are going. "History is not simply a record of events," Walton writes, "but a justification of them. . . . History is simultaneously a process of social production that looks backward at 'what happened' and forward at the importance for the future of 'what is said to have happened.'"

This chapter has presented a brief and incomplete telling of the historical events in Berkeley and Oakland that gave rise to and inspired the creation of the North Berkeley and West Oakland Farmers Markets. Events were selected based on those referred to by farmers market participants, and with the goal of contextualizing current efforts to create alternative food systems.

But the local histories invoked by farmers market participants are partial. There are, of course, other events and actors that have created the physical and social landscape in which the farmers markets exist, but none live larger in the collective memories of market participants than the social movements and countercultural values of the New Left and bohemians in Berkeley and the legacy of urban renewal and the Black Panthers in Oakland.

Additionally, market participants' invocations of these predecessors are themselves partial. The most striking omission is in their approach to economics. Both the BPP and Berkeley's student activists were radically opposed to capitalism. The farmers markets' strategy of promoting green economic exchange represents a stark departure from this orientation.

The Black Panther Party's opposition to capitalism differentiated them from other black organizations of their day and caused them to depart from the then-dominant philosophy of cultural nationalism. Though membership was originally restricted to blacks, the party's rhetoric and action often focused on class. In his book *Seize the Time*, originally published in 1970, Bobby Seale explicitly describes the BPP's dedication to socialism: "Working class people of all colors must unite against the exploitative, oppressive ruling class. Let me emphasize again — we believe our fight is a class struggle not a race struggle" (1991, 72). Indeed, Seale explicitly invoked the Free Breakfast for School Children program to create links to other exploited communities "living below subsistence: welfare mothers, poor white people, Mexican-Americans, Chicano peoples, Latinos and black peoples. This type of [free breakfast] program, if spread out, should readily relate to the needs of the people" (ibid., 414). Seale sought to build connections between marginalized communities through their shared experience of hunger.

In his online history of the Black Panther Party, Sundiata Acoli, a former party member, further describes the effects of the Black Panthers' socialism on party members' understandings of social life:

> The BPP theories and practices were based on socialist principles. It was anti-capitalist and struggled for a socialist revolution of U.S. society. On the national level, the BPP widely disseminated socialist base programs to the Afrikan masses. Internationally, it provided Afrikans in the U.S. with a broader understanding of our relationship to the Afrikan continent, the emerging independent Afrikan nations, Third World nations, Socialist nations, and all the Liberation Movements associated with these nations. Overall the ideology provided Afrikans here with a more concrete way of looking at and analyzing the world. (Acoli n.d.)

Acoli is critical of the party's adherence to socialism, writing, "They often gave the impression that to engage in any business enterprise was to engage in capitalism and they too frequently looked with disdain upon the small business people in the community" (ibid.). This critique demonstrates how paramount socialism was to the BPP's ideology.

"We do not fight exploitative capitalism with black capitalism," Bobby Seale wrote in *Seize the Time*. "We fight capitalism with basic socialism" (1991, 71). And yet, despite tracing its lineage to the Black Panther Party, black (and green) capitalism seems an accurate description of what the West Oakland Farmers Market works to create. Faced with small numbers of African American farmers, the West Oakland Farmers Market works to create increased sales outlets for their goods. Additionally, the farmers market seeks to rebuild the neighborhood's tradition of locally owned businesses, seeing itself as a venue in which local craftspeople can reach potential clients. Though the farmers market draws on the Black Panthers' notions of black pride and community self-sufficiency, it explicitly rejects their revolutionary goals.

Berkeley's New Left also embraced socialism, as well as communism. The free speech movement's immediate goal — procuring the right to engage in political activity on campus — resulted from the administration's restriction of political fundraising to the Republican and Democratic clubs. That policy had originated in the 1930s in response to a "communist-influenced student movement gaining momentum on the campus" (K. Fischer 2006, 260). Indeed, most of the free speech movement's leaders were active in socialist organizations:

[Mario] Savio had been a member of both SNCC and the Young People's Socialist League; Jackie Goldberg, a red-diaper baby, was an active communist, and so was her brother Art Goldberg, who described himself as a "Commiejewbeatnik"; Bettina Aptheker, daughter of the communist theoretician Herbert Aptheker, proposed a plan for the Free Speech movement that was based on communist popular front organizations of the 1930s; Sydney Stapelton was active in the local Young Socialist Alliance. (ibid., 264)

Through these leaders, the free speech movement was firmly rooted in opposition to capitalism.

The counterculture rejected capitalism as well, embracing an anarchist philosophy instead. The Diggers distributed food during their daily feeds. Their cry of "it's free because it's yours" rejected the notion that food could be a commodity. Even their recipe for whole wheat bread, which they baked in aluminum cans, contained the phrase, "Please take this recipe home and start making bread. The only stipulation is that you always *give it away*" (Digger Archives n.d., emphasis in original). The Diggers' rejection of capitalism was not limited to food. They are perhaps best remembered for their Free Stores,

Former Digger David Simpson looks on as Chris Sollars bakes Digger bread at the fortieth anniversary party for Chez Panisse.

which simply gave away their inventory. This is a far cry from the expensive produce featured at the North Berkeley Farmers Market.

The counterculture aimed to live rather than speak their opposition to capitalism. Bohemians and hippies embodied their resistance by residing in communal houses and rural communes in which they shared food and other household goods, eschewing private property and lessening their engagement with the capitalist market. In the city, these houses often provided meeting places for groups organizing demonstrations and protests, such as those leading to the seizure of People's Park.

People's Park itself was also explicitly anticapitalist, as it declared that the land belongs to those who use rather than those who own it. Indeed, during that struggle, activists referred to the park's creation as the liberation of corporate land. Tom Hayden, the former president of sds and eventual California state senator, who at the time lived in one of Berkeley's communal houses, referred to spaces like People's Park as "free institutions . . . building blocks of a new society from which we confront the system more intensely" (quoted in Echols 1994, 160). The building of institutions to support transformative social change is a far cry from the farmers markets' neoliberal emphasis on voting with dollars.

Although members of the Berkeley counterculture founded several small businesses, these were largely collectively owned and even worker-owned, and thus not straightforwardly capitalist enterprises. Cultural historian Maria McGrath describes the nature of the food co-ops and conspiracies of the 1960s and early 1970s:

> As experiments in participatory democracy, anti-capitalist countercultural business, and centers for alternative foods consumption, co-ops acted as protean clearinghouses for multiple political and cultural concerns. . . . Most significant, for many 1970s cooperators, the creation of a haven and community for unorthodox folks (including revolutionary dissenters) was just as important as selling food. As a member of Washington D.C.'s Field of Plenty Co-op explained in the late 1970s, "Selling food isn't our goal. It's just a pretext for building, living, and breathing models of revolutionary change." (2004, 3)

Indeed, McGrath's research goes on to demonstrate that many cooperatives failed because they prioritized their political aims and nonhierarchical organizational forms over their economic survival.[6] Economically, vendors at the North Berkeley Farmers Market seems to have followed more closely in the footsteps of Chez Panisse, which began as a countercultural business and became quite a lucrative one.

Although the North Berkeley and West Oakland Farmers Markets are in many ways descended from the radically anticapitalist social movements and bohemian counterculture that permeated the Bay Area in the 1960s, they differ markedly from their ideological forbearers in their approach to economic exchange. The socialist New Left, the Black Panther Party, and the anarchist counterculture were all directly opposed to capitalism. The farmers markets, on the other hand, reflect the rise of the green economy; they aim to increase environmental protection and justice through the buying and selling of goods. This strategy necessitates that farmers market participants redefine the ideals of justice, sustainability, and community to be consistent with the promotion of economic exchange. The following chapters explore the discourses and practices through which farmers market participants define their environmental and social goals to be consistent with the logic of the green economy.

CHAPTER FOUR

Creating Just Sustainability

I want to be as connected with the earth and with the food I eat as possible. I want to have good live food in my stomach, and I want to support good farmers in the area, because I live in this area, and I want to act like I live in this area. [At the farmers market] you're giving money to people that are using sustainable practices, and you're not contributing to this overarching dynamic of unsustainable food practices.

— JAY, North Berkeley Farmers Market customer

I think that's one of the differences of the inner-city farmers market concept versus someone who just says, "Oh, we want to farm organically because it's more environmentally sound." Well, it is more environmentally sound, but how far does that link go? Does it link all the way to someone in West Oakland or East Oakland who can't spend three dollars for a basket of strawberries? How do you bridge that?

— DANA HARVEY, Codirector, West Oakland Food Collaborative[1]

NORTH BERKELEY: FARMING AS IF NATURE MATTERED

In the spring of 2006, the North Berkeley Farmers Market hosted a series of special events called "Shopping with the Chef." During these tours, chefs shared their thoughts on the day's produce and offered simple recipes and preparations. The series' inaugural event featured Jessica Prentice, a locally renowned chef, activist, and food writer and one of the originators of the term *locavore*. Prentice had recently released a book, *Full Moon Feast* (2006), which combines commentary and recipes for each of the thirteen lunar cycles of what she calls the agrarian calendar.

Jessica began the event by discussing her book and the various threads woven through it. These threads include ecological sustainability, her own experiences with illness and healing, and nutrition ("but not so much the federal government, USDA approach to nutrition," she elaborated, "much more what traditional peoples knew about nutrition that we kind of forgot"). She termed a fourth thread "cultural foodways," explaining that she is fascinated by how other cultures, particularly in the past, saw food as something "sacred and a gift, something that came from the divine and from a mysterious place." She hoped her writing and recipes would help re-create a sense of reverence and honor around food. "So those are the main threads that are woven through, along with the very practical thread, which is, What are we going to put on the table for dinner?" she continued, linking her writing to the day's event. "Because it's nice to talk about food in all these theoretical ways, but ultimately it's about what are we going to have for supper, and that's why we're all here at the farmers market because if these are our beliefs about food, then this is what we have to make it real, and this is the way that we make it real."

Jessica began to lead a group of about twenty-five market patrons from table to table. She introduced these customers to Ben Lucero and Karen Toombs of Lucero Farms. Here she described Lucero's second-year "wild" strawberries, which are smaller and sweeter, and joyfully accepted a basket we could all sample. She told the crowd how Ben had been farming since childhood, including picking cotton alongside his parents at the age of five. As children of Native American migrant farm workers, Ben and his brother had contests to see who could grow the most vegetables. She also conveyed Ben's experience that only farmers market sales allowed him to garner some stable income. "Definitely wonderful farmers to support," she concluded. "Local, organic, truly organic in the deepest meaning of the word." Although the term *organic* refers only to a set of production practices, Jessica's description of Ben and Karen as "truly organic" invokes the kind of small, environmentally minded, ethical farming revered by the North Berkeley Farmers Market.

Continuing the tour, Jessica moved the crowd through the various stands, combining discussions of the food itself with anecdotes about the farmers. Listeners learned that two of the farmers' families had been on the land for generations but had only recently made the switch to organic. Another farmer, Jessica noted, was vehemently opposed to USDA organic certification, which he believed would dilute standards and include large, industrial farms. Rather than pay for certification, this farmer offered a thousand dollars to anyone who could find a farm more organic than his.

Between these tidbits, Jessica outlined basic recipes for a summer squash frittata, a simple hollandaise sauce for steamed asparagus, and a soufflé of mixed greens. She also described the way the past winter's rains, which were severe, would affect the summer's stone fruit crop. "Cherries," she said for example, "are going to be few and expensive, just like petroleum in the coming decades. They're only getting about 20 percent of what they normally get off the trees, so be prepared for cherries to be very special this year."

Jessica Prentice's presentation embodies many of the North Berkeley market's central themes. Most notable is its dedication to environmentalism. Allusions to the beauty, spirituality, and biodiversity found on organic farms invoke the wilderness ethic that has historically dominated the U.S. environmental movement but use it to describe cultivated farmland instead of wild places. Through this narrative strategy, the consumption of local organic food becomes a way for customers to develop the kinds of personal connections to planetary health that Jay describes in the quote that introduces this chapter. This connection, according to North Berkeley market managers, vendors, and customers, can inspire an ethic of sustainability that will lessen human material demands on the natural world. It is through this narrative that environmentalism becomes part of the commodities that North Berkeley shoppers are encouraged to purchase.

Attention to issues of social and racial justice are also present at this farmers market, as symbolized by Jessica's description of Ben Lucero's heritage and childhood. But this theme is much less prominent than environmental ones. The West Oakland Farmers Market, on the other hand, takes an environmental justice approach to the politics of food through its focus on food access and its celebration of black identity. In West Oakland, environmental issues are incorporated into the market's goals but play a secondary role. Taken together, these two farmers markets demonstrate that just sustainability — the intersection of environmental sustainability and social justice — is a complex endeavor that can be imagined and pursued in a variety of ways. Although each farmers market attends to both environmental and social justice themes, they do so unevenly, prioritizing the issues more traditionally associated with their social locations.

The Wildness of Organic Farms

As noted in chapter 2, classic environmental texts, such as the writings of John Muir, depict the natural world as a beautiful, wild place that nurtures the human soul. Environmentalists have long drawn upon striking images of nature in order to argue for the preservation of wilderness (see, for example, Worster 1994). Managers, vendors, and customers in the North Berkeley Farmers Market reflect this tradition by praising the beauty and spiritual potential of local organic farms.

Farmers' displays often emphasize idyllic landscapes, invoking the wilderness imagery associated with the environmental movement. One Thursday evening, for example, a young white woman admired two photographs that stood among Lone Oak Farm's brightly colored oranges, plums, and pomegranates. One depicted rows of trees with gracefully pruned branches, each dusted with delicate white flowers. The other showed a river running through the verdant, rolling hills behind the orchard. Marleen, the white woman working at the stand, whose brother-in-law owns the farm, told her customer that her family plans to open a bed-and-breakfast there. "That sounds so lovely," exclaimed the customer, smiling broadly. Organic farms certainly function as productive spaces in that they create food. But the increasing emphasis on agro-tourism among organic farmers also defines these lands as vacation destinations. As the latter, they allow those who can afford it the ability to relax and recharge, a feature nature writers often attribute to the wilderness. Organic farms can serve this function only in the context of a broader narrative depicting them as romantic, idyllic spaces. This narrative is common to agrarian authors, such as Wendell Berry and Michael Pollan, and is invoked and reproduced through the everyday interactions at the North Berkeley Farmers Market. It invites North Berkeley customers not only to visit but to protect such places through their purchases.

Environmentalists' regard for wild landscapes is often deeply spiritual. John Muir wrote of the Hetch Hetchy Valley, for example, that "no holier temple has ever been consecrated by the heart of man" (1912, 249). Proponents of farmers markets also draw from this spiritual regard for nature. Invocations and allusions to spirituality were common explanations for participants' attraction to local organic food. For example, Judy LaRocca, a biodynamic grape farmer and winemaker, expressed that for her, "farming is like a religion, something similar to Wicca. My husband is born Roman Catholic, and he might identify as a Christian, but he's really a farmer." Farmers, she went on to explain, create and sustain life through their daily work. "After all, soil and soul have the same root." Judy expressed great admiration for the work of Rudolf Steiner, who is often credited with founding biodynamic agriculture, though many of its techniques have long been used by indigenous peoples. These techniques include not only organic cultivation but also the use of fermented herbs and composts and a planting schedule guided by an astronomical calendar. In addition, Steiner developed the philosophy of anthroposophy, which states that the spiritual world can be accessed through imaginative, intuitive, and direct observation of the natural world.

Farmers market customers often expressed similarly spiritual inspirations for their devotion to the farmers market. One regular customer sees it as "a chance to offer my children an honest reality, to show them how sustenance happens." Though she did not directly express this as a spiritual sentiment, her words connote a regard for the maintenance of human life. More directly, Jessica Prentice hosts monthly "Full Moon Feast" dinners. During one such event, which ninety individuals each made a thirty-five-dollar donation to attend, Prentice opened with the following prayer: "Before we start, I want to give a moment of thanks. To all of you for coming tonight, to the farmers, to the ranchers, and to the animals that died so we may live. And to the big mother of them all, the planet Earth, who gives us everything that we need" (quoted in Hunnicutt 2006). Her prayer invokes a sense of reverence and gratitude, adding a spiritual dimension to the cultivation and consumption of food. Additionally, while it may be merely metaphor, many North Berkeley customers commonly describe their regular trips to the farmers market as their "weekly ritual" or "spiritual practice." In this sense, the worldviews of many farmers market participants echo the themes of beauty and spirituality often called upon to inspire wilderness preservation. Purchasing food from the farmers market becomes a way for urban consumers to connect to these ideals and to ensure that beautiful and spiritually nourishing farms can continue to flourish.

Biodiversity

While environmentalists have often used beauty and spiritual connection as literary tropes, ecologists offer a parallel argument in favor of biodiversity. North Berkeley market farmers emphasize their agricultural biodiversity, further connecting their productive landscapes to the wilderness ideal that has inspired many environmentalists and further linking their green economic practices to environmental protection. Most market farmers produce an array of crops, aiming to mimic the vast genetic diversity found in nature. While cultivating numerous varieties is a practical strategy to avoid environmental hardships and their economic consequences, farmers also emphasize the importance of biodiversity for ecological sustainability. For example, the website of Riverdog Farm, which grows a wide variety of produce, lists "promote biodiversity" among various reasons to choose organic foods, offering the following rationale: "Vast areas of land planted in only one crop — called monocropping — without interspersed diversity of vegetation makes that crop more susceptible to pests. This, in turn, makes large-scale conventional farmers more reliant on pesticides" (Mueller 2006). Through this quote, farmer Tim Mueller describes agricultural biodiversity as essential to the avoidance of harmful chemicals.

In addition, environmentalists often argue that any threat to biodiversity can endanger the existence of entire species. In contrast to industrial agriculture, which tends to produce a small number of hybrid varieties bred to withstand transport to market, many North Berkeley market farmers collect a wide variety of seeds and promote heirloom (nonhybrid) varieties. This practice positions market farmers as stewards of genetic diversity and ecological health.[2] Additionally, market managers draw additional links between organic farming, biodiversity, and threats of species extinction by taking a strong stand against genetically modified organisms (GMOs). GMOs are not allowed in any fresh or prepared foods sold at the farmers market. Many market customers support this opposition as well. For example, when a vendor applied to sell homemade cakes and pies, Kirk, a white customer and market committee member, spotted the use of corn syrup and baking powder in the vendor's recipes. He and the committee insisted that these two ingredients be certified organic (prepared foods need use only 80 percent organic ingredients) because of the probability that they would otherwise contain genetically modified corn.[3] To educate consumers on these issues, the farmers market even held a promotional event at which Deborah Koontz Garcia sold and signed copies of her anti-GMO documentary, *The Future of Food*.[4]

Farmed salmon, another threat to biodiversity,[5] are not allowed at the North Berkeley Farmers Market. One exception, I discovered, is the filling in the smoked salmon ravioli sold at a stand featuring homemade pasta. This exception provoked outrage by one regular customer, a white man in his early thirties. Although more emphatic than many conversations, his response combines concern for environmental protection with regard for "pure" food in a manner common to North Berkeley market participants:

> "Ooh, smoked salmon ravioli," he said to the woman beside him, gazing longingly at the pasta displayed in front of him.
>
> "It's Atlantic smoked salmon," she responded warily.
>
> If there were a soapbox around, he could have climbed right on. "Atlantic Salmon is all farmed and really bad for the environment," he said to the woman working. "The only salmon that's any good from an environmental standpoint is Alaskan. It's all wild. It's like real fish! And they have good governmental protection in Alaska so it's good to support that. In the Atlantic, though, it's all farmed. They keep the salmon in cages in one place, which has a disastrous effect on that bit of ocean, and then move the cage to another. It's like slash and burn!"

Farmed salmon is not only environmentally dangerous but described as something other than "real" fish. This customer aims to support Alaska's high

North Berkeley
Farmers Market
customers peruse the
produce at Riverdog
Farm's stand.

environmental standards by refusing to purchase Atlantic salmon and by encouraging others to do the same. Like many North Berkeley customers, he
invokes the wilderness ideal that pervades the environmental movement, discursively linking market food to ecological health.

Proponents of biodiversity, particularly those motivated by deep ecology,
argue that all species have a right to exist regardless of their usefulness to humans (Naess 1973). Respect for biodiversity and opposition to farmed salmon
has motivated collective direct action. The Coastal Alliance for Aquaculture's
"farmed and dangerous" campaign, for example, aims to end salmon farmers'
environmentally damaging practices through collective action protests outside
major supermarkets. In the green economy, however, support for biodiversity
becomes as simple as buying food from those who seek to increase it through
organic farming, or refraining from purchasing farmed fish and genetically
engineered foods.

Connection to Place

As described in chapter 2, discourses of sustainability move the locus of environmental action from the wilderness to the habitats humans share with other species. The North Berkeley Farmers Market emphasizes connection to place through its dedication to local and seasonal food. While the U.S. Department of Agriculture (USDA) mandates only that produce sold at a farmers market must be grown within the state, the Ecology Center envisions a *foodshed* (Kloppenburg, Hendrickson, and Stevenson 1996), an area encompassing the cultivation and consumption of food, in which most vendors travel less than one hundred miles. When I asked managers, vendors, and customers why the farmers market was important to them, a desire to "know where your food comes from" was nearly always their first response. In the popular literature on alternative foods, "coming home to eat," as Gary Paul Nabhan calls it, allows eaters to relate to the local landscape and to viscerally understand and embody such natural features as soil structure, weather patterns, and the local seasonal availability of various crops (Nabhan 2002; see also Berry 1990 and Kingsolver 2007). At the North Berkeley Farmers Market, vendors often educate customers on the importance of connection to the local landscape:

> "There are no flowers in your salad mix," said a white, female customer to Adam, a white man in his early twenties who sells produce for Happy Boy Farm. "I miss all the bright oranges and yellows."
>
> "It's hard to grow nasturtiums in the winter," he replied.
>
> Adam later told me that he was sorry to disappoint his customer, but liked the opportunity for education. "She'll appreciate them so much more when spring comes," he said.

By teaching about the seasonal cycles that accompany local eating, Adam links his customers' food choices to the local environment. Other customers need no education. During my fieldwork, I often overheard excited exclamations of "Ooh, summer squash already" or "Wow, you still have asparagus," evidence that shoppers understood the local growing cycles of various foods.

Many North Berkeley Farmers Market patrons regard produce as a vehicle through which they can connect to place. For example, Nikki, a white woman customer who works as a chef at Chez Panisse, describes her connection to a local farm:

> I've even gone to Laura's farm to plan a supper club. I took notes on the produce and planned the menu around it. It was mind-boggling to go out and see where my food is grown. . . . It's amazing to have a sense of where the food comes from because I can feel the energy of that space in the food.

Nikki feels that through the consumption of local, organic food, she can connect to the place where it was grown, again reflecting a theme common to the popular literature and activism on sustainable agriculture. However, Nikki does not have to return to the farm to feel that connection, because the "energy of that space" is embodied in the food itself. Accessing locally grown organic food through the green economy becomes a way for Nikki, and shoppers like her, to connect their own physical sustenance to the land. Bringing environmentalism into the daily lives of urban dwellers links it to their local places and to everyday activities like buying and eating food.

Sustainable Practices

The Berkeley Farmers Markets are well known for their dedication to environmental sustainability. Linda, a mixed Latina and white market manager, effectively summarized this goal, stating, "Dealing with food is one of the best ways we have to go about saving this planet." Indeed, though the other two Berkeley Farmers Markets contain a small number of nonorganic growers, North Berkeley is the first farmers market in the country to feature only organic produce, and prepared food items must be at least 80 percent organic. Many vendors are quite proud of their sustainable practices and can be heard discussing crop rotation, cover cropping, and other common organic strategies with customers. Farms with online presences detail these techniques. Lucero Farm, for example, offers the following information:

> SOIL: Depending on the parcel, the soil types vary from a light sandy
> loam to a rich, dark, crumbly loam. Each is amended with an organic
> compost that contains no animal products. Fish emulsion and cover
> crops enrich the soil with nitrogen, a key plant nutrient. Crop rotation
> also helps to prevent depletion of minerals in the soil.

> PEST MANAGEMENT: Crop rotation, selection of resistant varieties,
> hand removal, creation of habitat for beneficial insects, owl boxes
> to control rodents. (Center for Urban Education about Sustainable
> Agriculture n.d.)

This description of the farm's fertilization and pest management strategies helps its customers "know where their food comes from," giving customers a connection to place and reassuring them that their food is being grown in an environmentally sustainable manner.

The Berkeley Farmers Market offers customers many ways to reduce their ecological footprint.

In addition to promoting the environmental health benefits of organic production, the Ecology Center aims to make the farmers market itself a sustainable event. Building on their experience managing Berkeley's curbside recycling program, the oldest in the state of California, they not only offer the regular glass, plastic, aluminum, and paper recycling but also gather food scraps for compost and collect used plastic bags.

When spaces in this lucrative market become available, applicants are evaluated based on environmental criteria, including local production and the use of organic growing practices. Potential prepared food vendors are assessed on their use of organic, seasonal, and farmers market–purchased ingredients, as well as environmentally friendly packaging (bulk sales, reusable or recyclable containers). Additionally, market managers staff a table offering literature on environmental programs, protests, and events and sell green products such as organic cotton T-shirts, canvas shopping bags, and reusable water bottles.

During the winter, when there are fewer vendors, market managers offer extra space to organizations and individuals promoting sustainable practices. For example, one afternoon a young woman set up a small table to give away free oil-change kits. These included a receptacle to store the used oil as well as a list of places in Berkeley that accepted used oil for disposal. Otherwise, the volunteer explained, oil was often left in the street where, after a rain, it was washed into the nearest creek and eventually into the bay. Because the North Berkeley Farmers Market advocates environmental protection, this volunteer selected it as an appropriate site for kit distribution.

Farmers also encourage customers to adopt sustainable practices. Frog Hollow Farm, for example, which charges the same price per pound for different kinds of fruit, often displays a sign reading, "Save the Earth. Use One Bag if You Can." Conscious of this message, North Berkeley Farmers Market patrons also express their environmental concerns. For example, one afternoon, a white woman approached the Quetzal Farm stand carrying one mesh bag and several plastic bags full of produce. She asked the farmers for an additional bag, insisting, "We re-use our bags, so it's okay."

Customers also try to encourage environmentally beneficial practices in one another. For example, one afternoon, a white man in his mid-thirties strolled up to the market managers' table wheeling a shiny orange bicycle with banana handles. Market manager Herman Yee complimented the flashy, fun bike. "I try to ride around in style," the customer responded, "so I can inspire all the people driving their cars." North Berkeley customers also push market managers to engage in even more sustainable practices, requesting, for example, the elimination of plastic bags and silverware or the addition of a drop-off site for batteries and other hard-to-recycle objects. For its part, the Ecology Center attempts to respond to these pushes by, for example, aiming to make the farmers market a zero waste event. Indeed, a new market manager hired in 2007 was chosen explicitly for his experience diverting waste.

Environmental discourses pervade the North Berkeley Farmers Market, linking the products bought and sold there to efforts to lessen pollution and protect the planet. These discourses invoke wilderness preservationists' regard for nature as beautiful, spiritual, biodiverse, and in need of protection from humans. In this farmers market, however, that protection comes not from excluding human economic activity, but from the cultivation of green products. Through the consumption of local organic food, customers learn about and come to intimately embody their local regions. This embodiment, according to proponents of farmers markets, will inspire a sense of place and a responsibility to engage in other sustainable practices. Through this narrative, North Berkeley customers understand their farmers market purchases not only as food provisioning but as protecting the environment.

Visions of environmentalism that resist commodification are largely absent from the farmers market. For example, while many deep ecologists and farmers market participants share a regard for biodiversity, the farmers market does not espouse a vision of nonhuman nature as possessing an intrinsic worth or as having a right to exist beyond its use to humans. Indeed, the landscapes most lauded at the North Berkeley Farmers Market — organic farms — are valued precisely because they support human life through the production of food. Additionally, the social ecologists and eco-marxists described in chapter 2, who argue against the commodification of land, find their vision of environmentalism outside the farmers market's purview. The farmers market pursues neither the collective, policy-oriented action commonly associated with wilderness protection, nor the radical direct action often leveraged in support of biodiversity. Instead, it offers its vendors and customers a way to pursue environmental goals through the green economy.

Environmental Justice in North Berkeley

In addition to their environmental goals, many participants believe that the North Berkeley Farmers Market, and others like it, promotes a broad vision of social and environmental justice. For example, when I asked market manager Linda what kind of environmental goals were embodied in the farmers market, she began by talking about the effects of local food on carbon emissions but quickly shifted her focus.

> The Ecology Center tends to put environmental goals together with social goals. At the same time as saying sustainable agriculture is a really important part of preserving our planet, [we also emphasize] sustainable employment practices. A lot of farms use really cheap labor and the people who are working on the farms live in horrible circumstances.

She went on to describe several farms featured in the Berkeley Farmers Markets that use unionized labor, that rely solely on the labor of farm owners, or that have financed the purchase of land by their former farmworkers.[6] The owners of the farm that helped their workers purchase land also participated in the 2007 May Day immigrant-rights protests, supporting their workers' decision to strike. Rather than cancel that day's market, white farm owners and interns arrived with one small table full of produce and a statement claiming that this meager amount was what they were able to accomplish without the help of their Latino/a workers. They also wrote an article in their community-sponsored agriculture newsletter describing the situation.

However, while individual farm owners' and market managers' support for farm workers is important, the issue is somewhat outside of the Berkeley Farmers Markets' purview. Participating farms are screened for their environmental credentials. While the Berkeley Farmers Market guidelines also mention farm labor practices, that criterion is much less often applied in the screening process. Nor are the exemplary farms Linda describes given preference within the farmers market. Indeed, one evening, a white woman approached the managers' table to ask why Swanton Berry Farm, a vendor at the Saturday farmers market and the first organic farm in the United States to sign a contract with the United Farm Workers (UFW), was not present on Thursdays. Limited spots at the small Thursday market were offered on a first-come, first-served basis, explained Rosalie, another market manager. "We totally support the UFW. It's just that they didn't apply." Despite managers' individual support for this farm's exceptional labor practices, no institutional effort was made to extend them this opportunity. Additionally, the Ecology Center does nothing to encourage other market farms to follow this example.

Moreover, not all farmers market participants share these managers' support and sympathies for farm workers. When I asked one farmer, a white woman in her early fifties, why she sells at the farmers market, she replied, "The extra money is important." I expected her to elaborate on the financial difficulties of the small farm, but she blamed her economic hardships on her labor force. "They fake injuries," she claimed, "in order to go on unemployment, which then raises my insurance." This response demonstrates that small, local, organic farmers are not always supportive of farm workers' rights, a finding that Guthman (2004) has systematically advanced.

The North Berkeley Farmers Market's high-cost produce also puts it at odds with the social justice concern for increased food access among low-income people and people of color. Indeed, critics of the high cost of local organic produce, like what is sold at the North Berkeley market, sometimes refer to the produce as "yuppie chow" (Guthman 2003). Ecology Center staff members acknowledge this problem and work to address it. Indeed, when the state of California changed from paper food stamps to electronic benefits, thus preventing recipients from using them at farmers markets, the Ecology Center developed a mechanism through which they could accept the new cards. Ecology Center staff later trained managers from other farmers markets, including West Oakland, to adopt this system as well. In addition, several organizations involved in the North Berkeley market are dedicated to making fresh, organic food available to low-income people. As was mentioned in chapter 3, the activist group "Food Not Bombs" collects huge food donations each week in order to prepare and serve free meals at People's Park.[7] Market managers also emphasize that money earned at the Berkeley farmers markets goes to support other Ecology Center programs, such as Farm Fresh Choice, which market

The Farm Fresh
Choice logo.

manager Herman Yee described as the farmers market's "sister program." These examples demonstrate how some North Berkeley Farmers Market participants envision the green economic exchange they promote as supporting both sustainability and justice.

Nevertheless, the discourses that predominate the North Berkeley Farmers Market do not always include issues of justice, and some market participants regard them as less important than environmental priorities. For example, when the volunteer farmers market advisory committee had the opportunity to select a new cooked food vendor, they chose a collective that included Jessica Prentice, the chef described above, whose concept of a community-supported kitchen offering seasonal stews made with farmers market produce embodied, according to market manager Rosalie, "exactly our values." Two of the other vendors the committee had considered were people of color aiming to start small businesses. When describing the selection process, Rosalie conveyed that she and Linda tried to advocate for the inclusion of people of color, but the committee favored Prentice because her food used the most organic and local ingredients. Although Rosalie, herself a white woman from a racially mixed family, was consistently sensitive to thinking about race in the context of the farmers market, she also understood that, for the committee at large, "our values" meant local and organic food rather than diversity.

In another example, when challenged concerning the high cost of organic food, one local celebrity, the featured speaker at a farmers market special event, offered a snappy response. "Just because some people can't afford something doesn't mean that those who can shouldn't have it," she said. "I don't think we need to degrade everything so that *they* can afford it." Her statement clearly places the concerns of nonhuman nature, which she believes is degraded by nonorganic farming methods, over those of low-income people. Moreover, this statement naturalizes the high cost of local organic food while regarding low-income, food insecure people as others whose need for low-cost food is responsible for environmental degradation.

In sum, many participants envision the North Berkeley Farmers Market as a way to improve both environmental and social conditions through green economic exchange. However, environmental themes are prioritized and are thickly interwoven with the farmers market's institutional policies and culture. In addition, many market supporters, most notably the Ecology Center staff, also work to include issues of social and environmental justice. These, however, remain secondary and more partial and are at times contradicted by the speech and behavior of individual vendors and customers.

In West Oakland, the reverse is true. Issues of social and more specifically racial justice are most prominent, as the West Oakland Farmers Market represents an environmental justice approach to the politics of food. Environmental sustainability underlies this market's work — the creation of a local organic alternative food system — but is discussed only occasionally; explicit support for environmental themes is more partial and mixed.

WEST OAKLAND: PRODUCE TO THE PEOPLE

On a Saturday afternoon in the middle of June, the West Oakland Farmers Market celebrated the African American holiday known as Juneteenth. Though it is rarely known outside of African American communities, Juneteenth is a recognized holiday in thirty-seven states. It marks the day, nearly seven months after the Emancipation Proclamation was supposed to have taken effect, that Union general Gordon Granger and two thousand federal troops arrived in Texas to inform the former slaves of their freedom. The holiday's celebration began in 1865 but fell out of favor until it was revived by civil rights leaders in the 1960s.

During this celebration, instead of the usual DJ, market patrons were greeted by a row of musicians lining the entrance to the market. In front of the musicians, two men crouched low, swaying back and forth in time to the music, preforming a cross between dance and martial arts known as capoeira. Capoeira is quite popular in the Bay Area; several schools offer regular classes, and it is often formally or informally preformed at music festivals.

While capoeira is popularly associated with Brazil, market founder David Roach made sure the crowd was aware of its African roots:

This music is from Angola and has been preserved through slavery. Capoeira was a way that slaves preserved their cultures under watchful eyes. Masters mistook for dancing what was really a martial art. Capoeira is also tied to the Yoruba religion and became a way for slaves to secretly perform religious ceremonies. So the practice of capoeira is really a symbol of resistance. Resistance against those who would erase our culture. That's why developing our link to black farmers is so important. Their agriculture is part of our culture, and we need to make sure it continues.

After the music and speech, the crowd wandered out into the market. Many stopped to grab lunch from HuNia's Divine Soul Kitchen. Founded by Oakland native and African American entrepreneur HuNia N. Bradley, who wanted to protect her family from diseases like hypertension and diabetes, this microbusiness provides vegetarian soul food catering in order to "introduce the African-American community to a healthier way of eating." Interestingly, HuNia would later become one of the managers of Farm Fresh Choice, the Ecology Center's food justice program. Market vendors and patrons lunched on barbecued tofu and "fried fish" (a breaded, sautéed soy that tasted convincingly fishy). Side dishes, including ginger yams and collard greens prepared without meat, were sourced from local and organic farms. After lunch, the market returned to its regular pace. Customers strolled from table to table, stopping to shop and get to know market vendors.

The Juneteenth celebration captures many of the West Oakland Farmers Market's important themes. It constructs and celebrates black culture as both resistance against oppression and a tool to promote healthy communities and environments. Unhealthy patterns that plague many urban black communities — including high rates of diet-related diseases and lack of infrastructure and economic development — are described as the result of institutional racism. In response, this farmers market draws on and rearticulates black foodways and farming traditions to imagine other ways of being. Environmental justice activists are traditionally concerned with the disproportionate burden of environmental toxins borne by low-income people and people of color. The West Oakland Farmers Market is in some ways the inverse of this. It is concerned with providing access to environmental benefits — healthy food and public space — through the creation of a local food system.

Resisting Racism through Sustainable Agriculture

The goal of the West Oakland Farmers Market is to address two sets of circumstances resulting from institutional racism: declining numbers of African American farmers and the absence of fresh food in low-income black com-

Farmer Michelle Scott restocks the produce at her family's booth. Photo by David Hanks.

munities. For example, the website of Mo' Better Food, one of the nonprofit organizations sponsoring the farmers market, lists a number of questions that highlight the issues at hand:

> Who grows the food? Who owns the land? Who determines the fate of both? Where does that food go? And who gets it? These simple questions have the same answer: not us!

With this statement and others like it, the West Oakland Farmers Market's literature links the declining number of black farmers to the relative unavailability of fresh produce in West Oakland and similar neighborhoods. This discursive association sets the stage for the market to address these problems simultaneously, creating green economic opportunities for black farmers to supply fresh food to residents of a neighborhood with few other options.

The Last Plantation

In the early 1900s, more than nine hundred thousand black farmers owned over 15.6 million acres of land. By the end of the twentieth century, just eighteen thousand farmers owned only 2 million acres (United States Department of Agriculture, National Agricultural Statistics Service, 1999). While African American–owned farms were disproportionately small farms, and small farms generally fared more poorly in the intervening years than their larger counterparts, size alone cannot explain this decline (ibid.). White landowners often took advantage of the heir property laws that governed landownership in the absence of a clear will, buying black-owned farms at inexpensive prices. Additionally, black farmers were (and are) much less likely than whites to participate fully in government programs and subsidies, either because they were unaware of them or because they were denied some or all of the benefits (Gilbert, Sharp, and Felin 2002). The USDA's racism has been so egregious that the agency is sometimes referred to colloquially as "the last plantation."

Although the overwhelming majority of African American land loss occurred in the rural South, those farmers' descendants are scattered throughout the country. Indeed, southern heritage is so common among vendors and managers at the West Oakland Farmers Market that, as one vendor put it, "If you're not from the South, your parents are." The most prominent market farmers were raised in Oklahoma and Arkansas, and other vendors' families come from Florida, Louisiana, and North Carolina.

In 1997, a class-action lawsuit filed on behalf of almost fifteen thousand African American farmers claimed systematic discrimination by the USDA (Wood and Gilbert 2000). The lawsuit, which the USDA settled, claimed that black farmers were given false information about government programs, denied loans, and given insufficient or arbitrarily reduced loans. Despite this seeming victory, 86 percent of those seeking to claim a portion of the settlement have been denied. Black farmers have complained that the USDA's process through which individuals access their share of the settlement is difficult to navigate, leading to further disempowerment (Black Farmers and Agriculturalists Association 2004). A second lawsuit was settled in February 2010, instituting measures to reform the process through which black farmers and their descendants make their claims. In addition, some evidence suggests that USDA practices have not changed substantially. A 1997 USDA internal audit revealed that contemporary loans filed by blacks were reviewed three times slower than those filed by whites and that black farmers were treated with "bias, hostility, greed, ruthlessness and indifference" (Williams 2002).

The West Oakland Farmers Market features African American farmers, both to support them materially through green economic exchange and to raise awareness of the situation described above. The potential for merging racial politics with sustainable agriculture is recognized by Will Scott, a West Oakland market farmer and veteran of the civil rights movement, who claims, "This market fights the systems that are in place to keep down sharecroppers like my father and grandfather." By linking local food to this legacy of racism, West Oakland Farmers Market participants create a notion of the environment that is deeply intertwined with issues of racial inequality. This approach, like other environmental justice efforts, connects environmental issues to the lived experiences of low-income people and people of color (Bullard 1990; Novotny 2000).

Life in a Food Desert

Traditionally, the environmental justice movement's primary objective has been organizing low-income people and people of color in opposition to the noxious land uses that disproportionately harm their communities. The West Oakland Farmers Market, however, is concerned not with an abundance of environmental hazards but with the lack of environmental benefits such as healthy food and vibrant public space.

Not only have African Americans been stripped of their abilities to produce healthy, culturally appropriate food, they are also unable to purchase these items. When research began in 2005, West Oakland contained only one grocery store to serve its twenty thousand residents. This store closed the following year. On the other hand, the neighborhood contains over forty liquor stores, more than 150 percent of the City of Oakland average (California Alcoholic Beverage Control 2006). These statistics make West Oakland a prime example of a "food desert" (Wrigley et al. 2002).

Dana Harvey, the white codirector of the West Oakland Food Collaborative,[8] whose words are featured in the introduction to this chapter, describes the community's unmet food needs. The grocery store "has poor sanitation and high prices. Many residents rely on convenience stores that do not offer the affordability, quality, and selection of food choices appropriate to cook nutritious meals. For the most part, the convenience stores are well stocked with soda, candy, and alcohol instead of fresh produce and grains." For Dana, healthy food is a benefit that West Oakland residents cannot access through either chain supermarkets or locally owned corner stores. This lack fuels her desire to bring healthy food to the neighborhood through the farmers market.

A typical West Oakland corner store. Photo by Nathan McClintock.

Many West Oakland participants explicitly linked the absence of grocery stores to racism, referring to the process through which supermarkets left urban neighborhoods as *supermarket redlining*. Food First!, an Oakland-based nonprofit food policy organization working to support grassroots food justice activism, defines this phenomenon in the following way:

> Redlining usually evokes images of insurance companies, realtors, and banks refusing to grant fair insurance policies, mortgages, or loans to residents of certain neighborhoods. Now these images include the decaying shells of inner city supermarkets. The supermarket industry has drawn boundaries defining where fresh, nutritious, competitively-priced food is and is not provided for communities throughout the country. (Heany and Hayes n.d.)

From this perspective, racism becomes the cause of scant access to fresh food in low-income neighborhoods like West Oakland, allowing farmers market participants to call attention to the racialized geographies that determine who lives where and who has access to which environmental benefits (Kobayashi and Peake 2000). The farmers market encourages shoppers to respond to this racism through the purchase of green products from black farmers and other vendors. Participants believe that a lucrative farmers market can ensure that

farmers and vendors earn enough income to continue to sell in this neighborhood, making fresh food available in a food desert.

In this vision, it is not the responsibility of the state to provide food when
it cannot be accessed through the market. Indeed, Dana does not even mention food banks or other emergency food programs as possible food sources,
even though many West Oakland residents depend on these programs. Instead,
the community is empowered to respond. Market vendors in particular take
on this challenge, selling their goods at discounted prices in order to improve
access to healthy food. For example Latino/a farmers Sr. and Sra. Garcia[9] sell
certified organic strawberries for $2.50 a box. When I told Sra. Garcia that
they were selling for $4.00 in Berkeley, she replied, "We know. We sell them
cheaper here because people need it."[10] At the West Oakland Farmers Market,
the lack of access to fresh produce is an important part of the local environment, illuminating not only the neighborhood's lack of resources but also the
social processes through which race and class affect access to environmental
benefits.

The farmers market links West Oakland's poor food access to the decline of
African American farmers. As David, the market founder, has said numerous
times, "Why is there fresh food in Latino and Asian communities? It's because
they still have farmers." While it is true that, like African Americans, Latino/s
experience high rates of food insecurity, visitors to predominantly Latino/a
neighborhoods like Oakland's Fruitvale or the Mission in San Francisco will
find many small, Latino/a-owned markets carrying a good selection of produce. More important than his statement's literal accuracy, however, is that it
links African Americans' lack of opportunities to participate in food production to their lack of access to healthy food consumption, and links both to
institutional racism. By framing the West Oakland Farmers Market as a way
to address the effects of racism, market participants integrate environmentalism with justice and pursue both through the purchase of market produce and
other products.

The West Oakland Farmers Market as Racial Performance

The construction and performance of racial identity is an essential feature of
the West Oakland Farmers Market. Indeed, because farmers and other vendors
are predominantly black, and because of the featured foods, special events,
and everyday conversations that infuse this market's atmosphere, it is casually
and commonly referred to as a "black farmers market."[11] Although my survey
revealed that the market draws nearly equal numbers of black and white cus-

tomers, most customers cited support for black farmers as the most important reason for attending the market.[12] This pattern was true for both blacks (59 percent) and nonblacks (45 percent), who are encouraged to celebrate blackness as well. When asked why they support the farmers market, African American market participants offered responses indicating racial solidarity, such as "helping my brothers and sisters." This finding is consistent with both scholarship describing the environmental justice movement, which describes how movement actors often invoke racial empowerment as a resonant frame (Bullard 1990; Pulido and Peña 1998), and sustainable agriculture research demonstrating that customers shop at farmers markets to support "their" local farmers (Hinrichs 2003).

Food, Music, and Special Events

Vendors often market their green products through appeals to black identity and specialize in items that reflect the African American cuisine commonly known as soul food. Farmers cultivate greens, okra, and other vegetables that are staples of this way of eating. When they are available, the Scott Family Farm hangs a large sign that exclaims, "We have black-eyed peas!" This sign reflects the Scotts' perception that this is the kind of food West Oakland residents want to eat. In addition, during a vendor meeting, Mr. Scott further emphasized the importance of soul food cuisine, stating, "The foods that fortified the men and women who built this country were black-eyed peas, okra, and greens." This statement not only invokes soul food but emphasizes the often overlooked role that enslaved blacks played in early U.S. history, interweaving foodways with a racialized consciousness.

Additionally, the Oakland Based Urban Garden System (OBUGS), a nonprofit organization that sponsors cooking demonstrations, emphasizes similar foods. Although the employees who help prepare the dishes are largely white, their most common dish was sautéed greens topped with vinegar, a food commonly associated with southern black cuisine. Other common dishes included barbecued tempeh and African spinach and peanut butter stew, demonstrating a creative take on black cuisine and incorporating pan-Africanism. In this way, the farmers market creates an inventive food tradition, infusing dishes familiar to their African American customers with vegetarian alternatives to traditional high-fat ingredients. Additionally, HuNia Bradley, while a pioneer, is not the only chef promoting vegan soul food. Well-known African American eco-chef Bryant Terry moved from Brooklyn to Oakland in 2007, and several vegan soul food restaurants opened in the first decade of the twenty-first century.

Market manager David Roach
spinning records at the West
Oakland Farmers Market.
Photo by David Hanks.

Nonfood products also help construct this farmers market as a place to create and celebrate black identities. Many black customers are familiar with the
shea butter products sold by Dis_Scent Natural Healing Body Products. Shea
butter is derived from a seed native to Africa and is common in beauty products marketed to African Americans. Indeed, this business's name, coined by its
twenty-something, black, female owners, is based on speech patterns common
to many urban blacks, as well as an allusion to subversive politics. During the
farmers market, the "Hungry DJ Posse," which includes market founder David
Roach, spins soul, funk, reggae and jazz in order to "create an atmosphere that
brings out the community" (Mo' Better Foods n.d.). Much of the music featured is from black artists or speaks to black struggles, but it is often familiar to nonblack customers as well. One memorable afternoon, for example,
Michael Jackson's "Thriller" prompted farmer Leroy Musgrave to moonwalk
down the double yellow lines that run through the center of the market. In

addition, Reggie, a local artist, sells portraits of famous African Americans ranging from Malcolm X to Snoop Dogg. This market's food and music selection comprises performances of blackness, implicitly encouraging black customers to express their own black identities and nonblack customers to celebrate the black community.

Racial consciousness is also displayed in the choice of special events celebrated at the farmers market. In addition to the Juneteenth celebration, special events have included Black History Month commemorations and a fundraiser for the victims of Hurricane Katrina. During the former, the Scott Family Farm set up a display honoring important figures from black history. During the first market of that month, David Roach took a break from spinning records to give a short speech about the history of black farmers, highlighting the contributions of George Washington Carver to American agriculture. Later that day, I noticed that several of the vendors were wearing elaborate ribbons of red, black, and green, the colors of the Pan-African flag. Vendor Charlotte Coleman, a black woman who specializes in homemade jams, had simpler versions of the same ribbons available for purchase. The fundraiser for Hurricane Katrina victims was organized by two African American customers, in conjunction with market managers. These women arrived with a variety of nonfood goods for sale, including T-shirts that read "Kanye was right," referring to rap musician Kanye West's assertion that "George Bush doesn't care about black people." In addition, market manager Jason Harvey (no relation to Dana Harvey) had arranged for a performance of African highlife music, and for catering by HuNia. Like vendors' choices of products, these special events served to emphasize the market's black identity and to integrate blackness into the market's vision of the green economy.

Race and Racism in Everyday Life

At the West Oakland Farmers Market, black identity is not only explicitly constructed and performed through the attention given to the struggles of black farmers and food desert residents and through the selection of products, music, and special events. In addition, black managers, vendors, and customers regularly invoke their racial identities through casual conversations. For example, one particularly warm afternoon, a middle-aged black woman approached Ms. Charlotte Coleman's Pots-to-Jars canned goods stand. "Hot enough for you?" the customer asked. "Better than in Africa," responded Ms. Charlotte (as she's most often called by younger market participants) before going on to discuss, among other things, Al Gore's then–recently released film, *An Inconvenient*

Truth. Although Ms. Charlotte has never been to Africa, this response serves as a way to highlight her blackness and the importance of blackness to this farmers market. In another example, portrait artist Reggie introduced me to an old friend of his, who had come to the farmers market to visit him:

> "I've known this woman for eighteen years," he said to me. "She's like an ancient Egyptian queen. And I'm like _____."
>
> He said a name I didn't recognize, and thus didn't record. But when I asked who it was he replied, "An ancient Egyptian King. He was a powerful guy. They had a lot of power back then."
>
> "We had a lot of power back then," his friend corrected him.
>
> "We gotta get that power back," he continued, "economically, educationally . . ."
>
> "And spiritually, too," she concluded.

Prominent black popular intellectuals such as Marcus Garvey have argued that ancient Egyptians were black Africans but that white society disputes this fact in order to avoid associating the accomplishments of this ancient civilization with blackness (Garvey and Blaisdell 2005). By depicting themselves as Egyptian royalty and referring to ancient Egyptians as part of a collective "we," this vendor and his friend assert their African American identities and reassert the role of Africans in world history. In this way, they perform their black identities through everyday conversation.

Other conversations overheard at the market address individual and institutional racism. For example, one afternoon, three people — one white man and two white women — came to document the farmers market for San Francisco's newly opened Museum of the African Diaspora. One black regular customer was quick to approach them.

> "Why don't you have any Africans taking these photos?" she asked the man.
>
> "It's because the museum is in San Francisco," he answered. He had a strong European accent and may not have understood the implications of her question.
>
> She rolled her eyes and began to question one of the women, who explained, "Even though all three of us here today are white, there are many African Americans involved in planning the museum." She even mentioned a few names that the customer seemed to recognize. With this the customer seemed satisfied, and the two talked cordially for a few moments.

This customer's challenge to the museum employees reflects a history in which African Americans have been the subject of white inquiry and representation rather than participants in conveying their own experience, or, as market founder David Roach has put it numerous times, "Black people are on the table rather than at the table."

Perhaps the most striking discussions of racism occurred on the Saturday immediately following Hurricane Katrina. Market managers and vendors candidly discussed their shock concerning the abandonment and derogatory media treatment of black victims. One vendor referred to this as "proof that racism is alive and well in the United States." Dana, the white codirector of the food collaborative, was concerned for her father-in-law, who was black and lived in New Orleans. During this conversation, three young black boys, perhaps junior-high-school aged, entered the market. When one of the vendors asked who they were, Dana answered, "They look like looters to me," sarcastically referencing the common media construction of African American victims as criminals.

Leroy, an African American farmer, took her remark one step further. "Look at Sally," he said. "She's getting food for her family. Isn't she industrious and hard working? Now look at Leroy. He's looting. Let's shoot him." Not only does this comment decry the injustice of the situation, but by using his own name, Leroy demonstrates his identification with its victims.

Alexandra (Xan) West, an African American female vendor who would later spend weeks volunteering in New Orleans, drew similar parallels between that black community and her own. "If it happened here, people in West Oakland would be left just the way people in New Orleans were," she said. Leroy agreed that Oakland had no plan for how to handle a disaster of that magnitude.

Dana, the only one of this group who had worked on more traditional environmental justice campaigns, added that West Oakland was particularly at risk because of all the toxins remaining from its industrial past. "If that happens," she said, "I'm going to follow Leroy, because he has seeds and he knows how to grow things."

"I'm gonna become a capitalist!" Leroy joked in response, trying to lighten a dark conversation.

Interestingly, Leroy's grim humor reveals that he thinks of himself as something other than a capitalist. While he garners little profit and is constantly in danger of losing his lease on the land he cultivates, Leroy's farm is certainly a capitalist business. The strategies vendors use to create distinctions between the exploitation they associate with capitalism and their own green economic practices offer an important window into how individuals align their social change goals with neoliberal strategies. This theme is taken up in more detail in chapter six.

At the West Oakland Farmers Market, purchasing local, chemical-free food from African American farmers becomes an everyday practice of environmental justice and antiracism. The market atmosphere constructs black identity through food, music, and special events. Everyday conversations also embody the market's dominant themes of race and antiracism. This approach, in which race is invoked to motivate actions that would otherwise be perceived as environmental, is consistent with the environmental justice movement (Novotny 2000; Taylor 2000).

There are currents of environmental justice thinking and activism that aim to confront capitalist exploitation directly. These visions, however, are incompatible with the logic of the green economy and are absent from the West Oakland Farmers Market. Most foundationally, as in North Berkeley, there are no vestiges of eco-marxism, eco-socialism, or similarly radical environmental traditions. Socialism is not something one can vote for with one's dollar, and it is thus outside the vision of justice that farmers markets can create. In addition, the West Oakland market's emphasis on justice might suggest an emphasis on workers' rights. Workers' rights campaigns have a strong tradition in California agriculture (Pulido 1996; Daniel 1981); however, neither the struggles of migrant farmworkers nor workers' rights more generally were mentioned at this farmers market. Indeed, because the market emphasizes the needs of entrepreneurs of small businesses, which implies the absence of nonfamily employees, any potential emphasis on workers' rights or even working conditions is made invisible. The high regard for green entrepreneurship throughout both these farmers markets, and the green economy more generally, encourages its supporters to see themselves as owners, however struggling, rather than workers. Lastly, the green economy created by farmers markets produces a vision of social justice that at worst opposes and at best ignores the entitlement programs that function as an (albeit diminishing) safety net for low-income people. The notion that a more just society can be brought about through the buying and selling of particular goods is antithetical to the provision of basic needs outside of market exchange. Market founder David Roach has even argued that federal entitlement spending could be better used to support small business development.

The West Oakland Farmers Market creates a vision and everyday practices of social justice that can be realized through the green economy. For the most part, their strategies and goals are also compatible with environmentalism, though this theme is much less prominent than in Berkeley.

Environmentalism in West Oakland

The West Oakland Farmers Market creates a local food system that develops a consumer base for black, chemical-free farmers. While its primary emphasis is on racial inequality and identity, some limited attention is paid to the environmental benefits of this endeavor. Farmers have at times spoken about their opposition to GMOs, alluding to the same concern for biodiversity evidenced in North Berkeley. Nonfood vendors, such as the women who make soaps and other body products, tout their goods as natural, plant-based alternatives to those available at grocery, drug, and liquor stores. It is this attention to environmental as well as racial issues, that makes the West Oakland Farmers Market an example of just sustainability rather than only of environmental justice.

The kind of wilderness aesthetic common to the North Berkeley Farmers Market can also be found in West Oakland, although here it is not officially incorporated into market discourses and practices. Market farmer Leroy Musgrave, for example, describes organic agriculture in terms that resemble those of North Berkeley farmers. "I came from Arkansas. I started doing what I'm doing now when I was four years old. Now, they call it organic farming, but actually it's just trying to get as close as possible to nature." Leroy can often be heard describing the beauty of his farm and the river that runs through it. His self-published book of poetry (Musgrave 2005), which he sold at the farmers market, included the following short poem:

WATERMELONS

Give melons a good
Watering just before
New moon of July
The vines will grow under the filling moon
They need the water there in earth
When their Spirit runs and fills its belly with seeds.

In this poem, the cultivation of food fosters a spiritual connection to the earth. The imagery of a pregnant melon drawing in water supplied by the farmer to create the next generation of life offers farming as a path toward a life lived in harmony with, rather than in opposition to, biological life cycles. Through his presence at the West Oakland Farmers Market, Leroy provides the environmental benefit of local, organic food and also encourages low-income people of color to connect to the earth through their eating practices. Thus his approach

West Oakland farmer Leroy Musgrave on his farm. Photo by David Hanks.

to farming fuses environmentalism with environmental justice and seeks support for both through the green economy.

Similarly, Communities United Restoring Mother Earth (CUREME) is a home-based business and education project that sells herbal medicine. Its proprietor, Iyalode Kinney, distributes a pamphlet describing her goals in the following way:

> Through our need for progress and wealth, we have become
> GREEDY AND DESTRUCTIVE
> We are killing ourselves, our children, our future
> OUR MOTHER EARTH
> We must remember the old ways before the end.
> Communities United Restoring MOTHER EARTH, CUREME,
> is our remembering the beginning.

On her small property in Richmond, the predominantly low-income African American neighboring city to which she moved when extensive termite damage caused her to sell her West Oakland home, Iyalode cultivates numerous species of botanicals and then creates salves, oils, and perfumes from them. She also offers free classes in herbal medicine. Like Leroy's organic farming and poetry, these practices and the ideology they reflect invoke themes common to the environmental movement. However, Iyalode's embodied presence as a black woman, and her desire to use her ecological knowledge to enhance the health of the low-income African American community in which she spent the bulk of her life, fuses that knowledge with racial empowerment. And again, she pursues both environmental and environmental justice goals by selling products in the green economy.

West Oakland participants also evidence the notion that firsthand experience with local landscapes and creatures inspires support for environmental sustainable living. Ms. Charlotte, who specializes in jams, infused vinegars, and other preserves, described her experiences procuring local food.

> We used to go crabbing underneath the Golden Gate Bridge, and sometimes in Pacifica. One time, I was out there in the pouring rain, and I didn't have a rain hat, but I had just had my hair done and I had a plastic garbage bag over my head. And I thought to myself, either I'm crazy, or I must really love being out here. And it's fun to be out there with the water and all the people.

Later, Ms. Charlotte discussed her knowledge of crab varieties and support for sustainable practices.

> You're not supposed to take the market crabs, the Dungeness crabs, but there are red crabs and brown crabs and they're just as good. Brown crabs are all brown with black claws. Some people don't have any respect for the environment and just take anything. They even take the tiny crabs, and I'm thinking "throw that one back, he needs to grow up."

Ms. Charlotte's joyful experience of directly engaging with nonhuman nature, as well as her knowledge of ecologically sound harvesting, resembles the philosophy embodied by the North Berkeley Farmers Market.

The West Oakland Farmers Market does not, however, emphasize local resource conservation and waste reduction practices to the extent that its North Berkeley counterpart does. Only one garbage can is present; recyclables and compost are not sorted and are sent to the landfill. Although samples from the cooking demonstrations are served on reusable dishes, other prepared food is distributed in foam and plastic packaging. While the produce is chemical-free, the cooked food sold by local entrepreneurs, which has included barbecued chicken, ribs, cookies, and pies, rarely contains organic, free-range, or local ingredients as they do in North Berkeley. In addition, nonfood vendors are present in West Oakland. More typical of flea markets than farmers markets, these individuals are encouraged to sell clothing, trinkets, and used books because of the market's commitment to encouraging local entrepreneurship.

JUST SUSTAINABILITY IN THE GREEN ECONOMY

The North Berkeley and West Oakland Farmers Markets support both environmentalism and environmental justice by promoting green products. In North Berkeley, managers, vendors, and customers commonly argue that local organic food decreases the need for pesticides and fossil fuels. North Berkeley Farmers Market participants tend to draw upon wilderness preservationists' idealized images of nature to depict market farms as beautiful, spiritual, biologically diverse landscapes with which urban dwellers can connect through the consumption of organic food. Some managers, vendors, and customers also evidence strong support for environmental justice concerns, such as farmworkers' rights and food access, while others believe those issues to be less important than strictly environmental ones. In West Oakland, on the other hand, race and racism are the farmers market's central themes. This market aims to address two instances of institutional racism: discrimination against African American farmers and the lack of access to healthy food in urban black communities. The market reflects an environmental justice approach because it links racial empowerment to access to environmental benefits. Some attention is paid to more traditional environmental concerns, but everyday discourses most explicitly frame the purchase of produce as support for racial empowerment and local economic development. Thus, while both farmers markets enact Julian Agyeman's notion of just sustainability, they emphasize the aspects most commonly associated with their neighborhood's social location.

Both the West Oakland and North Berkeley Farmers Markets have, by design, conceived creative green economic practices that participants believe will further environmentalism and social justice. The North Berkeley Farmers Market certainly prioritizes environmentalism. However, had the Ecology Center not sponsored Farm Fresh Choice, and had individual participants not evidenced support for farm workers' rights and increased food access, the market might merely supply environmental benefits to its wealthy patrons. If that were the case, the green economic exchange promoted by this farmers market would advance environmental protection while increasing inequality. It is only because the Ecology Center staff and other participants view both environmentalism and justice as paramount that they have created ways for their farmers market to incorporate issues of inequality. However, their strategic choice to pursue these goals through the green economy prevents more radical streams of environmentalism, such as deep ecology and eco-socialism, from informing the vision they create. Similarly, if West Oakland Farmers Market managers, vendors, and customers were concerned solely with inequality, they may have adopted strategies other than a farmers market. Instead, they created a project that pursues the racial and economic empowerment of black farmers and West Oakland residents through the creation of a local, organic food system. This strategy fuses justice with sustainability. However, their reliance on green economic practices to pursue their goals limits their approaches to those consistent with neoliberalism. Vendors are constructed as entrepreneurs rather than workers, and there is no demand that the state provide adequate food.

These findings stand in contrast to previous scholarship, which tends to regard just sustainability as an all-or-nothing proposition. In other words, earlier work views environmentalism and social justice as either inherently compatible or inherently contradictory (Agyeman, Bullard, and Evans 2003; Sandler and Pezzulo 2007). Examining efforts to create just sustainability through everyday practice reveals instead that bringing these goals together with one another, as well as with economic growth, requires the imagination and active work of actors on the ground. While the farmers markets themselves promote discourses and practices that pursue justice and sustainability, not all participants in each farmers market favor both sets of priorities. Efforts to create justice and sustainability through green economic exchange certainly dominate each market, but they are also sometimes contested by participants who feel that one goal is more worthy than the other.

The next two chapters focus on the tensions and compromises that characterize each farmers market's efforts. Chapter 5 explores market participants' discourses and practices of building community as a lens through which to investigate how race, class, and gender affect who is and is not included in efforts to achieve just sustainability. Chapter 6 investigates market participants' understandings of how local economic exchange can foster social change. This chapter also includes instances in which economic goals cannot be reconciled with environmental and justice priorities, a tension that market managers, vendors, and customers generally attempt to ignore.

Chapter 4 has examined the visions and practices of justice and sustainability produced by managers, vendors, and customers in each farmers market. It draws from participants' worldviews to offer a new understanding of just sustainability as a set of diverse and uneven discourses and practices. The following chapters deconstruct participants' worldviews to explore more deeply the relationships between environmentalism, justice, and identity in the green economy.

CHAPTER FIVE

Who Participates in the Green Economy?

We like what happens socially at the farmer's market, which is quickly
emerging as the new public square in this country. If you compare
what happens in the aisles at the grocery store with the farmer's market,
think about what a world of difference that is. People politic. They
have petitions. They schmooze. It's just an incredibly vibrant space.
> — MICHAEL POLLAN, "Beyond the Bar Code: The Local
> Food Revolution"

No matter how casually it is used, then, the notion of community
may be doing sociological and ideological work — work that ranges
from simply reinforcing the status quo to challenging systems of
oppression. . . . Collectivity and exclusion are two sides of the same
coin. . . . Community is the coinage.
> — GERALD W. CREED, *The Seductions of Community:*
> *Emancipations, Oppressions, Quandaries*

To spend an afternoon at the West Oakland Farmers Market is to be surrounded by hugs, handshakes, and other expressions of familiarity. Many vendors and customers know each other by name and exchange familiar greetings. David Roach, the market founder, stresses the importance of this face-to-face interaction as a key purpose of the farmers market: "People come there to talk. They might buy just a little food, but they know each other. They sit there, listen to the music, and they'll talk for a long time. [They'll see] somebody else who they haven't seen in a long time." Examples of this kind of community building were common when I attended the market. One afternoon, an elderly black man named Kofi approached Jason, the market manager, telling him he had recently met his mother. "And now I've seen David at the market with his father and realized I know him too," Kofi continued excitedly. He then became a regular customer, spending many Saturday afternoons talking with the farmers and other vendors.

Similarly, one afternoon in North Berkeley, a white high-school student walked through the market with headphones on. "Hi, neighbor," said a tall white man, tapping him on the shoulder. The boy took off his headphones and smiled at the man, and then waved to the infant the man carried on his back. They continued to discuss the man's family, the boy's school, and the upcoming SATs. Nikki, the Chez Panisse chef who visited an area farm to plan a supper club, described the North Berkeley Farmers Market as "the most tangible community I have access to." Of the one hundred customers surveyed at each farmers market, 38 percent in West Oakland and 28 percent in North Berkeley reported seeing friends and neighbors every or almost every time they visited.

A VIBRANT PUBLIC PLACE

These are the kinds of practices that farmers market proponents, including popular writers like Michael Pollan, draw on to envision farmers markets as vibrant public spaces (2006; see also McKibben 2007). Market proponents believe that by buying and selling to one another, neighbors will become acquainted and develop relationships. This narrative evokes what Raymond Williams calls the "warmly persuasive" connotations of the term *community* (1975, 76). The desire to create social ties through face-to-face interaction at farmers markets is rooted in, and responds to, a nostalgic notion of "community lost" embedded in influential strands of U.S. social thought.[1] According to this perspective, urbanized, industrial society is inherently alienating, and the good life can be found only in small, rural towns (Park 1925; Wirth 1938; Lofland 1998). This "community lost" narrative is commonly invoked by conservative politicians lamenting the loss of traditional values, as Sarah Palin has done through references to the "real America." Conversely, it colors the thinking of the back-to-the-land movement and agrarian authors. Wendell Berry, for example, the farmer and poet to whom Michael Pollan dedicates *The Omnivore's Dilemma*, writes that "A proper community . . . answers the needs, practical as well as social and spiritual, of its members — among them the need to need one another" (2006, 63). It is this degree of interaction and interdependence with known people that many observers believe is missing from urban lifestyles. Romantic notions of community, coupled with nostalgic assertions that it has somehow been lost, prompt farmers market participants to interact in ways that simultaneously construct and claim this unquestioned good.

For proponents of farmers markets, creating community is not only socially fulfilling but a part of their efforts to create just sustainability. While some advocates of the green economy seek to reduce the ecological footprints of large organizations such as Wal-Mart, many believe their environmental and social goals can be achieved only by the replacement of massive corporations with small, locally owned businesses. According to this logic, local supply will reduce the ecological impact of transporting goods and local control will ensure a diversity of enterprises. Additionally, this way of thinking holds that local green businesses will be directly accountable to their neighbors, who can ensure that they meet the highest environmental and social justice standards (McKibben 2007; Pollan 2006).

Farmers markets become sites through which this sense of community is enacted, in part, by invoking a sense of ruralness represented by farmers themselves. For example, one afternoon in West Oakland, African American farmer Will Scott spoke with an African American customer, both of whom had been raised in Oklahoma. "When I was younger, there was a farm family and they had eleven sons and two daughters," the customer told the farmer. "They supplied all of our food. We didn't have Safeway." By becoming acquainted with Mr. Scott, she creates an urban proxy for the rural community she describes. Similarly, Daniel, a white regular customer who lives just a few blocks from the market, expresses his appreciation for the relationships he has developed with both farmers and neighbors: the farmers market is "a point of community connection. . . . The numbers of people that I've met that live here locally or even the farmers. Leroy [a market farmer] and I have developed a friendship that I never would have anticipated from going to the market to buy food. It's been extremely rewarding." By becoming acquainted with their neighbors and local farmers, urban customers can create a notion of community grounded in face-to-face interactions and more often associated with rural life. Twenty percent of West Oakland customers surveyed claimed that they were acquainted with vendors or managers prior to attending the market, and an additional 42 percent reported becoming acquainted through their participation.

North Berkeley customers and managers also value their relationships with farmers. One afternoon, a farmer and a customer, both white men, exchanged a particularly pleasant greeting. They asked about one another's families in ways that were even more intimate than the warm conversation that typically colors this farmers market. The farmer later explained that the men had seen each other at Yosemite National Park the weekend prior to the market and had enjoyed the chance to get to know one another outside the market setting. While only 6 percent of the North Berkeley market shoppers surveyed knew

Farmer Will Scott sorts produce to put out at the West Oakland Farmers Market. Photo by David Hanks.

managers and vendors prior to attending the market, 24 percent report having become acquainted through their attendance. In a tragic example of these important connections, Rosalie, a market manager, reacted to a farmer's suicide by erecting a small altar in the space where her stand had been. Customers left vegetables, stones, and other trinkets as a memorial to the farmer. For many customers, this farmer was not just a service provider but also a fond acquaintance. This informal ritual suggests that North Berkeley Farmers Market participants develop meaningful relationships with one another, creating community through their consistent if casual interactions.

Some farmers encourage customers to meet their neighbors by sharing food, fostering the notion that rural people understand community while urbanites must work toward it. For example, toward the end of the market day, Jeff, a white male North Berkeley vendor, offered a white woman customer a complimentary third set of greens in addition to the two she'd already bought.

"I'll just waste it," she answered, turning him down. "It's a good way to meet your neighbors," he responded, implying that she could pass the gift on to those living near her, "but I guess that's hard in the city." Through this conversation, Jeff constructs himself as the rural bearer of a sense of community and tries to impress its virtues upon his urban customer. In addition, several West Oakland customers responded to an open-ended survey question with praise for the market's "small-town atmosphere" and the ability to "build a rapport with farmers." These results also depict community as a "small-town value" available to urban residents at the farmers market.

Farmers market participants tend to emphasize a place-based sense of community that, despite their urban settings, invokes the romantic imaginary of rural small towns. Community, in this sense, indicates direct, personal, face-to-face interactions with others sharing the same public space. But, as anthropologist Gerald Creed (2006) contends in one of the epigraphs introducing this chapter, community is about both collectivity and exclusion; an in-group must define itself in reference to an out-group. Locally based identities are often constructed through race (Haynes 2001), class (Walton 2001), and lifestyle (Rosenbaum 2007). In this sense, community can also be thought of as a common identity, a set of imagined "impressions of a thinking and feeling that 'we belong together'" (Blokland 2003, 209), rather than mere co-presence in the same physical space (see also Gusfield 1975; Hunter 1974; Suttles 1972).

Community membership is not equally granted to all who arrive at each farmers market. In West Oakland, race is the most obvious attribute that includes or excludes someone from the market community. Blacks are immediately regarded as insiders, although nonblacks who perform respect for the market as a black space are also welcomed. However, this emphasis on race masks concerns about class, gender, and lifestyle that also serve to include or exclude participants in the farmers market community. In North Berkeley, on the other hand, market participants acknowledge that community members are more easily accepted if they perform a countercultural lifestyle. The present-day incarnation of Berkeley's countercultural past is less strident than during the 1960s but remains supportive of leftist causes and a so-called natural or hippie aesthetic. The focus on lifestyle allows participants not to see the ways in which race, class, and gender are deeply intertwined with farmers market participation.

Understanding who feels themselves to be, and is considered by others, a part of the farmers market community has important implications for participation in the green economy. After all, not only do farmers market participants co-create a warm, friendly atmosphere, but the market also gives them access to high-quality food. In addition, many participants in each of these farmers markets feel a strong sense of belonging and, by selling or shopping there, come to define themselves as people who care about the environment, their community, and social justice. They develop what Horton (2003) calls "green distinction" through the performance of green identities in everyday life, but especially through the buying and selling of goods. Those who feel like outsiders to the communities these farmers markets create, on the other hand, are subtly excluded from participation in the green economy and from access to the economic, environmental, and social benefits it can bring.

RACE (AND CLASS, GENDER, AND LIFESTYLE) IN WEST OAKLAND

The West Oakland Farmers Market is constructed as a "black market" by managers, vendors, and customers, evidencing what Mary Patillo-McCoy (2002) calls both reactionary (responding to racism) and nonreactionary (celebratory) racial consciousness. As described in chapter 4, choices in featured foods, music, and other events demonstrate a particular performance of black identity. While West Oakland contains growing populations of Latinos and whites, the farmers market's community building practices emphasize blackness. These practices can be read as a deliberate reaction to the pervasive whiteness in local food system activism (Slocum 2006; Guthman 2008a, 2008c) and to racial oppression in general.

David, the market founder, is a strong proponent of equating the West Oakland Farmers Market's community with the black community. His nonprofit organization, which holds the permit and insurance for the market, distributes an online newsletter called "Feeding Ourselves." "Ourselves" does not refer to West Oakland residents; the food featured at the market, while local compared to food available in supermarkets and liquor stores, is not grown in the neighborhood. Rather, it is grown by African American farmers. David further stresses the importance of a link between black farmers and the black community by asserting that other low-income communities of color have healthy food available because there are farmers from those communities to provide it. When he claims that the absence of available produce in West Oakland is because "our farmers are so few," the *our*, again, refers to African Americans. Even the name of David's nonprofit (The FamilyHood Connection) and its food justice campaign (Mo' Better Foods) reflects the African American community in which it operates through the use of African American linguistic idioms.

Sociologist Elijah Anderson (2011) describes two orientations through which African Americans regard racial interaction in public places. He argues that an "ethnos" approach emphasizes loyalty to one's own group as defined by ascribed characteristics such as skin color. In contrast a "cosmos" perspective highlights individuality and achievement. Anderson is careful to note that these orientations are not mutually exclusive, and that most blacks "code switch" depending on how they read, and are read in, a particular situation. In the examples above, David demonstrates an ethnos approach to the farmers market.

This ethnos approach is attractive to black customers, approximately half of whom travel from more racially integrated neighborhoods and relish this chance to be in a place that celebrates black identity. For some, the market is a place to buy foods not commonly found at other farmers markets, such as okra or purple hull beans. In this way, the market is reminiscent of the re-emergence of interest in soul food in the 1960s. During that time, many blacks used food to proclaim their own racial authenticity (Wit 1999). More than half of the West Oakland customers surveyed listed support for black farmers and businesspeople as their primary reason for farmers market attendance, and many black survey respondents referred to the market as "more culturally comfortable," in the words of one man, than other Oakland farmers markets. If racial identification is a process rather than a biological absolute (Omi and Winant 1986), then participation in the farmers market can be seen as a path through which individuals embody and perform their own blackness. Previous studies have found that racial identities can be produced by environmental justice activism (Sze 2006) and by association with racialized places (Haynes 2001). By attending the West Oakland Farmers Market, black customers whose lives may otherwise embody a more "cosmos" perspective perform their identities as a part of the black community.

Many scholars, most notably feminist women of color, have noted that antiracist struggles produce identities other than racial ones (Moraga and Anzaldúa 2001). For example, many black feminists argue that the black identity produced by the civil rights and black power struggles was implicitly masculine and heterosexual (Hull, Scott, and Smith 1982; Robnett 1997). By defining the market community as black, participants produce a narrative about what blackness is, which in turn shapes who is and is not attracted to the farmers market. Because it works to create a local food system, a strategy most often aligned with forces deemed countercultural or left of center, the West Oakland Farmers Market largely attracts customers with this worldview. Besides their connections to the Black Panther Party described in chapter 3, vendors have participated in a variety of political activities ranging from the civil rights movement to local antigentrification campaigns to protests against international development agencies such as the World Bank. Through the West Oakland Farmers Market, participants cultivate a collective identity that is both explicitly black and rooted in leftist social movements.

This leftist political orientation is also evidenced through casual conversation during the market. For example, Tola, a young African American woman raised in West Oakland, reacted strongly to one of Reggie's portraits of African American celebrities. "What's that doing here?" she asked rhetorically about a painting of Condoleezza Rice. "This is a black market. We don't want to see that." For this woman, Rice's politics make her a figure that, despite her heritage, does not belong at the market. Tola constructs the West Oakland Farmers Market community as both black and politically left, demonstrating how an "ethnos" orientation can intersect with "cosmos" identities such as political affiliation.

Moreover, the West Oakland Farmers Market features many elements of the countercultural food movement. For example, Leroy Musgrave of Goodfoot Farm can often be overheard giving herbal medical advice. While herbal medicine has long been practiced by Africans and African Americans (Covey 2007), Leroy's prescriptions give the farmers market a "new-age" feel, despite the fact that the new-age community is often perceived as white. Even the market's emphasis on supporting black, chemical-free farmers closely parallels the food movement's focus on small, organic farmers. Additionally, mobilizing the green economy to address injustice, by encouraging people to spend money to help those who are struggling, further amplifies the farmers market's political ideals. This particular construction of black identity as aligned with leftist counterculture provides an avenue through which nonblacks, while not a part of "the community," can still play important roles in the market.

Identity without Exclusivity: Roles of Nonblacks in a "Black Market"

Despite its focus on black identity, the West Oakland farmers market draws nearly equal numbers of black and white customers, as well as smaller numbers of Asian and Latino/a shoppers.[2] While celebrating black identity is the market's central theme, participants are careful not to explicitly exclude other potential customers. David, the market founder, explains the relationship between blackness and inclusivity using a metaphor that draws from another progressive social movement.

By saying "African American farmers" you limit yourself to the support of other farmers as well, and it's not like we're anti-farmers. We're for all small farmers, but we have just been wanting to say, for example, that "Save the Whales" doesn't mean you don't like other fish. It's just that you're letting the public know that there's a crisis here. . . . The whales are dying. The whales are getting shot at.

In this excerpt, David tempers his "ethnos" orientation with a more "cosmos" sensibility.

Similarly, when I asked an African American vendor how she understands David's and others' description of West Oakland as a "black market," she responded with the following comment: "I think what he means is that it's for the people in the community that are still majority black. I don't think he means that it's just for us. I think we're putting it on for us, but everyone is welcome." While their approach allows for nonblack participants, it maintains a concept of the community the market seeks to build as black.

Again, nonblack vendors have participated in the market. The most prominent of these were Bertenice and Jose Garcia, a Mexican couple who sold strawberries and other produce. One of the Mo' Better Foods newsletters highlighted their contributions to the market, claiming, "They come because they know we need good food." Whereas the African American farmers are part of the col-

Farmer Bertenice Garcia and her husband Jose sell strawberries at the West Oakland Farmers Market. They are considered important allies by market managers. Photo by David Hanks.

lective "we" who are "feeding ourselves," Latino/a farmers are defined as allies. Similarly, while Latino/as make up 12 percent of the market customers surveyed and 16 percent of West Oakland residents (Alameda County Department of Public Health 2005), food, music, advertising, and special events are not aimed at this population.

Some nonblack customers do, however, feel closely connected to the market. During an interview, Daniel, the farmers market's steadiest white customer, describes the roles he feels he can play. "I can go and give them [the vendors] my money. I mean, more than they ask sometimes. I can go and work on Leroy's farm sometimes just 'cause I want to. I can go be a positive member of a black community and contribute something good to it without taking away from its blackness." By evidencing a desire to help struggling businesses and alluding to the joy of volunteer farm work, this customer highlights a connection to the market community based in a shared countercultural worldview. Through relationships such as the one that developed between Leroy and Daniel, the farmers market bridges its "ethnos" and "cosmos" orientations.

Contesting Community

While whites are appreciated as customers, other roles are more closely contested. For example, Daniel is a musician. Jason, the market manager, had invited him to play music during a black history celebration. When Daniel arrived, however, guitar and amplifier in tow, David asked him not to play, claiming that it was inappropriate to feature a white musician at this particular event. Jason was disturbed by David's decision, evidencing conflicting social constructions of community. A mixed-race black and white man who describes himself as "two-thirds oppressed and one-third oppressor,"[3] Jason suggests that the term *community* is often used to denote blacks in situations where overtly racially specific language would draw accusations of black nationalism. In other words, he believes that through the word *community*, some West Oakland market participants feign a more socially acceptable "cosmos" perspective rather than revealing their "ethnos" approach.

> The word [*community*] gets thrown around so much, in my opinion, at the farmers market because it's a disguised word. I can talk about something in a very general sense and layer it with other coded words so when I'm talking to you about it, you know exactly what I'm talking about. But if I were to just say that I'm doing this solely for this specific group of people, then, you get called a racist and all these other words that bring out so much emotion. But if you can just say *community*, you're disguising it.

In a compelling example of the very phenomenon he describes, Jason uses the phrase "this specific group of people" to denote blacks.

Perhaps the most prominent example of tensions between "ethnos" and "cosmos" definitions of community involved the dissolution of the West Oakland Food Collaborative (WOFC). Codirected by David Roach and Dana Harvey, a white food and environmental justice activist, the collaborative worked to develop a local food system in West Oakland and provided funding to support and expand the farmers market from 2003 to 2006. Its most ambitious goal was to found a worker-owned cooperative grocery store. During this process, however, David and several others felt that Dana was playing too strong a role, and they withdrew from the collaborative. Several collaborative members explicitly voiced that blacks should instead shoulder some of the responsibilities she had taken on. Dana, who is married to a black man and mother to four mixed-race children, consistently attended the farmers market, largely playing an unofficial managerial role. In several instances, arguments between Dana, David, and vendors aligned with each of them disrupted the market's celebratory atmosphere, eventually causing many of the vendors to withdraw. Notably, vendors did not take sides along racial lines. With the exception of the Garcias, all of the regular vendors are African American, and roughly half of them sided with Dana.

This conflict exposed the competing definitions of community at play in the market. David discursively coded the market community as black by using racialized language to describe the situation. The market, he claimed, had been "colonized" by the collaborative. Working within a white-led organization was "like being a black man in America because people are trying to keep you down." By describing the conflict in this way, David marks himself as an African American community insider while criticizing whites not only as outsiders but as exploiters.

By contrast, for two African American West Oakland vendors, Xan West and Jada White, race is relevant but not the sole marker of insider status. They draw a distinction between market participants paid by nonprofit organizations, including David, and those struggling to make a living through the market. "NGOs get so caught up in foundation funding that they don't really pay attention to the communities they are supposed to serve," Xan lamented. "Then there are all these turf wars between the NGOs, and the community gets marginalized." Rather than assuming that David's blackness makes him part of the community, these vendors imply that he profits at the community's expense. While these vendors identify as coming from middle-class backgrounds, they draw boundaries around a community in-group based on income, arguing that

TABLE 3
Demographic Comparison of West Oakland and the West Oakland Farmers Market

	WEST OAKLAND	FARMERS MARKET
Black	77%	33.7%
White	9%	39.5%
Latino/a	15%	9.2%
Asian/Pacific Islander	9%	5.1%
Percent completing college	11%	48.7%
Percent earning below $35,000/year	45%	34.2%

Sources: West Oakland demographic profile and author's survey data.

those who get paid for their nonprofit work are different from those for whom they advocate. Their "cosmos" perspective, however, is tempered by their use of racialized allusions to describe the situation. "From being colonized," said Jada, "[David] learned that power was something to hold on to and defend, rather than share." While the presence of racial imagery suggests just how deeply racial identity characterizes the market, these vendors display a notion of community rooted in both race and class.

Bringing Class and Gender Back In

The market's dominant focus on black identity works surreptitiously to marginalize class differences not only between vendors and NGO employees but also between market clientele and West Oakland residents. In other words, the identities performed at and conferred by the West Oakland Farmers Market are not only explicitly black and dedicated to just sustainability but also implicitly middle-class. Sixty-five percent of black customers surveyed live outside the neighborhood and are much wealthier and more highly educated than local residents. Eighty-two percent of black customers surveyed hold college or postgraduate degrees. Sixty-four percent live in households earning more than $60,000 per year.[4] Interestingly, white customers are more likely to be from West Oakland (41 percent), less likely to have a college or graduate degree (61 percent), and less likely to live in households earning more than $60,000 per year (23 percent). White customers who are West Oakland residents tend to be in their early twenties and to have lived there for relatively short periods of

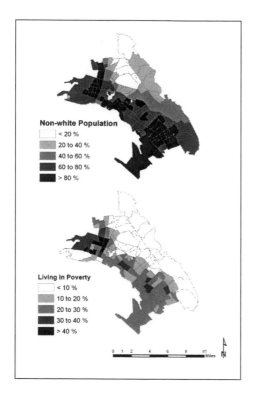

Maps of Oakland by race and percentage living in poverty. Created by Nathan McClintock.

time. Despite their lower incomes, their speech and mannerisms imply middle-class backgrounds. West Oakland is rapidly gentrifying, and many of the market's white customers are young artists who see the neighborhood as a cheaper alternative to San Francisco.

In contrast, the neighborhood's median household income is $23,366, and only 14 percent of residents hold a bachelor's or advanced degree (Alameda County Department of Public Health 2005). Only three of one hundred survey respondents identified as black, from West Oakland, and earning less than $30,000 per year. The market managers' and vendors' emphasis on race makes these class discrepancies less visible.

Some vendors and managers are aware of the discrepancy between their clientele and local residents. When asked by a customer if the market was reaching "the community," Xan and Jada, the two vendors described above, immediately said no. "Activists aren't asking what the community wants," Jada explained, asserting that local concerns were more focused on police brutality. "If you want someone to go to your meeting on Thursday, you'd better be doing their laundry on Wednesday," Xan added, implying that it is the responsibility of food justice activists to work with local residents to encourage their participation. Vendors and managers have tried unsuccessfully to address this gap. For example, one nonprofit sponsored cooking and science demonstrations, which drew a number of local grade-school-aged children but failed to draw their families as customers.

Class-based tensions among African Americans are, of course, not new and are evidenced by other studies of the black middle class (Haynes 2001; Poe 1999). Neither is this the first time that class tensions have played out in debates and campaigns related to food. What is commonly called "soul food" is often traced to the so-called slave diet, which included discarded parts of animals consumed by slave owners (but see Carney 2010). Diet was one mechanism through which urban blacks distinguished themselves from poor African American migrants as they immigrated to northern and western cities. Black nationalist leaders have urged a departure from traditional "soul food" cuisine because of its connotations of filth (Poe 1999). The 1960s saw an interest in soul food among the black middle class, though radical leaders sometimes criticized such a diet as bourgeois slumming (Cleaver 1969; Wit 1999).

Neither is this the first time that gender has been ignored by activists focused on racial empowerment, a theme common to the writings of many feminist women of color (Hull, Scott, and Smith 1982; Moraga and Anzaldúa 2001; Robnett 1997). Women are disproportionately poor and more likely to populate predominantly black, underserved communities, in part because black men have considerably shorter life expectancies and are more likely to be incarcerated (Gilmore 2007). West Oakland Farmers Market managers and vendors seem largely unaware that the overwhelming majority of low-income, black West Oakland residents they seek to serve are women and children.

The marginalization of class and gender issues provided a useful frame for Dana Harvey, the white activist described above, to continue her work toward the establishment of a worker-owned cooperative grocery store. She defined the community her work sought to build in a way that epitomizes the "cosmos" orientation, highlighting class and willingness to work against social and economic inequality. The worker-owners, who include several African Americans but also Latino/as and whites, began by operating a farm stand at a nearby senior center, where they resold produce grown by both black and white small farmers. In the summer of 2008, just as the West Oakland Farmers Market was closing, the cooperative procured a space just across the street, and Mandela Foods Cooperative opened. It tends to draw a predominantly young, white

A worker-owner at
Mandela MarketPlace.

customer base but provides an important source of income as well as shared ownership and managerial control to its worker-owners.

Originally drawn to the West Oakland Farmers Market by an interest in black nationalism, Jason moved toward a more "cosmos," multiracial definition of community as well. The most important thing, he said, is to support "farmers who have some kind of social justice frame, who are willing to take a hit [financially] and hang in for a while" in order to build demand in low-income communities. Jason eventually left the farmers market to found the Oakland Food Connection, a nonprofit organization sponsoring school garden and food service programs in Jason's native East Oakland. Though he currently employs two African American program associates, many of the student interns he has hired have been Southeast Asian or Latino/a.

In addition, Dana cultivated close relationships with several older female African American vendors, claiming that their talents and dedication to the market were previously overlooked in favor of younger, "hipper" male activists. Many of their discussions focus on the need to provide healthy lives for their children, echoing a frame used by many environmental justice activists (Brown and Ferguson 1995). In addition, Dana has begun to purchase food for her farm stand and store from a white woman farmer, who, she argues, also faces increased obstacles. Dana and those who side with her define the community economically and politically, and they incorporate a gendered perspective rather than focusing on race.

But minimizing the importance of race is particularly problematic in a place like West Oakland, whose very geography is shaped by racial oppression. It is not only poor neighborhoods but particularly African American neighborhoods that experienced redlining, were bulldozed by federal projects in the name of urban renewal, and now contain few places to buy fresh fruits and vegetables (Morland et al. 2002; Self 2003; Rhomberg 2004). Dana's approach serves to redraw the community boundaries with her inside, which is in some ways fitting considering her indomitable dedication to food justice in West Oakland. At the same time, this approach denies the realities of racism and serves to re-entrench the dominance of white cultural practices (Frankenberg 1993; Kobayashi and Peake 2000). In one example, the white woman farmer who had begun to supply produce to the food co-op spoke at a 2006 fundraiser for Oakland Food Connection. During her talk, she argued that life in general was better during her grandparents' time. Xan shot me a troubled look, and I saw several other audience members exchange glances. While the farmer was referring to life before the advent of processed foods, invoking a narrative common to the writings of Michael Pollan and Wendell Berry, she neglected to realize that her grandparents' time occurred during Jim Crow, and that most of her audience would have been subject to a host of racial exclusions and violence. Mandela Foods Cooperative has since decided to work primarily, but not exclusively, with farmers of color.

In sum, the West Oakland Farmers Market creates a community centered around a leftist, food- and eco-conscious, African American green identity, subverting a potential intersectional perspective incorporating class and gender (Collins 2000 [1990]). Lack of attention to class and gender enables middle-class blacks and nonblacks to be deemed community insiders, which yields them a vibrant public space and access to one of the neighborhood's few sources of fresh produce. The absence of the low-income African Americans in whose interest the farmers market began, the majority of whom are women and children, is sometimes lost amid this emphasis on race. Low-income people are therefore not integrated into the farmers market community, and their nonparticipation in this local green economy, as well as their continued lack of access to the environmental benefit of fresh food, often goes unnoticed. Other efforts attend to class and gender but resort to a color-blind approach that obscures historical and present-day racial oppression.

LIFESTYLE (AND RACE, CLASS, AND GENDER) IN NORTH BERKELEY

At first glance, North Berkeley Farmers Market participants seem to have a more inclusive, cosmopolitan notion of community than the multiple and contradictory definitions evidenced in West Oakland. This farmers market community, quite simply, consists of the vendors, patrons, and market managers who comprise the farmers market. In other words, the community is anyone who participates in the local green economy the market creates.

Perhaps the most obvious commonality among many of these individuals is a knowledge of or interest in some form of counterculture, which underlies the green cultural scripts that develop and inform casual conversation. The characterization of local food systems as a way in which urbanites can connect to and preserve beautiful, biodiverse local ecosystems, as described in chapter 4, invokes a sort of new-age spirituality. Geoff, a white regular customer, described the community as "hungry people . . . and also the soil, the air, the land" necessary to produce food. This response indicates the inclusiveness that characterizes explicit definitions of the market community as well as its countercultural roots.

As described in the introduction and previous chapter, the North Berkeley Farmers Market invokes an agrarian, back-to-the-land ideal embodied by the writings of authors such as Wendell Berry and Michael Pollan. This narrative brings together a nostalgic admiration for small farms, a spiritual reverence for biological cycles, and an individual moral imperative to turn away from cultural forces that it claims separate humans from nature. In fact, books by these and similar authors are often prominently displayed at the Ecology Center's information and product sales table. Less well known but similar local authors, such as Mike Madison (2006), have been featured at North Berkeley Farmers Market special events. The food movement's roots in the 1960s back-to-the-land movement also serves to link the Berkeley market to the counterculture.

Participation in the contemporary countercultural scene often creates connections between vendors and customers. For example, recall the farmer and customer described earlier in this chapter who had seen each other hiking in Yosemite National Park.[5] Vendors, managers, and customers have often visited the same places, volunteered for the same organizations, and attended the same events, and they often know people in common. Those who have participated in the counterculture are more likely to share these experiences and will more easily feel comfortable at the farmers market. These patrons are more likely to have the cultural knowledge necessary to deploy the proper green scripts and to define themselves as the kind of people who choose to support small farmers and the local environment. As in West Oakland, inclusion in the farmers market community can promote participation in this local green economy, ensuring access to the environmental benefits contained there, including a vibrant public place, connection to local landscapes, and access to high-quality organic produce.

Race, Class, and Gender in a Gourmet Market

The countercultural agrarian ideal invoked by the North Berkeley Farmers Market is raced, classed, and gendered in very traditional ways. While West Oakland participants also invoke a kind of agrarian nostalgia, the popular writings of the agrarian authors cited in North Berkeley implicitly interpolate white family farmers rather than black sharecroppers or immigrant farm laborers. In this way, the North Berkeley Farmers Market's seemingly "cosmos" notion of community masks an unconscious "ethnos" approach. Wendell Berry's writings, for example, tend to romanticize a preindustrial era, ignoring the circumstances of people of color at that time (1990). And Michael Pollan's instruction to eat the way our great-grandmothers did, which is the first of his 2009 *Food Rules*, presumes that "our" great-grandmothers were free individuals with access to the foods they considered culturally acceptable.

Additionally, the small family farm idealized by agrarian writers often maintains traditional gender relations. For example, Joel Salatin, the hero of Michael Pollan's *Omnivore's Dilemma*, advertises two-year-long apprenticeships on his Polyface farm website. The apprenticeships "offer young men the opportunity to live and work with the Salatins." Beginning in 2007, the farm will also offer an additional part-time, three-month summer internship to "six young men." The photo that accompanies this text depicts fourteen young white men in matching shirts, all of whom have been interns between 1995 and 2005. Polyface calls itself a "family farm," and, according to its website, both men and women family members work there full-time. However, it is only Joel who is profiled in Pollan's book and who can be hired to speak publicly for a three-thousand-dollar honorarium (Polyface Farms n.d.). While Polyface Farm is in Virginia rather than Northern California, Michael Pollan is both widely read and occasionally spotted by Berkeley farmers market customers, and he was the keynote speaker at the Berkeley Farmers Market's twentieth anniversary celebration in 2007. I have never heard him challenged, either directly or in discussions of his work, for idealizing a farm with such a traditional approach to gender. Additionally, authors like Pollan and Berry idealize the heterosexual, two-parent family much the way conservative politicians do, with the (presumably unintended) consequence of opposing women's empowerment and failing to acknowledge queer perspectives and experiences (Coontz 2000). Pollan has even laid responsibility for the rise in convenience foods at the feet of working women, without acknowledging the economic realities that necessitate dual-income families (Clark 2010) or the fact that the so-called second shift of housework falls disproportionately to women (Hochschild and Machung 2003).

While North Berkeley market managers, vendors, and customers rarely discuss the raced and gendered nature of this agrarian ideal, some do recognize that social class limits market patronage. Nearly one-third of North Berkeley clients I surveyed have household incomes over $100,000 and 78 percent have earned college or advanced degrees. Two-thirds live in North Berkeley, a neighborhood with a median home price of over $700,000. In West Oakland, opposing notions of community based on race, class, and locality led to conflict among market participants. In North Berkeley, however, the wealth and whiteness of the clientele, as well as the neighborhood itself, cohere to produce a notion of green identity that is implicitly affluent and white. This exemplifies what geographer Rachel Slocum (2006) means when she writes that when white bodies cluster around property and privilege, they become viscous, covering the space and coding it as white. This process, she argues, can subtly preclude low-income people and people of color from participation in the farmers market community and the local green economy this community creates.

Affordability

Rosalie, a white, female North Berkeley market manager in her late twenties, described the farmers market as "somewhat of an exclusive community [because] if you don't have the money to come to the farmers market" you will not be a part of it. She does claim, however, that this exclusivity is somewhat ameliorated by "gleaners" who arrive near the end of the market to receive reduced prices on or donations of produce that farmers cannot resell the next day. While some gleaners are individuals procuring food for themselves and their families, others, as described in previous chapters, are a part of Food Not Bombs. Each evening, as the market closes, two white men in their early twenties arrive on bicycles, towing large carts behind them. Their torn, black clothing, sometimes held together by patches and safety pins, signifies their countercultural identities. When they leave, their boxes are filled with pounds of produce; farmers tend to donate everything that will not last for future markets. This food is then brought to various collective houses, where other volunteers prepare and distribute it at nearby Peoples' Park. The food also provides a substantial part of these collective houses' grocery needs. While this opportunity for discounted food is something rarely available in traditional grocery stores, it is also dependent on relationships between the gleaners and farmers, who often share racial, class, and countercultural identities. Although many gleaners are low income, they tend to be college educated and politically leftist individuals choosing not to pursue more lucrative careers. In this way, gleaning introduces a broader spectrum of incomes but reinforces notions of the farmers market's community as white, middle–class, and countercultural.

Affordability is a somewhat contentious topic at the North Berkeley Farmers Market, as I learned when I told a white, male vendor that six dollars for half a dozen eggs was beyond my price range. "People don't like to pay," he responded angrily, "but at Safeway, you pay later. You pay for it with your health; you pay for it with the kind of culture you create." While he claimed not to blame consumers of agribusiness products, his response expresses no sympathy for low-income people. "Instead of talking about low wages and other constraints," he said, "we need to rethink the percentage of our budget that we spend on food. Only when people are willing to pay for it will our relationship with the land become more sustainable." In this response and other similar statements I heard during my fieldwork, North Berkeley shoppers are regarded as ethical because they are willing to pay the high cost of local organic food, with no acknowledgment that they must also be wealthy enough to do so. In addition, structural factors such as wages are ignored, and the consumption of organic food is reduced to an individual choice.

This vendor's response is no doubt colored by his economic need to sell what he produces. However, market customers whose rational self-interests presumably lie in keeping prices low offer similar, if less charged, versions of the same argument. Commonly, customers respond to questions about food access by emphasizing the need for education. Jordan, for example, a white man, offers the following response:

> The thing is you have to educate people. And whether folks want to take the time or are willing to listen, that's the question. You know one concept that's helpful to talk about is price versus cost. The price being what you pull out of your wallet and hand to the guy for a bag of apples, and the cost being the political cost, the

environmental cost, the cultural cost . . . the things that come back and bite you
on the butt two years later. People don't think about those. Those happen some-
where else, in the landfill or in Central America. . . . Those things are behind the
screen of the TV set.

When pushed to think about issues of access rather than education, which
was the original question, Jordan responded by probing the spending habits of
low-income people.

People who complain about the price of some of the items, I'll bet you a hundred-
dollar bill, are out there spending money on all kinds of crap that frankly doesn't
taste that good but looks cheap. If they stopped buying it all, and added it all up,
they could afford to buy some decent food.

This statement problematically sees access to expensive, local, organic food
as a result not of income or other structural inequalities, but of individual
choice. And although this statement was made several years before debates
about restricting the autonomy of food stamp and other entitlement recipients
to choose their own foods, it is easy to see how its logic provides support for
that position.

Many market participants respond to similar concerns by offering the kind
of analysis of the political economy of agriculture that Michael Pollan so elo-
quently lays out in *The Omnivore's Dilemma*. The problem is not that organic
food is too expensive, the argument goes, it is that conventional food is unrea-
sonably cheap. While this critique rightly alludes to the huge subsidies the federal government gives conventional agribusiness, of which market managers,
vendors, and many customers are well aware, it ignores the financial concerns
of low-income people. Many North Berkeley market participants also espouse
an apocalyptic view of the corporate-dominated food system. As market manager Max told an African American customer in response to her questions
concerning the high price of market food, "When we hit peak oil and have
to pay the true cost of food, organic and local will be the same or cheaper."
By dismissing immediate financial needs in favor of lofty moral values, this
explanation avoids a relevant class critique, reinforcing the notion that a local
green economy is the province of those who can afford it. It also reaffirms the
liberal worldviews of market participants, charging them with the education of
those who do not understand the "true" nature of the industrial food system
while attributing lack of access to ignorance rather than material inequalities
(Minkoff-Zern 2010).

White Markets, Race Matters

Issues of class do emerge in the farmers market, albeit problematically, through questions of affordability. The relationship between whiteness and market participation, however, which also works to identify the market as a site of environmental privilege, is almost entirely ignored. More than three-quarters of market customers surveyed (77 percent) identified as white. But attending only to the proportion of whites that frequent the market deemphasizes the important role that people of color do indeed play in this market. One of the four Ecology Center staff members is Chinese American, and another is mixed Latina and white.[6] Five of the approximately twelve year-round vendors, though only two of the farmers, are people of color as well. In an attempt to minimize the market's predominant whiteness and environmental privilege, managers celebrate the "diversity" that does exist, emphasizing, for example, the large number of languages spoken by vendors.

The North Berkeley Farmers Market constitutes a white space not simply because of the preponderance of white patrons, but because the green identities and community construct acted out in this market embody a set of cultural practices that reflect white histories and present-day realities. According to Guthman (2008a), farmers markets "conform to white ideals" by exhibiting what Frankenberg describes as a cultural dimension of whiteness. White American culture "carries with it a set of ways of being in the world, a set of cultural practices often not named as 'white' by white folks, but looked upon instead as 'American' or 'normal,'" or, in this case, countercultural (Frankenberg 1993, 4). Although participants understand the establishment of a local food system as a way to question and resist a number of practices associated with what they call "mainstream" or corporate-dominated culture, whiteness remains unnamed and therefore largely uncontested. Because race and class are intimately related, this cultural whiteness reinforces (and is reinforced by) the practices and performances of the market's affluent and highly educated patrons. The intersection of whiteness and affluence subtly works to construct the North Berkeley farmers market community as a site of race and class privilege, as well as of the environmental privilege that provides access to landscapes and green goods not available in other communities (Park and Pellow 2011). This constellation of privileges can deter the participation of low-income people and people of color.

At the North Berkeley Farmers Market, gender also reinforces the market's race and class identity. Nine of the twelve farmers and prepared food business owners who regularly attend the market are men.[7] In fact, when reacting to the

The North Berkeley
Farmers Market is a
popular destination for
mothers and children.

farmer's suicide mentioned above, Rosalie lamented the loss not only of her personal connection but also of "one of our only woman farmers." Customers, on the other hand, are disproportionately women with young children. Many vendors and customers' descriptions of the market align with Rosalie's statement that the market is "Kid mania! All the moms come with their kids." Mothers often planned to meet each other at the farmers market so that one could watch the children while the other shopped. An informal "mom's group" consisting of about five women used the farmers market as their weekly meeting place in the spring.

The presence of so many mothers and children genders the market, underscoring the traditional association of food provisioning as women's work. Moreover, the mothers who bring their children to this weekday afternoon market appear to be predominantly middle class and white, which is not surprising given the strong correlation between whiteness and income in the

United States, and presumably either do not work outside the home or have flexible work schedules. This clustering of race and class privilege reinforces the farmers market as an affluent and white space.

Perhaps the most pervasive example of the North Berkeley farmers market's white culture is the association between local organic and gourmet food as described in chapter 3. Elite restaurants and celebrity chefs feature prominently in the literature promoting farmers markets. This theme is particularly strong at the North Berkeley market due to its location near many of Berkeley's elite eateries. And although the neighborhood features cuisines from many parts of the world, the most renowned restaurants employ the "California French" tradition pioneered by Alice Waters in the 1970s. Not only do neighborhood restaurants tend to have European influences, they are also quite costly, providing an example of the mutually reinforcing interaction between whiteness and affluence.

The farmers market's informal association with the Italy-based Slow Food movement also works to characterize it as affluent and white. Slow Food's website describes its goal as "to counteract fast food and fast life, the disappearance of local food traditions and people's dwindling interest in the food they eat." Like the vendor described earlier, this organization emphasizes individual choice in decision making, rendering invisible the experiences of those who make food decisions based primarily on need. Members of the Slow Food movement seek to identify "old world" foodways, which broadly indicates European culinary traditions, as a counter to what they see as a degraded, global fast food culture (Gaytan 2004). One regular customer can often be heard talking to farmers about her participation in the local *convivia*, or chapter, and two market farmers attended the organization's 2006 conference in Italy. People of color are much less likely to be able to reach back to their European roots to provide or construct food traditions that fit within this narrative, and may thus be discursively excluded by the North Berkeley Farmers Market's reverence for things European. Additionally, given the strong correlation between race and class, many people of color are unlikely to be able to be a part of this farmers market community, and through it to participate in the local green economy, simply because they cannot afford it.

Another striking absence from the North Berkeley Farmers Market is that of the predominantly Latino/a migrant farmworkers who populate and cultivate the fields of California agriculture. Farmers do hire workers to sell at the market, but these individuals are largely young, white, and college educated. Some lived on the farms as volunteers, interns, or apprentices and regard farmers markets as an opportunity for paid work. Others lived in or around

Berkeley, and farmers markets comprised their only agricultural employment. In contrast, 97 percent of California agricultural laborers are foreign born (Philpott 2008).

In addition to the physical absence of these workers from the farmers market, there are several ways in which the literature describing local and organic food serves to metaphorically erase this group from the image of community that farmers markets construct. The market's directive to "build community with the people who grow your food," as one manager put it, emphasizes connections between farmers and consumers but ignores the laborers performing much of the actual cultivation. Indeed, the food movement's reverence for small, family farms mistakenly convinces many customers that market farmers do not employ nonfamily labor when nearly all of them do. In addition, while all of the food at the North Berkeley Farmers Market is local, those who cultivate it are not. Farmers markets' emphasis on the local obscures the difficult, costly, and sometimes even deadly journeys of those who travel thousands of miles in order to produce the food found there (Alkon and McCullen 2010). The physical and metaphorical absence of low-income people of color who are integral to the creation of a local food system combines with the presence of white, predominantly affluent customers and middle-class vendors to construct the farmers market as a white space, revealing its unspoken but powerful "ethnos" orientation.

In sum, North Berkeley Farmers Market participants' visions of community make it a ripe setting for the performance of green countercultural identities that are implicitly raced, classed, and gendered. Market participants' explicit desires to create community hide deeper layers of meaning that constrain the participation of working-class and nonwhite potential consumers in the green economy. While many market participants recognize that income can limit participation in their market, they predominantly characterize this as a reflection of individual choice rather than structural constraints. Moreover, participation in this farmers market can also be seen as a process of racial formation, though, as is common to whites, race is learned and performed in implicit yet powerful ways. Participating in farmers markets comes to be seen as something that affluent white people do, as is reflected by the inclusion of farmers markets on Christian Lander's well-known satirical list of "stuff white people like" (2008). Associations between farmers markets such as this one and notions of affluent whiteness can subtly preclude the presence of even those people of color who can afford the farmers market's high prices, minimizing their ability to reap the benefits of participation in the green economy.

Emphasizing Social Justice: A Challenge to Environmental Privilege

Despite the pervasiveness of affluent whiteness in the North Berkeley Farmers Market's discourses and practices, there are some ways in which participants work to integrate social justice concerns. For example, lower-income market participants often mock the farmers market's elite, gourmet character, as Rosalie does when she characterizes it with invented terms like "shnitzy" and "glam-o." Additionally, those employed by farmers to sell at farmers markets describe this as the "most service oriented" of any farmers market they sell at. "People really expect to be waited on here," said Jeff, a young white man who works for Blue Heron Farm. Both managers and farm employees have confided that they prefer other markets where the clientele is more racially diverse and less well-off. One employee, who had recently taken a Challenging White Supremacy workshop, even described his practice of charging people of color lower prices. Farm owners, on the other hand, have described North Berkeley's customers as more "enlightened," in the words of one, because they are willing to pay high prices for food.

North Berkeley market managers also work to discursively mark the absence of both farm laborers and food insecure people. Recall, for example, market manager Linda's statement emphasizing farmworker issues in describing how sustainability plays out in the farmers market. Additionally, managers stress that farmers market profits go to support the Ecology Center's food justice program, Farm Fresh Choice, which works to raise awareness of the relationship between institutional racism and food insecurity. Using a frame that emphasizes race, Farm Fresh Choice adopts a discourse similar to that of the West Oakland market. "We're not serving the community, we're serving *our* community," stated Tiffany, the program's African American director. In a personal conversation, she described the process of hiring a codirector. Nearly all of the applicants were white. With the full support of the Ecology Center, she insisted on running the program alone until a "qualified person of color" could be found (eventually hiring a Latino man). Support for the activist priorities of people of color represents a strong antiracist stance through which the Ecology Center creates space for people of color to participate in, and reap the environmental and health benefits of, the local green economy.

Many North Berkeley Farmers Market participants who emphasize the importance of social justice ideals continue to promote high-priced local organic food for those who can afford it. Christina, a white female farm employee who also volunteers for a food justice organization, described her frustration with a customer who complained about the high cost of the food. "She had one of those big, six-dollar bottles of Pellegrino under her arm," she told me. Todd, a white man employed by his aunt and uncle at the stand next door, overheard us and agreed. "What I really love is when they're holding their four-dollar Starbucks latté, but they complain about the price of fruit," he said sarcastically. These examples differ from the previously described vendor because they acknowledge the customers' ability, rather than mere willingness, to purchase local organic food. These employees understand that the food they sell is not accessible to everyone, but they expect those with enough disposable income to afford luxury food items to prioritize supporting small organic farmers. Programs such as Farm Fresh Choice are expected to fill the gap between high cost and food access for low-income consumers and are often referenced by North Berkeley market managers when questioned about the high cost of market produce. However, one African American market customer suggested that such programs are stigmatizing. "Why do we need a program?" she said when informed of Farm Fresh Choice. "Why can't it just be affordable?" As supplements to the farmers market, these programs do nothing to resist the pervasive environmental privilege that characterizes the North Berkeley Farmers Market, which works to code the green economy as racially and economically exclusive.

COMMUNITY IN THE GREEN ECONOMY

Popular writing promoting farmers markets tends to highlight their ability to create local community among those who inhabit the same locale. In that community, individuals espouse and reinforce each other's support for everyday green economic practices such as the production, distribution, and consumption of local organic food. Both the North Berkeley and West Oakland Farmers Markets explicitly work to create a sense of community grounded in face-to-face interactions. However, market managers, vendors, and customers engage in green performances that implicitly define their community with regard to race, class, gender, and lifestyle. These definitions affect whether and how various groups can imagine themselves as a part of the farmers market community and as the kinds of people who participate in local green economies.

In West Oakland, community building practices emphasize blackness, though nonblacks are also accepted in a variety of supporting roles. However, an implicit alliance with leftist counterculture makes the market palatable to middle-class blacks and nonblacks rather than to the low-income, food-insecure West Oakland residents on whose behalf it was founded. In using race as the litmus test to determine insider and outsider status, market participants fail to address the economic disparities between their clientele and local residents, and therefore to recruit low-income West Oakland residents to take part in the green economy. West Oakland Farmers Market participants also emphasize race at the expense of gender. Given the feminization of poverty, gender could act as an important lens through which to view the struggles of food-insecure West Oakland residents. Some participants challenge the West Oakland Farmers Market's emphasis on race, explicitly relying on political orientation, economic need, and gender. These efforts, however, often fail to account for the paramount role that race plays in shaping the economic and environmental conditions faced by low-income blacks in neighborhoods like West Oakland.

In North Berkeley, community is explicitly defined as all those attending the farmers market. Community building practices draw on the relationship between sustainable agriculture and 1960s counterculture, as well as on Berkeley's history of radical politics. Participants often invoke an agrarian ideal that, while emphasizing progressive opposition to large corporations, also embodies traditional notions of gender and ignores the histories and lived realities of people of color. Some participants do acknowledge that income limits participation in the farmers market community because of the high price of the food sold there. But while many are concerned with class as well as racial diversity, market participants fail to interrogate their implicitly affluent and white performances. Attention to social justice represents something of a challenge to this pervasive affluent whiteness, but fails to explicitly discuss racial and economic inequalities. In this way race and class continue to subtly inform who sees themselves as a part of the farmers market community and thus who participates in its green economy.

Many progressives have embraced the "warmly persuasive" connotations of the term *community* since the social justice struggles of the civil rights era (R. Williams 1975; Gusfield 1975). Creed (2006) argues that *community* became a substitute for the term *culture* after the latter was critiqued as essentialist. *Community*, however, can also essentialize diverse groups of actors and mask within-group power differentials based in race, class, and gender. Claims of community cannot be taken for granted and must be deconstructed to reveal the multiple and sometimes conflicting meanings that can contradict explicit definitions. Analyzing the discourses and practices used to create community in each farmers market helps explain why they attract the customers they do. In each farmers market, participation in the green economy is limited to the middle-class individuals who see themselves as a part of the farmers market community and who can deploy the proper green cultural performances.

Restrictions on low-income peoples' participation in the green economy are not only cultural but also economic. The next chapter explores and deconstructs the frameworks through which farmers market participants align justice and sustainability with local economic exchange. It examines how market participants come to see the green economy as an appropriate strategy for social change goals and analyzes the ability of this strategy to challenge environmental degradation and racial and economic inequality.

CHAPTER SIX

Greening Growth

I really have a lot of faith — and I know that it's considered naive
by some people on the left — that consumers can change things.
I have seen too many cases of what happens when consumers decide
to inflect their buying decisions with their moral and political values.
It brings about change.

— MICHAEL POLLAN, *Progressive* magazine, November 2008

To be sure, it is necessary for individuals to struggle to organize their
lives so that in their consumption they live more simply and ecological.
But to lay too much stress on this alone is to place too much onus on
the individual, while ignoring institutional facts.

— JOHN BELLAMY FOSTER, "Global Ecology and the Common Good"

The Ecology Center, which manages the North Berkeley Farmers Market, is a nonprofit organization seeking to facilitate urban lifestyles that contribute to ecological sustainability, social equity, and economic development. In a letter to its members, director Martin Bourque described the relationship between the farmers market and these goals. "The Ecology Center measures our success on the success of the small family farmers who grow our fresh fruits and vegetables all year long," he said. By shopping "at the Berkeley Farmers Markets, you're safeguarding a way of life while feeding yourself: protecting family farms and rich topsoil." Bourque depicts buying from the North Berkeley market farmers as a way to ensure environmental sustainability (healthy topsoil) and the economic viability of small businesses (family farms). Moreover, when market managers refer to the Ecology Center's food justice endeavor, Farm Fresh Choice, as the farmers market's "sister program," they imply that support for the farmers market contributes to social justice as well. Profits from the farmers market are used to subsidize the availability of healthy produce in lower-income Berkeley neighborhoods. Broad social goals become a rationale for farmers market purchases.

Several months later, West Oakland Farmers Market founder David Roach emailed a similar message to his constituents. In it, he described the need to purchase food grown by black farmers.

> In our efforts to re-develop a direct connection between Black farmers and [residents of the] East and West sides of Oakland, we ask that you shop weekly at the Mandela Farmers Market. I cannot tell you how gratifying it is to see the same people each and every week, rain or shine, supporting our farmers, by shopping at our market.

As in North Berkeley, customers come to the farmers market not solely because they want to buy a product, but also because they believe in the market's social and environmental goals. Through the purchase of local organic food, customers are asked to ensure the livelihoods of struggling farmers and vendors, which in turn provide environmental and social benefits. Additionally, West Oakland customers are asked to help sustain the market itself so it can continue to provide for a food-insecure community.

THE LOGIC OF SUPPORT

Activists explain their embrace of the green economy through a set of discursive strategies emphasizing the ethics of sustainable consumption while eliding instances in which economic, environmental, and social goals remain at odds. Primarily, they justify this strategic choice through what I call the *logic of support*. This narrative emphasizes the environmental and social benefits of green products and compels consumers to ensure the economic viability of producers through their purchases.

In order for this logic to cohere, proponents of local green economies such as farmers markets need to separate the kind of capitalism they aim to create from the critiques of big business that continue to dominate progressive activism. Through this process, they provide a strong example of what economic sociologists call a moral system of exchange (Biggart and Dellbridge 2004). In this system, ethical values, rather than cost-benefit analyses of products and prices, are the primary drivers of economic activity.[1]

Human Need Not Corporate Greed

Farmers markets such as those depicted in this book often describe their vendors as primarily concerned with providing services to their communities rather than garnering profit at all cost. This narrative contrasts vendors with large corporations, which are personified as ruthless and greedy. Indeed, farmers market participants' indictment of corporations taps into a spirit of resistance that has fueled global protests against the World Trade Organization, International Monetary Fund, and World Bank. Drawing on and extending the work of political economists, political ecologists, and world-systems theorists, anti–corporate globalization activists highlight the ways in which international lending institutions have imposed neoliberal policies that force poor nations to eliminate protective tariffs. This practice destroys local markets while increasing opportunities for multinational corporations, including agribusiness. People throughout the global South must then compete for low-wage jobs producing commodities whose profits accrue to corporate headquarters in rich nations. For many supporters of farmers markets, the anti–corporate globalization movement's slogan, "Another world is possible," represents a vision of local communities in which members provide many of one another's needs in a just and sustainable manner, without exploiting other communities and environments. This vision, according to market participants, can be partially fulfilled at farmers markets. Given this approach, it is not surprising that Linda, a mixed Latina and white market manager, describes the North Berkeley Farmers Market in the following way:

> [The market is] a way to counter the corporate globalization that's going on really fast right now by creating a local economy where the money that you put into your community goes back into the community and not some corporation that wants to take your money away.

According to this logic, negative consequences of capitalism — including the concentration of wealth — are attributed only to large corporations. Farmers market participants view local green economies, on the other hand, as motivated by concern for local people and place and therefore able to provide a less destructive, less exploitative alternative to environmental destruction and human exploitation. This narrative elides any recognition that local economies still engage in capitalism, as well as discursive histories of the local as a site of exclusion (DuPuis and Goodman 2005).

In West Oakland, participants similarly align the farmers market with local communities in opposition to large corporations. Dana, the white activist who convened the West Oakland Food Collaborative, articulates this logic:

> [The West Oakland Farmers Market is about] finding a way to make a living in a community from our own innovation and talent. Building a network within the community, which is equal to building a community that takes care of each

other's needs. We can self-sustain outside of the dominant system. I feel like all the systems around us are breaking down. Trying to build a community where we're focused on health and morals and values and neighbors instead of consumerism, and how to build that and make it self-sustain.

[Our] consumerism isn't profit driven. It's more meeting needs driven. And it's true, we are trying to get each other to consume. And we do want to buy and sell from each other. But I think it's more on a scale of more, if we consume in a way that helps us sustain our neighborhoods or our communities, that's different than consuming in a way that sustains a megabusiness that's separate and distinct from us. I think our bottom line is a little different. It's not all profit motive.

Like many farmers market participants, Dana views local economies as motivated by "health, morals, and values," while she characterizes other types of capitalist exchange as not only destructive but fated to collapse.

Even the mission statements of businesses themselves emphasize differences from large corporations. For example, Dis_Scent Natural Healing Body Products bills itself as "the end of dependence and the beginning of resistance." In its literature, the company's founder, Xan West, a mixed-race African American woman, describes its goals:

> On the real, we ain't bout capitalism or wage-slavery but we are about freein us (and others) from an oppressive system which says that our work has to make someone else rich. We bout owning the means of production, teaching people how to free themselves from reliance, and getting people some real natural healthy-ish.

Readers familiar with the writings of Karl Marx will recognize some of the phrases Xan uses, such as *wage slavery* and *the means of production*. Xan's language is a product of more than a decade of radical activism of various forms. And yet if forced to label it, Xan would describe her political worldview as anarchist rather than socialist. Her goal is not to create a strong state capable of restraining corporate power, but to construct a self-reliant DIY (do-it-yourself) alternative. Additionally, although Xan recognizes the contradiction inherent in trying to have an anticapitalist business, she mentally separates her own work from capitalism by emphasizing her desire to take care of herself and her community and to survive without becoming alienated from her own labor.

Similarly, during a meeting of West Oakland managers and vendors, several speakers conveyed a belief that the moral nature of their work was consistent with their economic success. Farmer Will Scott said, "The purpose of the market is to bring valuable product to this community. We come here not only to sell our wares." A moment later, manager Jason Harvey offered similar sentiments:

> We all want to present something good to the community," he said. "But we all want to make money. . . . Bottom line. All their food is gone (glancing at the Scotts), money in y'all's pockets (indicating the rest of the venders), community served.

These statements depict selling quality products as a way to serve a community.

This logic of support, in which local business is cast as providing an essential community service, contributes to a worldview that sees the local green economy as means to social change. Indeed, creating entrepreneurs is one of the explicit goals of the West Oakland Farmers Market. Founder David Roach is a former high-school business teacher and was heavily influenced by Booker T. Washington's model of black empowerment through economic development. David promotes local entrepreneurship because he believes it can create a vibrant local economy in which both commerce and employment can occur.[2] He describes the farmers market as "a way to get your business started outdoors, and we're working to get you indoors" — that is, more permanently established. The West Oakland Farmers Market seeks to create local entrepreneurs in order to empower West Oakland residents to depend on one another rather than on the dominant, corporate system Dana describes above.

According to participants in each market, growing numbers of community and environmentally minded local entrepreneurs can provide a competitive challenge to corporate capitalism. Kirk, a middle-aged white man who works as the North Berkeley market special events director, deploys the anticorporate discourse described above. "We do not want to see our food supply controlled by corporations," he explained emphatically. "They're blowing it in so many other ways and they already control so much of the food supply!" Farmers markets such as the one in North Berkeley allow him to participate instead in what he depicts as an anticorporate food system. "I can know where [my food is] coming from so that I don't have to be a part of that," he continued, "so that I can find an alternative to that and feed that [alternative]." Kirk envisions his farmers market purchases as diminishing corporate control of the food system and supporting ways of farming that are more sustainable and just. By attributing only to corporations the destructive qualities that previous generations of activists assigned to capitalism, Kirk and others who share this point of view align farmers markets with their social change goals.

Even more utopian is the belief, held by many farmers market participants, that local green entrepreneurs will eventually force destructive corporations out of business. For example, one African American West Oakland customer described the motivations behind her own entrepreneurial goals. "Everyone has to put out a product," she said excitedly. "That's how we're gonna beat the big boys and overthrow the corporations. We need to put out a product!" While this may seem naive, market participants' confidence in the superiority of their products, as well as the commonly shared belief that the industrial food system is fated to collapse, yields a worldview in which market demand will inevitably shift to locally produced products. This is precisely the revolution through attrition promised by the natural capitalists described in chapter 2.

Many participants in the North Berkeley and West Oakland Farmers Markets subscribe to a worldview in which support for green producers, through the purchase of local and organic food, creates an alternative economy advancing social and environmental goals. Through this narrative, the survival and success of green businesses becomes essential to the creation of just sustainability.

Sacrificing for the Cause

For the most part, farmers market proponents describe the creation of justice and sustainability through the green economy as a joyful thing, as it encompasses not only social change goals but also high-quality food and the formation of community. This portrayal differs greatly from accounts of social movements as sites of struggle and sacrifice. Think, for example, of the contrasting connotations embodied by Alice Waters's "Delicious Revolution" and social movement theorist Francesca Polletta's evocation of drudgery in *Freedom Is an Endless Meeting*. And yet, proponents of farmers markets do evoke a narrative of sacrifice in their characterizations of farmers and other producers. These producers are described as ethical individuals who willingly forgo more lucrative careers to work at the farmers market, thus bringing the joys of fresh food, community, and ethical consumption to urban dwellers. In West Oakland, customers and managers attribute additional regard for vendors who willingly sell at this less profitable market. This narrative of sacrifice further constructs the idea of the markets as distinct from exploitative forms of capitalism and aligns the green economy with social change goals.

For market managers and customers, the decision to farm organically reflects a willingness to forgo more lucrative financial opportunities to contribute to the larger social good. When I asked market manager Herman Yee to describe his decision to work for the farmers market, he said he wanted to better understand "the practical side of farming, what it takes to run the farm as far as, for example, business and marketing and how to stay afloat as a farmer, because it's hard to make a living." While some farmers have confided that they're able to live middle-class lives, others stress the financial difficulties of farming. When asked why she farms, one young woman farmer, who comes from a wealthy family, replied, "I think probably all of us do it [because] we gain some deep emotional satisfaction from it. Because we certainly don't make any money. We don't make shit."

Ted Fuller of Prather Ranch meats, who often laments his own financial woes, described the homes of several of the other farmers. One farm couple "doesn't live in a big house," he said. "They live in a small one." Another couple "lives in a trailer." The owners of another farm confided that they had experienced intense financial difficulties, including operating at a loss and losing bank financing. These statements strongly contradict a widely held U.S. belief linking economic gain to moral virtue. Long ago identified by Max Weber in his *Protestant Work Ethic and the Spirit of Capitalism*, this belief informs right-wing support for tax and other policies favoring wealthy elites. It also supports the existence of social sanctions against public discussions of financial struggle, particularly among those who are or aspire to be middle class. And yet for market farmers, the greater virtue lies in the kind of proclamation of economic hardships Ted conveys, as they support the farmers market's narrative of sacrifice. In contrast to U.S. mass-media depictions of low-income people as unworthy takers of government "handouts" and responsible for a host of social problems, struggling farmers portray themselves as forfeiting lucrative careers in order to provide quality products that embody sustainability and justice. This sacrifice narrative also serves to reinforce the market's class privilege by presuming farmers would, had they not chosen to farm, be entitled to high incomes. Indeed, the previously described young woman farmer began her career after dropping out of Berkeley's Boalt Hall School of Law.

Despite these hardships, many vendors in the North Berkeley Farmers Market gain significant economic returns; the largest farms gross more than one thousand dollars per market and sell at more than ten markets a week. However, many managers, vendors, and customers cast justice, sustainability, and community goals as more important than revenue. For example, the following conversation took place between Herman and Rosalie, two North Berkeley market managers:

> "Look at that," said Herman. "Bob [who works markets for Blue Heron Farm] is helping a woman to her car. Isn't he a nice, accommodating guy?" His tone was a bit melodramatic, but his respect for Bob was genuine.
>
> "Yeah, he's really nice," answered Rosalie. "And he's a public servant."

"It's great to have a public servant who's into helping people," Herman continued. "A lot of public servants aren't."

"What kind of a public servant is he?" I asked.

"He's on the BART [Bay Area Rail Transportation] board," Rosalie answered.

"But I always see him riding his bike," Herman joked.

We stopped our conversation so Rosalie could answer a customer's questions about the benefits of compact fluorescent light bulbs. But then she further de-scribed her regard for Bob.

> Bob is great. He's worked for Blue Heron farm for thirteen years or so, just 'cause he's friends with [the owners]. He doesn't do it because he needs to. Before he was on the BART board, he was the accountant for BART.

Market managers regard Bob's motivations, which are based on voluntarism rather than economic need, in a positive light. Though regard for individu-als who volunteer and participate in civic activity is certainly understandable, these comments also evidence a discourse of choice similar to that described in the previous chapter. Bob earns a level of respect unavailable to those farm employees for whom financial motivations are primary.[3] In addition, regard for volunteers serves to further depict farmers markets themselves as civic projects capable of creating social change.

In West Oakland, amid meager sales, vendors constantly reaffirm the preeminence of community and social justice over self-interested economic goals. For example, one afternoon I overheard market manager Jason, a mixed-race black and white man, describing a new vendor. "He just sees it as a business opportunity," he said. "I'm looking for people who do more than that." Many other farmers have participated in the market for brief periods of time but left due to meager sales. As one packed up early on his first day, Ms. Charlotte, a long-time African American vendor, remarked, "They wanted to make money, and that's not what this market's about." Despite these com-ments, there were always open spaces at the West Oakland Farmers Market. Vendors whose motivations were primarily financial would never have been asked to leave. They left because the financial opportunities were so meager.

As in North Berkeley, West Oakland vendors are eager to talk about the sacrifices they make to participate in this farmers market. Leroy, an African American farmer, views the market as an opportunity to provide healthy food and nutritional advice to a population in need. "There's a lot of people I love here, and they're sick," he says emphatically, referring to the neighborhood's high rates of diet-related health problems. "So I'm doing everything I can to be here."

"There are some times that we don't make no money, but there's something here," said Mr. Scott, another African American market farmer. "This connection [between black farmers and black urban communities] should have been made so many years ago. . . . Money is fine. I'd like to have a little more," he continued. "But some things are more important."

His daughter Michelle had perhaps the most poignant words on the subject. "When I get up at an ungodly hour to come here," she said, nearly in tears from weariness and frustration, "I think, 'How can I make Oakland better?' not 'How can I make money?'" Both she and her father describe their first priority as improving the lives of their customers. Profits, if mentioned at all, are a secondary consideration. In each of these statements West Oakland Farmers Market vendors and managers trumpet their dedication to their social change goals while criticizing those for whom economic motivations are most important.

Vendors and managers emphasize the economic sacrifices made by middle-class individuals who choose to become organic farmers and vendors selling at low-income and therefore less-lucrative markets. In this way, they distance the green economic exchange that takes place at farmers market from a capitalism characterized as exploitative of both humans and nature. This narrative of sacrifice, in addition to the previously described logic of support, serves to construct the farmers market as a space dedicated to economic exchange that fosters justice and sustainability.

A PRAGMATIC ALTERNATIVE

According to farmers market participants, the green economy is a site not only for moral systems of economic exchange but also for a new kind of political struggle. In participants' frameworks, the green economy is a pragmatic, workable alternative to organizing collectively for policy change. Against a backdrop of failed national and local policy campaigns, particularly during the George W. Bush era when this research took place, participants characterized the green economy as a way to build just sustainability in spite of, rather than through, a political system unable or unwilling to guarantee it. In this way, farmers markets are just one of a range of community organizations decrying "the inevitable failings of state provision of welfare, crime control, education and much more, and demanding that individuals, families, communities, employers take back to themselves the powers and responsibilities that, since the nineteenth century, have been acquired by states, politicians and legislators" (Rose 1999, 2). Farmers market participants acknowledge and accept a state that functions in this way, and they look to farmer markets to create just sustainability when the government will not.

An Alternative to Influencing Policy

Due to the overwhelming rollback of environmental regulation and entitlement funding that has occurred in the past few decades, it is not surprising that advocates of just sustainability have turned to strategies that seek to work around, rather than through, the formal political process. Many managers, vendors, and customers make statements similar to that of market manager Rosalie, who says, "I feel like I have more power with my dollar than with my vote." This, of course, is the very logic of the green economy — the idea that the purchase of products aligned with environmental and social goods can create social change. Unlike the customers in Andrew Szasz's (2007) *Shopping Our Way to Safety*, who buy green products merely to protect themselves, North Berkeley and West Oakland Farmers Market customers also see their purchases as a force for social improvement that can occur despite repeated political defeats. For example, Kirk, the white, male North Berkeley special events director, explains his decision to work for a farmers market rather than attempt to influence policy in the following way:

> I think that people continue to work on the government, but the government hasn't shown us anything good for an awfully long time. Democrat or Republican, they still don't get it. . . . With the government, it's like fighting fires with them. Trying to control the spread of GMOs and the release of the new most toxic chemical, like trying to stop the move from methyl bromide to methyl chloride or whatever it is. . . . We can't even get methyl bromide phased out, and that's been worked on for years! No matter how much money has gone into the organic market, it's just a small fraction of what agrobiz can muster.

For Kirk, as for many at the North Berkeley Farmers Market, the green economy is a pragmatic alternative to the perceived impossibility of policy reform.

Farmers market participants depict the federal government as captured by agribusiness interests. For example, a common defense employed by farmers market advocates against charges of elitism is to criticize U.S. farm policy for subsidizing commodity crops. Echoing Michael Pollan, they argue that federal subsidies make processed foods, whose ingredients are most often grown on large, chemically intensive monoculture farms, less expensive than organic and local food. As previously noted, this claim offers little sympathy to those who cannot afford market produce, yet it does serve to depict the federal government as favoring agribusiness, making it an unlikely ally in efforts to create a more sustainable or just food system. Similarly, farmers' market participants express distrust in the federal government's ability to create standards to certify organic products, which it became legally mandated to do in 2001. For example, the Ecology Center collects food scraps from the city and, a few times a year, brings finished compost to a downtown location to give to area gardeners. One customer asked market manager Rosalie if the compost was organic. Rosalie described the process they use in some detail. "It's certified for use by organic farmers," she concluded.

"By CCOF?" the woman asks. California Certified Organic Farmers is a nonprofit mutual-assistance and certification organization for organic farmers. Until 2001, they were the primary certifier of organic food in California (www.ccof.org).

"No," Rosalie answered. "Everything is done by the USDA now."

"The USDA," the woman grumbled, shaking her head. "As if they understand organic."

This customer's response demonstrates the distrust that many supporters of local and organic food feel toward the federal government. In addition, the two core West Oakland farmers, both African American men, name the expense and confusion of USDA organic credentialing as the reason they call themselves chemical-free rather than pursue certification.

North Berkeley vendors also recount instances in which government regulation prevents them from producing their product to the best of their ability. Ted Fuller, a white male cattle and lamb rancher, often describes how the intricate regulations for slaughter constrain his operation, preventing him from keeping up with the high market demand for his product. Similarly, Judy LaRocca, a white female grape farmer and winemaker, explains the various farming and alcohol production regulations with which she must comply, offering an alphabet soup of acronyms belonging to the agencies she deals with. "I had to go to law school for two years just to understand the administration," she joked to customers one afternoon. These complaints are not merely about convenience or economics. In the green economy, the production and consumption of green products is seen as the key to social change. By describing how government makes the production of green products more difficult, vendors convey a belief that the government is not interested in promoting justice and sustainability. Against this context, the green economy becomes a more attractive strategy for social improvement than attempting to change policy.

The perception that it is extremely difficult to create policy in the interest of just sustainability is amplified by several vendors' failed attempts to do so. Judy was active in Butte County's campaign to ban genetically modified organisms (gmos). Butte was one of four California counties whose voters failed to approve ballot initiatives in 2006. "We're gonna be eating some pretty scary things pretty soon," LaRocca told a customer during a market following the measure's defeat.

In another example, Yvette Hudson of Hudson Fish Company, North Berkeley's only African American vendor, worked with a coalition of activists to lobby the federal government not to renew Pacific Power's lease on the Iron Gate Dam on the Klamath River. While the dam produces a minimal amount of hydroelectric power, it blocks salmon runs, denying access not only to commercial fishermen but to Native American tribes who approach access to traditional fishing runs as an issue of food justice (Alkon and Norgaard 2009). When the Bush administration announced its plan to address declining salmon populations by eliminating the summer's fishing season, Yvette discussed the need to close the dam with farmers market customers:

> The feds killed all the salmon, so we're going out to protest so at least they won't renew the dam leases. I mean, if I have to sacrifice [through lost income during the summer season], it would be nice if the people who made the problem fixed it.

Despite their protests, the Bush administration declined to remove the dam.[4]

These examples support farmers market participants' widely shared belief that government-sponsored reform in the interest of just sustainability is unlikely. The improbability of political success lends credence to participants' desires to pursue their social change goals through green economic exchange.

Feelings of disenfranchisement experienced by North Berkeley participants pale when compared to the understandings evidenced by West Oakland Farmers Market vendors. In West Oakland, perceptions of political efficacy were so low that the state was never discussed as a potential ally. In fact, when minor safety violations occurred, such as customers bringing dogs or bicyclists riding through the market, vendors stressed the importance of rule enforcement because, in the words of African American farmer Leroy Musgrave, "The state would love to shut us down." African Americans generally tend to experience lower levels of trust in government than whites, and distrust was amplified by allegations of racially motivated voter fraud during the 2000 and 2004 elections (McLean 2006) as well as by the disparate treatment of black and white survivors of Hurricane Katrina. Indeed, recall how West Oakland vendors identified with the victims of both the hurricane and the government and media response to it, referring to themselves and one another as "looters." This is hardly a group who believes that the government will help them create a more just and sustainable community. Additionally, the discrimination faced by black farmers at the hands of the USDA, a core theme at this farmers market, gives credence to a worldview in which the state is a perpetrator of institutional racism rather than a potential ally in the establishment of food justice and economic empowerment.

Against the context of failed national and local political campaigns, federal agencies presumed to be captured by agribusiness, confusing bureaucratic regulations, and institutional racism, it is not surprising that vendors, managers, and customers at the North Berkeley and West Oakland Farmers Markets view the state as an obstacle to the creation of just and sustainable communities. Absent any belief that they can reform or transform the state, they seek to pursue their social change goals through moral systems of economic exchange. Supporters of the green economy view themselves not as apolitical, but as pursuing political ends through the green economy.

An Alternative to Nonprofit Organizations

In North Berkeley, the green economy is seen as a preferred alternative to policy campaigns because the state is perceived to be aligned with industrial agriculture (Magdoff, Foster, and Buttel 2000; Buttel, Larson, and Gillespie 1990) and efforts to change policy seem fated to fail. In West Oakland, the state is seen as a perpetrator not only of environmental degradation through unsustainable agriculture but of institutional racism. But in Oakland, the green economy is also compared favorably with a third social change strategy, the creation of nonprofit organizations that can advocate for social change.

While the West Oakland Farmers Market is managed by one nonprofit organization and several others sponsor booths, the market's central goal is to pursue just sustainability through local economics. Several market vendors are former nonprofit employees. For example, Leroy Musgrave was employed by two different nonprofit organizations to teach gardening to Oakland youths. Twice, his employment ended dramatically due to funding difficulties and interpersonal dynamics with program directors. In each case, according to Leroy, the land was sold, leaving him without a job and the youth without a garden they were beginning to learn from and enjoy. After these experiences, Leroy decided to farm on his own rather than work for nonprofit agricultural education projects.

As was discussed in the context of creating community in chapter 4, some vendors feel that the need to attract foundation funding prevents nonprofit organizations from serving the interests of their stated constituencies. Indeed, vendor Xan West refers to established organizations as part of the NGO-industrial complex (a term she borrowed from Incite 2007). After participating in radical political actions, including anti–police brutality campaigns, protests against the International Monetary Fund, and organizing with Anarchist People of Color, Xan graduated college with the goal of starting a nonprofit organization. She describes the process through which she became disillusioned with the nonprofit sector and came to adopt a for-profit business model:

> What I saw in the process of researching what it takes to do it [start a nonprofit] and working for them, I realized that most nonprofits are actually run like businesses. All the bureaucracy and dynamics. . . . Most nonprofits spend 60 percent of their time and energy fundraising, and that's just not a model I want to replicate. And I thought it would be interesting if you could just be a business, and I thought about a lot of the models from [the Black] Panthers allegedly selling drugs and guns to, now, the Huey P. Newton project that sells hot sauce.

While she still self-identifies as anticapitalist, Xan aligns small businesses with justice and sustainability by describing them as a preferred alternative to the nonprofit model. She alleges that the energy nonprofits necessarily spend perpetuating their own existence prevents them from truly working for those they purport to serve.

Additionally, there is often suspicion that nonprofit organizations may hire community members (in this case meaning African Americans from West Oakland) for particular tasks but remain controlled by outsiders. Vendor Jada White pointed to Ted Dixon as an example. Ted is an African American man who worked for a nonprofit urban garden organization, harvesting and selling flowers at the farmers market on the weekend. Although the nonprofit hired Ted for part-time work in the gardens, its full-time staff consisted predominantly of white middle-class women. "Ted is never going to become the head of [that organization]," Jada said emphatically. This demonstrates vendors' suspicions that nonprofit organizations were not really interested in empowering West Oakland residents — a suspicion that made small businesses seem a preferable choice.

Interestingly, vendors also see operating as a small business as a way to avoid the intense competition among nonprofit organizations doing similar work. After decades working for nonprofit organizations and after the demise of the West Oakland Food Collaborative, Dana, the collaborative's white codirector, began to develop a business model for the Mandela Foods Co-op, which opened in 2008. Dana contrasts the support she received from other area green businesses with her frustrations running a nonprofit.

> I'm thrilled that our retailer discount at the Food Mill [a small, locally owned health food store in East Oakland] allows us to break even and keep prices low, rather than sell at a loss. I'm used to dealing with nonprofits and having to beg granting agencies for money. But retail outfits have been really supportive. Thanksgiving Coffee [a regional organic roaster] offered to sell to us at bulk rates even if we only bought one pound per week.

Given the intense competition for both grant money and publicity among food justice organizations in West Oakland, Dana found the support and cooperation she received from green businesses refreshing.

Participants in the North Berkeley and West Oakland Farmers Markets describe the green economy as an attainable alternative to an increasingly reactionary state and frustration with nonprofit models. Business, according to this logic, is not only consistent with, but the most proper vehicle for, farmers market participants' social change goals. Through these narrative strategies, participants elide tensions between capitalist economics and just sustainability. But a closer look reveals that such tensions nonetheless remain.

WHEN GREEN MEETS GROWTH

Many scholars have been critical of consumption, no matter how ethical or green, as a substitute for political reform (Szasz 2007; Princen, Manites, and Conca 2002). Such a strategy, as stated by John Bellamy Foster in one of the epigraphs to this chapter, ignores the institutional realities through which capitalism functions. Despite farmers market participants' claims that just sustainability goals are compatible with green economic strategies, there remain situations in which vendors must choose between the two. Pellow, Schnaiberg, and Weinberg (2000) refer to instances when a decision must be made between competing priorities as "zero-sum moments." These moments occur more often with regard to social justice concerns than environmental ones because goods associated with environmental themes tend to garner premium prices. For this reason, tensions between green economic strategies and social change goals have particularly significant consequences in West Oakland, where issues of justice are most prominent.

Participants in the North Berkeley and West Oakland Farmers Markets have seldom considered the limitations of pursuing just sustainability through local green economies. When I asked Linda, a mixed-race Latina and white North Berkeley market manager, whether she felt that vendors' needs to succeed economically got in the way of their social and environmental goals, she replied, "No, I've never felt that." She paused a moment to think about this before deploying the logic of support. "Because part of the sustainability is being able to support the farmers," she said. "They should be making money for what they do." She depicts the economic success of local farmers and entrepreneurs as a key pathway to sustainability.

Despite this response, zero-sum moments do occur. For example, Antonio, who sells vegan, organic Mexican food at the North Berkeley market, uses his business to establish a just and sustainable food system. As a Mexican American man, he is particularly concerned about environmental and health issues among Latino/as. But when asked why he chose not to sell at the nearby Fruitvale farmers market, located in a largely low-income Latino/a neighborhood, he cited lack of sales. In Fruitvale, Antonio's products could serve as a healthier alternative to the neighborhood's many fast food establishments. Despite his genuine personal regard for issues of food access, the need to sustain his business demands that he cater to an affluent, largely white clientele.

In addition, while North Berkeley Farmers Market participants discursively differentiate their own vendors from businesses interested primarily in profit, several North Berkeley farmers describe sustainability largely in economic terms. The following quote represents the viewpoint of the farmer who was most extreme on this point.

> People talk about sustainable agriculture. The first thing I think about in sustainability is financial sustainability. . . . While a lot of the work is enjoyable and you can't put a price on it, some of it is frustrating and difficult so you need to be paid for your time. There's a number of things that I'm trying to accomplish. First and foremost is making a living.

Tellingly, while this farmer "made a ton of money" selling his first farm to a large organic industrial company, he continues to employ a largely undocumented labor force who receive no benefits and have no collective bargaining power, despite the fact that some of them have worked for him for over two decades. While he claims that an environmental ethic motivated him when he began farming over twenty years ago, this farmer expressed frustration with what he calls "the groove quotient," in which "starry-eyed kids" see organic farming as a kind of "drop-out, cop-out." For this farmer, a green business is primarily a business, rather than a means to create just sustainability. But because he hires employees to sell at the farmers market, it is impossible for customers to know how his values differ from the narratives that pervade the market.

Even those vendors professing justice and sustainability as their primary motivations remain limited by the capitalist market system, demonstrating that economic constraints remain even in the midst of deeply moral systems of economic exchange (Hinrichs 2000). Increasing numbers of industrial farmers use organic methods, and their size and wealth allow them to influence the rules by which farmers dedicated to just sustainability must compete. According to cultural geographer Julie Guthman, "The conditions set by processes of agro-industrialization undermine the ability of even the most committed producers to practice a truly alternative form of organic farming" (2004: 301). While the farmer quoted above could afford to supply benefits to his workers, neither the state nor his customers require it of him. Other farmers claim that they would prefer to supply benefits but are prevented from doing so by the need to succeed economically. Guthman (2004) describes the "conventionalization" of organic agriculture, in which, as the industry grows, it comes to increasingly resemble the industrial agriculture it originally sought to replace. This conventionalization trajectory is perhaps the most serious limitation of green economic exchange as a political strategy. Over time, green businesses tend to become more like conventional businesses and less concerned with being green. This is not merely because their proprietors lose their dedication to their social change goals, though some, such as the farmer described above, clearly do. The ever-increasing need for profit is essential to the capitalist mode of production.

MARKETING SOCIAL JUSTICE

While market managers and customers promote and support local organic producers in the interest of justice and sustainability, vendors must prioritize their own economic needs. To a certain degree, because organic products are priced highly, environmental goals are more consistent with the green economy. Social justice priorities, on the other hand, such as providing food to those without access and offering benefits to farmworkers, are inevitably at odds with increased profits. The former necessarily involves lowering income while the latter requires additional expenditures. In order to profit in a competitive market, vendors such as Antonio often find they must compromise some of their social justice ideals because adhering to them takes away from their financial bottom line.

In West Oakland, because justice concerns are the most prominent, reliance on market-based strategies has consequences for the farmers market's ability to continue. Although this market's farmers generously charge much lower prices than at other Bay Area farmers markets, their food remains more expensive than the processed and canned goods available at chain groceries. Only a small number of mostly middle-class black and low-income but middle-class white customers are able and willing to pay for food that embodies the market's social justice priorities. The low-income neighborhood residents in whose interest this farmers market began most often leave the neighborhood, sometimes taking multiple busses, to shop at large supermarkets because they want to purchase the cheapest possible food. This helps explain the findings of recent studies showing that installing a supermarket in a food-desert neighborhood does little to change residents' eating habits. They were already shopping at similar stores ("If You Build It, They May Not Come," *The Economist*, July 7, 2011).

Not only does the absence of long-term West Oakland residents limit the farmers market's ability to increase food access, but the neighborhood's small numbers of loyal and ethically motivated customers cannot make the farmers market lucrative for producers. For example, after several years selling strawberries and other produce in West Oakland, Bertenice and Jose Garcia, the Latino/a farmers referred to as important allies in chapter 5, left the market when offered a space in a more lucrative one. While they understood and sympathized with the West Oakland Farmers Market's goal to provide for those without other forms of access to fresh produce, they eventually felt that they had to leave in order to sustain their struggling business. Many other vendors came to West Oakland for only a few weeks before leaving, presumably because sales were so meager. These examples highlight a difficult component of pursuing justice through market-based strategies. Entrepreneurs are necessary to supply the product but cannot be compensated as they would be in wealthier locales. This underlines a tension between the West Oakland Farmers Market's goals of creating local neighborhood food entrepreneurs and increasing food access. Individual entrepreneurs might have to leave the neighborhood to achieve economic success. However, in doing so, they can no longer contribute to local food access.

Like Linda in North Berkeley, the West Oakland market managers remain unaware of how economic strategies necessitate privileging the financial bottom line over justice and sustainability. When I asked David Roach, the market founder, how his social change goals interact with capitalist strategies, he responded, "It's not about social change and capitalism because I don't like the word *capitalism*. Capitalism is about how do you capitalize on, a few people trying to capitalize on the majority of people, and that's not going to do anything for social change." Exploitation, according to this worldview, is rooted in individual desire rather than in the logic of the system. David's understanding of the West Oakland Farmers Market as something other than a capitalist venue prevents him from recognizing existing tensions between the market's social change and economic goals.

COMMERCE AND SOCIAL CHANGE IN THE GREEN ECONOMY

In choosing to advocate for just sustainability through green production and consumption, farmers market participants must negotiate an important contradiction. They are attempting to challenge capitalism's destruction of the environment and human communities through the creation of a market. Farmers market proponents, however, construct their markets as quite different from the capitalist economic system. They attribute environmental degradation and human exploitation to large corporations' increasing need for material resources. In contrast, local, green producers are described as embodying the moral values of the community and as sacrificing more-lucrative careers to produce sustainable products. Through these narratives, justice and sustainability become a part of the commodities for sale at the farmer market, and market purchases become a vote with one's dollar in favor of social change goals.

Farmers market managers, vendors, and customers also minimize tensions between local economics and just sustainability by positing the former as a pragmatic, workable alternative to policy change. They point to a federal and state government that subsidizes agribusiness and is increasingly hostile to issues of justice and sustainability. In West Oakland, the state is seen as a perpetrator of institutional racism rather than a potential ally. Additionally, several West Oakland vendors have turned to business models after disappointing efforts to pursue their social change goals through nonprofit organizations.

The circumstances cohere with Guthman's (2008b) description of food movements. On the one hand they are opposed to neoliberalism writ large, in terms of their work to counter the growing power of multinational corporations over various aspects of social life. On the other hand, because the locus of social change lies in the market rather than the state or civil society, this opposition is, paradoxically, neoliberal in nature. However, market participants fail to see how the neoliberalization of their social change goals constrains the success of their farmers markets. Attempts to achieve justice and sustainability through market-based strategies, which include not only farmers markets but also the green economy more generally, do so by pricing the environmental and social benefits of green products in a manner consistent with the philosophy of natural capitalism. Ethical customers are expected to support sustainable and just producers by paying this additional cost.

However, environmentalism and justice are not priced equally; the former often garners premium prices while the latter does not. In the North Berkeley Farmers Market, customers are willing and able to pay for the environmental benefits of the food sold there, making environmental goals cohere with green growth. Vendors' desires to contribute to social justice, on the other hand, by offering lower-cost food or paying better wages to workers, remain at odds with their economic goals. In West Oakland, however, the low-income residents in whose interest the market began are largely unable to pay for food that embodies social justice, and instead they leave the neighborhood to acquire the cheapest possible provisions. Market managers, vendors, and customers draw on the narratives described in this chapter to avoid recognizing these contradictions as consequences of their desires to pursue a collective, political goal — the implementation of a just and sustainable food system — through individual green economic exchange.

CHAPTER SEVEN

Farmers Markets, Race, and the Green Economy

Over the next ten years the green economy is going to change virtually every major aspect of our lives for the better. . . . It's clear from our inability to pass climate legislation that we're not going green because it's the right thing to do. We're going green because it's simply the smart thing to do.

— ANDY MANNLE, "Why the Green Economy Is Unstoppable"

Green capitalism is not the final stage of human development, any more than gray [industrial] capitalism was. . . . But we have to recognize that we are at a particular stage of history, where the choices are not capitalism versus socialism, but green/eco-capitalism versus gray/suicide capitalism. . . . I don't know what will replace eco-capitalism. But I do know that no one will be here to find out, if we don't first replace gray capitalism.

— VAN JONES, "Who Gains from the Green Economy?"

Farmers markets like those in North Berkeley and West Oakland represent the larger green economy because they advocate the buying and selling of local organic food as essential to social change. This social change includes environmental goals like healthy soil, biodiversity, and decreased use of fossil fuel and fertilizer. In addition, the green economy is often lauded as a creator of jobs. Farmers markets provide opportunities for small farmers and other small businesspeople to earn their livelihoods through direct sales. Small farmers would otherwise be unable to compete with an industrial agriculture that uses economies of scale and federal subsidies to make food cheap. The African American farmers vending at the West Oakland Farmers Market face not only the obstacles incurred by all small farmers but a legacy of institutional racism and discrimination by the U.S. Department of Agriculture. Thus this farmers market, and to a lesser extent Berkeley's Farm Fresh Choice, works to reverse a history that has prevented African Americans from controlling the means of food production and from consuming healthy food. This strategy explicitly brings issues of race and class into a food movement that has often been criticized as elitist and attempts to use local food systems to address racial inequalities.

In addition to jobs, the green economy is trumpeted as a creator of environmentally healthy lifestyles. The farmers markets depicted in this book offer the benefits of fresh, local, and organic and/or chemical-free food. Such benefits are often absent from low-income neighborhoods populated largely by people of color, such as West Oakland. Food justice activists and researchers argue that this absence is due to a history of institutional racism in land use planning, lending, and development and contributes to the high rates of diet-related illnesses such as heart disease and diabetes experienced by people of color (McClintock 2011). In West Oakland, one of the farmers market's primary aims is to provide access to healthy food. In Berkeley, profits from the farmers market support a program that does the same. Emphasis on inequality in both the production and consumption of food epitomizes efforts to deploy the green economy as a strategy toward both justice and sustainability. This strategy broadens the appeal of local organic food beyond the predominantly white farming and environmental communities, bringing the insights of the environmental justice movement to bear on the politics of food.

UNDERSTANDING THE GREEN ECONOMY THROUGH FARMERS MARKETS

The overall goal of this book has been to help readers better understand the complex set of meanings and practices that give rise to and make up the green economy, particularly with regard to food, and to examine how those meanings and practices intersect with racial and economic identities and inequalities. It traced the historical local, national, and global contexts from which the green economy emerged, keeping an eye toward various visions of the relationships between economy, environment, and equity. As a green ideology developed from its predecessor, sustainability, it came to embody a vision in which not only were economic growth and environmental protection compatible, but the former was posited as the key pathway to the latter. This neoliberalization of what were formerly social movement goals moved the locus of social change from the state to the market and shifted responsibility for this change from citizens to consumers.

The North Berkeley and West Oakland Farmers Markets provide opportunities to explore visions of justice and sustainability that can be pursued through the green economy. In these markets, actors choose from among competing narratives to envision and emphasize the spaces where buying and selling green products leads to environmental protection *and* social justice. The demographic differences between these cases lend insights into the ways that race and class can inform the meanings and practices that drive and constitute the green economy. Both farmers markets combine environmental and social justice goals in innovative ways, though the predominantly affluent and white North Berkeley market prioritizes environmental concerns, while its predominantly black West Oakland counterpart emphasizes issues of racial inequality and identity. This contrast shows that social location affects how just sustainability can be envisioned and pursued.

In addition, each farmers market lends insights as to how participation in the green economy can influence individual and cultural identity formation. The West Oakland Farmers Market creates an alternative food system rooted in the lived experiences of African Americans. This system makes visible racial inequalities in the production, distribution, and consumption of healthy food, as well as the structural causes for these inequalities. It also gives its predominantly African American participants an opportunity to fuse their performances of green and black identity. Simultaneously, though, the farmers market's failure to emphasize issues of poverty prevents managers and vendors from seeing class differences between their customers and neighborhood residents and from creating a market accessible to the latter.

In North Berkeley, on the other hand, the white cultural discourses and the affluent character of the neighborhood reinforce one another, creating an upscale market that reflects and highly regards European and Euro-American foodways. This association between local organic food and affluent whiteness is precisely what the West Oakland Farmers Market attempts to disrupt. Well-intentioned and important efforts to integrate social justice concerns do exist in North Berkeley, but these remain at the fringes of the farmers market. Although natural capitalists argue that green products are more efficiently produced and will ultimately become less expensive, they currently tend to cost more than their industrial counterparts. Thus the consumption of green products remains an expression of middle-class identity, even amid efforts to cast green products in ways that speak to the histories and cultures of low-income communities of color.

Furthermore, proponents of the social change potential of the green economy attempt to redefine capitalism not as an exploitative system that must be overcome or restricted in order to protect people and the environment but as a tool to create a more just and sustainable world. Managers, vendors, and customers in the North Berkeley and West Oakland Farmers Markets align green capitalism with their activist goals through narratives contrasting the good intensions of green producers with the greed and destructiveness of large corporations. In addition, they view the green economy as a pragmatic and doable alternative to working through the political process or nonprofit organizations. They argue that collective political participation remains an option but that the green economy provides an additional tool. Nonetheless, farmers market participants solely or largely devote their energies to economic strategies, pursuing environmental protection and social justice not through policy or direct action but through market exchange.

At the same time, while economic behavior at farmers markets is constructed as integral to social movement goals and performances of individual and collective identity, it remains guided by the need to purchase goods and garner profits (Hinrichs 2000; Block 1990). Farmers market participants ignore or explain away remaining tensions between these economic goals and their desires for social change by arguing that the economic survival of green businesses is a necessary step toward justice and sustainability. In North Berkeley, participants further explain issues of access in individual rather than structural terms, ignoring the realities of those, such as migrant farmworkers, whose needs are not served by the green economy. In West Oakland, managers, vendors, and regular customers fail to realize the broader social and economic contexts that constrain low-income neighborhood residents' food procurement strategies, instead professing a belief that residents will learn about local and organic food and begin regularly attending the farmers market. These narratives reveal how the broader context of neoliberalization pushes activists toward adopting green economic strategies, even as they profess visions of justice and sustainability that are strongly rooted in anticapitalist histories and traditions.

Taken together, these insights allow for a greater understanding of the green economy, the practices that compose it, and the meanings its supporters attribute to their actions. The remainder of this concluding chapter takes on the more pragmatic task of assessing the strengths and weaknesses of the green economy as a strategy for promoting justice and sustainability.

JUSTICE AND SUSTAINABILITY: A CROSS-POLLINATION

In some ways, the farmers markets depicted in this study are extraordinary because of their dedication to both environmental sustainability and social justice. Working toward these dual goals becomes possible, in part, because participants in each farmers market define environment and justice in ways that render them compatible with one another. In North Berkeley, the dominant environmental narrative urges consumers to connect to and protect beautiful, biodiverse landscapes (organic farms) through the consumption of locally grown organic foods. While this account does not explicitly discuss inequality, it moves the locus of environmental protection from the wilderness to human habitats, and it also attends to human health. Direct references to inequality come from Farm Fresh Choice, which uses profits from the farmers market to make subsidized market produce available in Berkeley's low-income, predominantly black and Latino/a neighborhoods. The West Oakland Farmers Market, on the other hand, defines the environment by linking culture and agriculture. Here, racial identity is paramount, and the farmers market uses food as a tool to empower people who have been marginalized. Protecting ecosystem health and human physical and cultural health are again linked, as the market's strategy of supporting local, chemical-free black farmers is good for both the environment and marginalized people.

The compatibility between sustainability and justice achieved at these farmers markets is not inherent. Farmers market managers, as well as some vendors and regular customers, actively work to conceptualize strategies that speak to both goals. A farmers market could easily work to promote black farmers and vendors without any regard for environmental sustainability. On the other hand, another market could promote environmental concerns through organic and local food without regard for food access (which many do). Although some participants in each farmers market have not adopted the goal of working toward justice and sustainability together, the markets themselves have successfully created strategies that do so.

These examples show that the green economy is not merely the backdrop against which this cross-pollination of justice and sustainability can be produced but an active player in its production. In a traditional social movement organization, tensions between factions who are supportive of both environment and justice and those strongly prioritizing one or the other goal would be cause for disagreement and debate. This might result in a compromise in which priorities were ranked, or even in one faction leaving the organization. On the other hand, one of the key claims of this book has been that environmentalism and justice themselves become regarded as commodities for sale in the green economy — the ideals become part of what consumers pay for when they buy a product from these farmers markets. But not every commodity must embody both goals. At the North Berkeley Farmers Market, environmental goals are primary. Thus, the Ecology Center mandates that all products be local, organic, and non-GMO. Social justice goals are secondary. Some products embody this second goal, such as produce from the two farms owned by former farmwork-ers, while others do not. Customers who use the farmers market as a venue to pursue both justice and sustainability, such as the customer described in chap-ter 4 who went out of her way to support a farm with unionized workers, can do so by choosing their products. Others, such as the vendors and customers who revealed striking disregard for the circumstances of low-income people, might only seek out products that contain environmental benefits. Conversely, in West Oakland, social justice is deemed most central, and all vendors present during this study were people of color. Here, customers pursuing both justice and sustainability might be delighted by the chemical-free produce grown by black farmers. They might also, however, avoid the nonorganic (and thus with-out environmental benefit) prepared foods provided by black entrepreneurs.

Because these venues are markets rather than traditional social movement organizations, tensions between environmental and social justice goals do not have to be worked through. Individual vendors and consumers can merely choose to produce or procure those commodities that embody their values and to forgo those that do not. The market context allows for the creation of compatibility between justice and sustainability without needing to convince those who remain wedded to the belief that they are irreconcilable or who favor one goal without attention to the other. For this reason, it seems as if the green economy holds promise for the continued development of just sustainability.

CONSUMPTION AND EQUITY

As participants in the North Berkeley and West Oakland Farmers Markets cre-ate meanings and strategies that foster both justice and sustainability, they help produce compatibility between the two. The presence of both ideals, however, does not mean that the broader marketplace treats environmentalism and so-cial justice equally. The green economy assigns widely different values to envi-ronmentalism and justice. Demand for commodities embodying the former is higher in the affluent, predominantly white communities like North Berkeley, whose residents are willing and able to pay premium prices for it. Thus, an or-ganic peach costs considerably more than a conventional one not only because of the higher price of its cultivation but also because customers are willing and able to pay for it. North Berkeley market farmers sustain this demand by promoting their food as a means to environmental protection. In part due to its environmental credentials, the market is quite lucrative. When a space for a new vendor becomes available — a rare occurrence — many applicants vie for it in a competitive process. The selection is based on vendors' environmental credentials.

Justice, however, does not carry the same premium price. While fair-trade products have successfully lured affluent consumers with promises of increased pay for peasant farmers, poor Americans are often regarded as "undeserving" (Katz 1990). Even in progressive cities such as Berkeley, few customers evidence any willingness to pay extra to support African American farmers or to create opportunities for locally led economic development in West Oakland. Indeed, proponents of farmers markets often romanticize the local, a mindset that can and often has resulted in affluent communities focusing on their own places while ignoring inequality between places (DuPuis and Goodman 2005).

Middle-class African Americans, however, do travel from wealthier neighborhoods to support the West Oakland farmers market, but not regularly enough or in high enough numbers to sustain it. And West Oakland's low-income residents do not attend the farmers market because their priority is to find the least expensive food, even if doing so requires multiple bus rides out of the neighborhood. This trend illuminates one difficulty of using the green economy to create environmental justice in marginalized communities: residents often do not have the economic means to support green products. Moreover, because the market draws few customers, it cannot fulfill its promises of creating economic opportunities for local entrepreneurs or increased revenues for African American farmers. For this reason, there is high turnover among vendors. Those who remain are tremendously dedicated. They often have other sources of income and see their participation in the farmers market as a form of community service. In the words of Will Scott, this market's original and most consistent farmer, "We have the paperwork to put in for a lot of other markets, but one of the things that keeps us at [West Oakland] is connection to the black community. . . . We don't have the support structure that those other markets have, and that's the truth." Mr. Scott, a retired engineer, barely sells enough produce to cover his transportation costs. He and others like him effectively subsidize the market in order to serve its few consistent customers in the hopes that local demand will grow.

While both farmers markets envision their work as creating justice and sustainability, it is in North Berkeley, where affluent shoppers are able to pay, that the market is economically viable. Here, dedication to justice exists largely outside of market exchange relations. Indeed, the Ecology Center formed Farm Fresh Choice, through which low-income youth of color purchase discounted food from market farmers and resell it in their own communities, only after efforts to create a farmers market in that neighborhood failed. Despite the food's discounted price, demand for it is low. Farm Fresh could not exist within the confines of the green economy; its staff is paid through foundation grants and with money raised from other Ecology Center programs.

Because the green economy rewards environmentalism much more than justice, it may hold negative consequences for the creation of just sustainability. Environmental justice activists have often been skeptical of the environmental movement, believing that environmentalists would willingly sacrifice the issues most relevant to marginalized communities in order to foster their own aims. The green economy may provide such an opportunity, as it is inherently undemocratic; influence depends on an actor's ability to spend money on green products. In other words, if the green economy is a way for individuals to vote with their dollars, then those with more dollars by definition cast more votes.

Thus green economic venues are more successful when they prioritize issues and products valued by affluent communities. This principle remains true even if affluent consumers do not consciously seek to direct the green economy but merely aim to fulfill their own desires and express their own political and cultural identities through their purchases. Low-income consumers cannot, by themselves, create profitable green economies. Moreover, affluent consumers may not be willing to pay premiums to advance the issues of justice most relevant to marginalized communities.

Additionally, the green economy does little to constrain the environmental and social degradation caused by polluting industries — in this case, industrial agriculture. Farmers markets may be the fastest-growing part of the food economy, but they do little to stop companies like Monsanto from patenting GMO seeds or farms in Florida and elsewhere from confining workers to conditions of modern-day slavery (Estabrook 2011). In other words, creating positive alternatives is not the same as preventing pollution and inequality.

Some scholars have even argued that the focus on creating alternatives itself draws energy away from what could be collective campaigns to regulate the destructive power of industrial agriculture. Guthman, for example, has asked if the energy that has gone into creating the food movement had been more focused on regulation, might it have succeeded in banning methyl bromide (personal communication). This hypothetically successful campaign would result in the removal of a poisonous chemical, a benefit to all eaters and especially to farmworkers, rather than the creation of a niche market whose benefits accrue largely to affluent whites. Guthman has also argued that the green economy undercuts collective campaigns not only through the diversion of activist energy, but by promoting the idea that the market is the proper venue to pursue social and environmental change (2008b).

This critique is both scathing and difficult to ignore. However, recent policy campaigns such as those described below have gained support from the green economy, suggesting that it has the potential to fuel the kind of broader and deeper social change efforts that can benefit all people.

THE GREEN ECONOMY AND COLLECTIVE ACTION

The green economy may siphon some of the energies of environmentalists and social justice activists away from broader collective campaigns, and it certainly implies that the market, not the state, is the appropriate site of reform. However, the rise of the green economy has not prevented campaigns demanding that the state promote green industries or constrain environmentally and socially harmful actors. This final section offers three examples of such campaigns, each of which has received support from the growing green economy and/or a food movement that prioritizes market-oriented strategies.

The (Food and) Farm Bill

Perhaps the most sweeping collective campaign rooted in the green economy was the 2007 effort to reform the U.S. Farm Bill. Prior to the food movement's growth, few U.S. citizens were aware of this important legislation. Initially designed to raise farm incomes during the New Deal, the farm bill has become the darling of agribusiness corporations and farm-state politicians. The commodity title, widely considered the core of the bill, provides a range of subsidies, as well as (de)regulatory and production policies, that dramatically affect agricultural markets. For example, the farm bill subsidizes, and therefore secures, the plentiful production of corn. Corn provides much of the filler for processed foods, as well as sweetener in the form of high fructose corn syrup (Pollan 2006). The export of subsidized corn to developing countries such as Mexico also makes small-scale farming economically difficult, often driving these farmers to cross the border and become immigrant farmworkers. The U.S. Farm Bill both decreases the cost of processed foods and increases corporate dominance over U.S. agriculture.

Many groups associated with the food and food justice movements sought to influence the 2007–2008 farm bill reauthorization. Advocates for rural communities, ecological integrity, public health, hunger relief, and immigration reform recognized that this important piece of legislation was germane to their interests. Public interest in the farm bill was considerably higher than in previous cycles. Not only did the above-mentioned constituencies include new voices but the *New York Times* and other widely read media featured a number of stories on this bill. Author Michael Pollan was among the best-known writers publicizing the issue.

In its report on the 2007–2008 farm bill, the Institute for Agriculture and Trade Policy describes progressive efforts as a "Christmas tree approach." Each of the aforementioned constituencies received an ornament, be it a provision that federally supported biofuel refineries guarantee union wages, increased funding for conservation stewardship, or a new diversity initiative designed to aid farmers of color. However, the tree—the commodity title and all of its agribusiness subsidies—remained unaffected. Guthman represents the views of many food and agriculture researchers and reformers when she writes that she "can think of no clearer path to a more ecologically sound and socially just food system than the removal of those [commodity crop] subsidies" (2007, 77).

This book suggests that without significantly reforming the farm bill to instead subsidize environmentally sound and socially just production, efforts to provide just and sustainable alternatives will remain niche markets serving only those who can afford, and choose, to pay the increased costs. Despite their predominantly economic strategies, food and food justice activists were important drivers of this collective effort for reform, and many are currently gearing up for the 2012 reauthorization of the bill. If this activism continues to grow, it may eventually be able to garner enough public support to influence the commodity title, potentially resulting in a sweeping restructuring of industrial agriculture.

Green Jobs as a Pathway out of Poverty

The rise of the green economy is also essential to campaigns seeking to create green jobs for low-income people and people of color. Activists such as those at Green For All, a national organization that lobbies state and local governments to build the green economy through legislation, define green jobs as well-paying, career-track jobs that improve the environment. Green For All and its allies have achieved a wide variety of successes at the local, state, and national levels. Mayors from Oakland to Newark have created training programs, as have states including Washington, Minnesota, New York, and Massachusetts. And in 2007, the federal government passed the Green Jobs Act, authorizing a $125 million training program with a special focus on low-income people. Although these job programs mostly focus on alternative energy, it is worth noting that the West Oakland Farmers Market defines some of its goals in similar terms — as creating meaningful, well-paying job opportunities for low-income people and people of color.

However, rather than relying entirely on the green economy to sustain these training programs, leaders in the green jobs movement are forging a new kind of hybrid goal that bridges the green economy and public policy. In lobbying for state investment, these advocates question the green economy's premise that justice and sustainability will come through economic exchange. As this book has demonstrated, working only through the market makes it difficult to address inequality, as even green businesses that value social justice must attract affluent consumers to stay afloat. Although it depends on the rollout neoliberalization in which states create favorable market conditions, government support for green jobs training can free such programs from the requirement to garner funding, allowing them to better attend to issues of equity.

Proposition 2: The Prevention of Farm Animal Cruelty Act

Lastly, in 2008, California voters passed Proposition 2, the Prevention of Farm Animal Cruelty Act. This law mandates that all veal calves, pregnant sows, and egg-laying chickens be confined in a manner that allows them to turn around freely, lie down, stand up, and fully extend their limbs. While California's law is the first to include chickens, it joins similar legislation passed in Florida, Arizona, Oregon, and Colorado. The California initiative was funded primarily by the Humane Society. Opposition was funded by agribusiness interests throughout the country, as well as farm bureau federations.

Clearly, this law is an attempt to regulate agribusiness practices in favor of animal rights. It is equally clear that the wide popular support this initiative received (passing 63 to 37 percent) was rooted in a food movement that has operated primarily through the creation of alternative markets. According to *Grist*, an online environmental magazine that often devotes coverage to environmental justice issues, voters were "sending a message that goes far beyond the relatively modest changes required by the measure: Consumers really do care where their food comes from and how it's raised, and they're willing to set limits even if the industry isn't" (Ness 2008). This measure harkens back to the limits-to-growth variant of environmentalism, in which citizens were willing to constrain industry profits in favor of environmental goals.

BEYOND THE GREEN ECONOMY

Granted, none of these collective campaigns coheres exactly with the issues raised by the farmers markets depicted in this book. The farm bill reform was minimal, and even commodity reform must be accompanied by new incentives if it is to guarantee food access. The green jobs bills have produced trained candidates but have been accompanied by neither policies to constrain the development of harmful energy sources such as oil and coal nor enough growth in green industries to create employment opportunities. And lastly, Proposition 2 is precisely the kind of animal rights regulation to which environmental justice activists often take offense because it fosters animal welfare while ignoring human welfare. As a whole, these three campaigns have been but small steps toward making the food system, and society in general, more sustainable and just.

Nonetheless, these examples point toward potential connections between the green economy and broader forms of collective action that can constrain, or someday even eliminate, the destructive effects of industrial agriculture. Managers, vendors, and customers in the farmers markets depicted in this book may envision the green economy as the most favorable social change strategy, but that does not seem to dissuade them, and others like them, from participating in policy campaigns. The desire to pursue both the green economy and broader policy campaigns is nicely summarized by one Oakland activist who stated that people should "buy [our] organic apples and nontoxic dish soap, but do so with the knowledge that it's not enough — and act accordingly" (Wiegand 2007). This acting accordingly can and should include participating in collective action and policy campaigns that can help advance just sustainability. It is through these campaigns that the green economy can make its strongest contributions to the visions held by those depicted in this book, and by many others who share their goals.

Reading, Writing, Relationship

I entered the field on a sunny spring Saturday morning. I biked to the local train station and boarded a southbound train. The train headed underground as we approached the downtown Oakland business district and then emerged again to make one final stop before it crossed the bay to San Francisco. I climbed off the train and looked over the railing before descending the steps. I could see the easy-ups common to outdoor farmers markets. A few dozen people milled around the various booths. Across the busy street sat a brightly colored, newly constructed, multistory building. The design was identical to other mixed-use complexes in rapidly gentrifying areas.

I carried my bike down the stairs, locked it to a nearby pole, and entered the market. For a few moments I stood off to the side, hands in my pockets, unsure what to do with myself. When I had moved to Davis, California, the farmers market was one of the first places I had sought out. It had immediately felt comfortable, and I had met some of my first friends there. But this market was different. I browsed each of the ten booths multiple times, listening to snippets of conversation. I wondered self-consciously if others had noticed my presence. I was not the only white woman shopping, but I still felt as if I stuck out. "What's this white girl doing here?" I imagined vendors and customers asking themselves.

What I was doing there, of course, was much more than shopping. My background in the alternative food movement, combined with my training as a sociologist, had led to research questions about how a farmers market would work in a low-income community of color. I knew that if I wanted to do research here (and to someday finish graduate school) I would have to overcome my initial hesitancies. I located Jason, the market manager, seated behind the information booth. By this time, I had several bags of produce in my hands, and I put them down on his table. I took a deep breath, and told him I was interested in doing research.

"What are we going to get out of it?" he asked me immediately. The question was not unfamiliar to me. My ethnographic training had paid great attention to

the issue of reciprocity with those we study. Still, I was momentarily stunned by his frankness.

When I reflect on the path my research has taken, this moment is always the first to come to mind. It encompasses many aspects of my research process ranging from ethical questions of reciprocity to the more mundane issue of how to participate in the research site. It reveals that the building of relationships is inextricable from the gathering of data.

Ethnographic research is an embodied craft. It is the researcher's physical presence in the social milieu she wishes to observe that enables her insights. How the ethnographer presents herself in the field and how she works with those she studies are crucial aspects of the research. These issues, however, are often made invisible in the final manuscript. In this study, the process of gathering data was mediated by my own body, which, as I discuss below, is raced, classed, gendered, and stylized in particular ways. This epilogue contains my reflections on my own research and writing process.

Much has changed since William Foote Whyte, frustrated by his difficulties finding "realist descriptions" of the ethnographic process, first published a methodological account to accompany his *Streetcorner Society* (1991[1943]).[1] My research has greatly benefited from the writings of ethnographers who conclude their manuscripts with tales of the personal, intellectual, and ethical processes that give shape to their text (see, for example, Grindstaff 2002; Duneier 1999; and Lavie 1990) as well as anthologies of feminist ethnographic reflections (for example, Wolf 1996; Bretell 1993). This body of work provides an important and inspiring public discourse about what is usually assumed to be a private struggle, and it leads to methodological, ethical, and theoretical insights.

Throughout my study, I have attempted to provide both accurate and evocative accounts of the everyday discourses and practices that constitute the green economy. I have thus far told the kind of "realist tale" (Van Mannen 1988) that dominates academic ethnography. The words and deeds of those I study are the evidence behind my arguments. Additionally, I have intermittently inserted myself as a presence in both observations and conversations. This is done not for navel-gazing[2] but to remind the reader of my own presence as author and my own role in translating the everyday experiences of those I study into a coherent and theoretically relevant argument. Any knowledge I've transmitted about the discourses and practices that make up the green economy was first filtered by my own understandings of the farmers markets depicted in this study and my own relationships with actors buying, selling, and working within them.

Here in the epilogue, I shift strategies to tell a more process-oriented, "confessional tale" (ibid.). I focus on my own embodied presence in the research site, my relationships with those I studied, and my writing process in an attempt to illuminate the ways in which they inform my analysis.

GAINING ACCESS AND COMMUNITY INVOLVEMENT

West Oakland

Confessional tales, including my own, generally begin with stories about gaining access to the research site. When Jason asked how my research could contribute to the West Oakland Farmers Market, he posed a question I would struggle to answer throughout my time in the field. The literature describes reciprocity as an internal struggle for ethnographers rather than a demand made by those being studied (Jackson 1987). Both Jason and I, however, were aware of the history of white researchers exploiting communities of color (for discussions on race and ethnographic research, see Mohanty 1991 and Twine 2000). I admired Jason's imperative to protect his vendors and customers from mistreatment.

My initial response to the question of "What are we going to get out of this?" was clumsy at best. I felt flushed as I stumbled for words to respond, eventually articulating desire for market participants to benefit from my study, as well as my openness to what those benefits would be. I offered to begin to brainstorm specific ideas and to incorporate any suggestions he had. I cannot imagine Jason was impressed by my immediate response. I did not come with a preformed plan because I wanted to first listen to the needs and desires of those with whom I would work. Still, I felt embarrassed at my inability to provide an answer. We exchanged e-mail addresses with a promise to continue the conversation.

Despite my embarrassment, I was also relieved that Jason had posed the question of reciprocity directly to me rather than maintain unstated expectations. While his question was intended, he would later tell me, to be off-putting, I also saw in it the potential for dialogue. Later that week, I wrote a short plan for community involvement and sent it to Jason, as well as to David, the market founder, and Dana, who codirected the West Oakland Food Collaborative. Because each of these individuals played (official and unofficial) managerial roles in the farmers market, I viewed them as gatekeepers whose permission to conduct my research would be essential. The plan was simple. I proposed to hire someone from West Oakland as a research assistant and to pay everyone I interviewed a small stipend.[3] I viewed paying informants as not only a way to ensure access but a symbolic gesture to convey my valuation of their time and my regard for them as lay experts on their own lived experiences.

I expected this plan to be the beginning of negotiations concerning my access to the farmers market and was pleasantly surprised when Jason, David, and Dana indicated that they were satisfied with it. Months later, Jason confided that his initial sharpness was a reaction to being "studied to death" by journalists and undergraduates who "come to the market once or twice, and then never even give us a copy of the paper." Moreover, he conveyed that the length of my study had also made it attractive. When he learned that I planned to attend the market weekly for at least a year, Jason began to see me not only as a researcher but as a regular customer in a market with dwindling attendance. In the most immediate sense, my purchases were an important contribution to the farmers market.

North Berkeley

When I began this project, my interest was only in studying how the food movement intersected with efforts to create racial and economic inequality in a low-income community of color. But as I became more interested in a comparative study, I quickly narrowed in on North Berkeley as an important and appropriate comparative case. As an exclusively organic market, North Berkeley's environmental standards were the strongest I had ever seen. I also knew anecdotally that the neighborhood in which it occurred was predominantly affluent and white, which would provide a strong contrast to West Oakland. Moreover, while it is more than twice the size of the West Oakland market, North Berkeley is the next smallest market in the area, which made for an easier comparison.

Like the Davis Farmers Market I had patronized for years, the North Berkeley Farmers Market felt immediately comfortable. Both Davis and Berkeley are predominantly white, middle-class college towns, and I hold the same relative social location as many farmers market's patrons (though as a student, my income was much smaller). Additionally, I recognized some of the names of the farms from my previous involvement in the food movement. Here, permission to conduct my study was immediate and unquestioned. I had met Herman, a Berkeley Farmers Market manager, months earlier when we both volunteered at a community garden managed by a food justice organization that works with the West Oakland Farmers Market. At that time, we had realized that we had a common friend with whom I had lived in a student cooperative in Davis. On my first research visit to the North Berkeley Farmers Market, I told Herman that I wanted to study this market in comparison to West Oakland. He agreed that it would be an interesting study. I was so comfortable at this market that I immediately asked a small favor — to leave my laptop in his truck while he introduced me to other managers and vendors. He agreed and seemed happy to do so. As would be common throughout my fieldwork, I ran into several more acquaintances that afternoon. Although the question of what to do with myself for four hours during a farmers market remained, in this setting I could easily blend in.[4]

North Berkeley managers, vendors, and customers were not at all reluctant to be studied. Many, however, expected me to be more interested in agro-ecology or agricultural economics (especially given that UC Davis is best known as an ag school). Vendors especially seemed surprised that a sociologist would study farmers markets. Because I wanted to gather data before deciding which aspects of my study were most important, answering the question of why I was interested in farmers markets was quite difficult. I generally described my study as concerned with the political and cultural aspects of farmers markets, which seemed to satisfy those who asked. Because I feared making market participants defensive, I did not initially highlight my interests in race and class. I eventually shared that aspect of my work, but only with those managers, vendors, and customers with whom I had established close relationships.

MAINTAINING RELATIONSHIPS

West Oakland

As ethnographer Laura Grindstaff writes in her reflections on her research process, "fieldwork is not a discrete, static event, but an ongoing process, typically accomplished over long periods of time" (2002, 284). In West Oakland, formal access from market managers was merely the start of a complex set of negotiated relationships with each vendor and regular customer. During my first visits to the farmers market, I bought from each of the food vendors, if only to have an excuse to engage in conversation. Within the first month of my fieldwork, I told each person with whom I spoke about my project; some seemed intrigued and asked questions, while others were more concerned with the immediate sale. The first vendors with whom I spoke at length were Xan West and Jada White, who, like me, were women in their late twenties. Both had been involved in a number of interrelated movements and protests, including struggles against corporate globalization and police brutality. Moreover, they maintained a strong political-economic critique of both the state and what Xan refers to as the NGO-industrial complex (a term she took from INCITE! 2007). It was this shared interest in radical politics and the difficulties of collective action that fueled our early conversations, though I initially played the interested novice, revealing little of my own activist background. Despite my status as a white researcher and theirs as African American members of the group I studied, I viewed our shared ages and interests as important commonalities. I spent many of my first hours of fieldwork at their booth.

My interest in researching farmers markets was rooted in my own participation in food activism throughout my early twenties. Given the scathing environmental justice critiques of environmentalism, as well as the ethnographic literature's emphasis on presentation of self in the research setting (Lofland and Lofland 1984; Wolf 1996), I was concerned about how much I looked the part. I took measures to prevent myself from being stereotyped as a young, white hippie, fearful that my appearance would align me with those whom EJ activists often criticized for caring more for endangered species than for low-income people of color. During my early fieldwork, I made sure to tie back my waist-length hair and to trade my long skirts and Birkenstocks for jeans and closed-toed shoes. In retrospect, I should have learned from Mitch Duneier's experience working among street booksellers on New York's Sixth Avenue. "I was wearing the same clothes I had been wearing in the classroom a few days earlier," he writes in his methods appendix. "Even if I had dressed differently . . . my speech and diction alone would have made me seem different. Had I tried to downplay these differences, [those I studied] would have seen through such a move immediately" (Duneier 1999, 336). Rather than see my presentation of self as deceitful, however, West Oakland Farmers Market participants treated my involvement in alternative foods movements and other activism, which I revealed slowly over my first few months of fieldwork, as something they gradually learned about me.

Indeed, despite my assumptions to the contrary, my experience with the food movement was an important way I connected to West Oakland Farmers Market participants. On my first day of fieldwork, upon hearing that I had previously lived in Davis, Dana asked if I had shopped at the Davis Food Cooperative, a member-owned supermarket that carries both organic and conventional food. When I answered yes, she invited me to sit in on meetings of the West Oakland Food Collaborative, which was working to open a cooperative grocery store. These meetings, which were my first exposure to the issues of race and power described in chapter 5, were an important source of insight into the broader landscape of West Oakland food justice activism.

Another connection was that both David and I had attended college (albeit ten years apart) in Atlanta, where we had the same favorite restaurant, a vegan soul food joint owned by a black, Hebrew-speaking Christian sect. This commonality gave the impression that I was aware, at least to some degree, of the politics of food in black communities. Similarly, the summer prior to beginning my research, I had begun learning to can jams, salsas, and other preserves. As I began to experiment with recipes and techniques, Charlotte Coleman, whose Pots-to-Jars home canned goods sold similar products, became an invaluable source of advice. Canning was often the topic of our early conversations and allowed us to build a relationship around this common interest. While racial difference continued to influence the research process,[5] I believe these common interests and experiences gave us a basis from which to build relationships. Perhaps the most important foothold I gained from my background in agriculture, however, was my relationship with Leroy Musgrave.

During my early fieldwork, I recognized that Leroy was happy to sell me produce but reluctant to engage in conversation. I was careful not to push, hoping he would eventually warm up to me, but things got worse. When I distributed my survey, he belittled it. He mocked the questions, reading them aloud and then giving what I imagine he thought would be the worst answers, such as "I ate no vegetables yesterday" or "I eat fast food every day." His comments prompted several customers, who had agreed to fill out the survey, to return them all or partially blank. My immediate response was to move to the other end of the market and continue. I worried, however, that Leroy would prevent me from continuing my study.

I waited months before asking Leroy for an interview, and was relieved (and a bit surprised) when he agreed. By this time, I had managed to do a few small favors for him, such as loaning my car to Jada so she could go help out on his farm. I drove the two hours to Leroy's farm while the sun was rising, in order both to beat the traffic and to get a few hours of work in before the Central Valley heat became overwhelming. We had agreed that I would come for the whole day and that, in exchange for the interview, I would help him with some basic farm chores. After spending the morning prepping beds, we walked to my car to get the lunch I had brought. I watched him read over my bumper stickers, his eyes moving from "Buy local, boycott corporate globalization" to "The problems we face will not be solved by the minds that created them." "I'm glad you're studying the market because you're a conscious person," he said, smiling. And while I had become increasingly convinced by my experiences at the West Oakland market that "buying local" was, at best, a limited approach to social change, I merely thanked him for the compliment and allowed it to set the tone for our interview.

As we sat on a carpet of wild grape vines beneath a giant oak tree, Leroy spoke at length about both his own life and his experience with the farmers market. Afterward, I asked Leroy about his response to my surveys. "I get suspicious when white people come around asking questions," he said. "White people come around the market asking for information pretty often. I try and wait them out a while before I trust anyone." I was flattered to have earned Leroy's trust.

Not all of my attempts to build relationships with West Oakland participants were so successful. The biggest challenge came during the managerial struggles described in chapters 4 and 5. I was very careful not to become involved, and, fearful that I would be perceived as aligned with Dana because we are both white women, I kept my distance from her. I had by this time become quite close to Xan, Jada, and Jason, all of whom are about my age, and whom I perceived as neutral during the conflict. However, as ethnographers often advise, early alignments can become problematic as conflicts among those we study shift (Lofland and Lofland 1984). As arguments about how the market should be managed continued, all three sided with Dana and began to actively work to establish a more collective approach to market management. I made certain to spend some time each week talking with David in order to ensure that he wouldn't feel as if I'd sided against him. While I believe I was largely successful in this respect, I suspect that some of the vendors and customers who were close to David ceased to see me as an ally. In the only instance in which this was verbalized, a regular customer and friend of David's asked me, snidely, how Dana was doing. "I don't work for Dana," I replied directly. "I'm here because I'm doing a research project." He nodded but had a kind of faraway look in his eyes that led me to believe he wasn't convinced. I would have liked to interview this customer but never asked to do so. Mistakes are an inherent part of the ethnographic process, and in this instance, my flawed negotiation of intergroup tensions affected my access to a potential interview subject.

North Berkeley

In North Berkeley, on the other hand, I could both literally and figuratively let my hair down. Not only did my appearance and personal connections suggest that I belonged in this farmers market community, but I was generally knowledgeable about the larger sustainable agriculture scene. Prior to beginning my research, I had worked as a farm apprentice; I had seen and met several vendors at the Ecological Farming Association's annual conference; and I had volunteered at the annual Hoesdown Harvest festival, a celebration of organic farming that several North Berkeley market farmers regularly attended. Indeed, years earlier, I had interviewed one of the owners of the farm that hosts that festival for a place-based guidebook to the bioregion in which UC Davis exists (Alkon 2002).

Even those vendors to whom I had no personal connections quickly felt like friends. As in West Oakland, I spent the bulk of my early fieldwork at the stand at which I felt most comfortable. In this case, it was the Happy Boy Farm stand. While many vendors and customers were regularly engaged in conversation, Happy Boy employed a young man named Adam who was particularly boisterous. It was through him that I first got a sense of the rhythm and flow of farmers market life. My other early home base was the Ecology Center table. Market managers Herman and Rosalie always offered me one of the empty chairs behind their table. This was an important spot from which to observe because many customers brought up environmental and social justice concerns with the market managers. From this vantage point, I also got a sense of the market community. When a vendor would miss a week of the market, customers would always stop by and ask after them. Eventually, I began to understand the workings of the market enough to participate in, rather than merely observe, these conversations.

In West Oakland, buying food from market vendors was both an important source of entrée and a contribution to the market. In North Berkeley, however, the greater number of vendors, combined with the higher cost of food, made that practice nearly impossible on a graduate student stipend. Indeed, once my presence became more established, vendors began to support me through discounts and freebies. The woman who owned the fish stand was especially generous, often referring to me as her "starving student." Additionally, I learned the art of gleaning, which I described in chapter 5. One evening, I offered to help the employees at Happy Boy pack up their leftover food and tables. Unexpectedly, they offered to trade me produce for this service. We continued to trade for much of the remainder of my fieldwork.

Because participants in the North Berkeley Farmers Market are generally affluent, I felt a lesser imperative to ensure that the community benefited from my research. In this site, I did not pay people for their interview time, and I even allowed those respondents who insisted to pay for food and drinks. I did, however, become one of the Ecology Center's most consistent volunteers, offering to slice and offer samples of various fruits in their season or to sell cider during the annual Holiday Crafts Fair. After completing my surveys and sharing the results with market managers, I also wrote a short article for the farmers market newsletter. These contributions were much less involved than those in West Oakland. I do not believe that my work in North Berkeley was studying up, in the sense of studying elites (Nadar 1982). North Berkeley managers, vendors, and customers may be affluent, but they are not "those who shape attitudes and actually control institutional structures" (284). Indeed, as I have demonstrated, North Berkeley participants are attempting to change oppressive social structure with regards to the food system. Nonetheless, the ethical dictates of feminist ethnography seemed less compelling at this site.

In North Berkeley, I appeared quite similar to other market participants. However, my sociological training, as well as my engagement with the West Oakland farmers market, led me to understand the ways the North Berkeley market was raced and classed. This awareness made my fieldwork in this site less comfortable, particularly in those instances when individuals made comments that demonstrated unacknowledged race and class privilege. There were many instances in which I wanted to question farmers who, for example, stressed individual willingness to pay the high cost of their food over wages and other structural constraints. In the classroom, I am accustomed to deconstructing similar statements. During my fieldwork, however, I knew that I would want to convey the ways in which privilege characterizes this market, and so I manipulated my presentation of self, resisting the urge to respond to such comments. In these instances, my nodding silences were likely interpreted as agreements and contributed to the marginalization of social justice issues. In this way, I became complicit in reinforcing this farmers market's environmental privilege.

COMMUNITY-BASED RESEARCH?

Early in my research in West Oakland, I asked each vendor if they had questions a research project could potentially answer. My conversation with Mrs. Scott of Scott Family Farms served to direct much of my approach. "We'd like to know how we can be more useful to the community," she said humbly. She, like all of the market's participants, was concerned with its low attendance. My first step toward answering this question involved creating a survey. If we could understand more about who shops at the farmers market, and why they do so, I reasoned, managers could better target their advertisements and promotions. I hired Tola Williams, a San Francisco State undergraduate who had been raised in West Oakland and who had been involved in a youth program run by one of the market vendors, to help distribute the surveys. I also used a bit of my fund-ing (provided by the UC Davis Small Farm Center) to purchase fruit from the Scotts. Tola and I distributed the surveys during stone fruit season, and mar-ket customers each received a peach or plum in exchange for their completed responses. I wrote up a summary of these survey results and shared it with market managers and vendors. Market participants were certainly interested, and even a bit surprised, by the survey results. The survey's key finding was that although the market had successfully educated consumers on the need to sup-port black farmers and to increase food access, it appealed mostly to middle-class blacks from outside the neighborhood, as well as to whites. Managers and vendors remained perplexed about how to reach the low-income, food-insecure community for whom the market had been founded.

Months later, I learned of a grant opportunity from the Poverty and Race Research Action Council for collaborative research between investigators and nonprofit organizations. I approached both Dana and David, each of whom was the executive director of a nonprofit, but only Dana was interested. We received the grant and with it were able to increase Tola's hours and tasks, as well as the stipends we would pay to those I interviewed. I also began to receive an hourly wage for conducting interviews. Most importantly, we conceived a series of focus groups with West Oakland residents who did not patronize the farmers market. Through these focus groups, we aimed to learn more about how West Oakland residents managed the constraints of food insecurity — where they procured food, what they ate, and how they made their decisions. I hired Xan West, a market vendor with strong facilitation skills learned through anarchist political organizing, to lead the focus groups. I taped and transcribed this data and again compiled a report to share with market managers and vendors. I also sent this report to directors of other food justice nonprofits who had confided similar problems to me. While my primary goal in conducting these focus groups was not academic publication, I may eventually use the data to that end.

I consider my survey and focus groups, which aim to address questions formulated by those I studied, community-based research. Community-based research is defined as research preformed "by, with or for communities" (F. Fischer 2000), though scholars have noted that these are distinct func-tions (Sze 2006). In the environmental justice movement, community-based research has largely consisted of professional researchers partnering with EJ organizations to collect public health data (such as air and water samples) that can then be used in making policy claims (F. Fischer 2000). Community-based research has become an important tool for EJ communities to quantify the toxicity of their neighborhoods (Corburn 2005; Brown and Mikkelsen 1997).

While my focus groups are quite different from this model, they follow what I believe are the two most important dictates of community-based research: that community members should be involved in each stage of the research, including the formation of research questions, and that research outcomes should benefit the community (Israel et al. 1998). While these focus groups are not formally a part of my research for this book, their results may be my most important contribution to efforts to achieve a just and sustainable food system.

INTELLECTUAL PROCESS

The questions that drive this book, however, are not those of farmers market participants, but arise from theoretical puzzles in sociology and related disciplines. Ethnographers often enter the field guided only by what Malinowski (1922) called "foreshadowed problems," our own best guesses and assumptions as to what will be important. Additionally, and somewhat paradoxically, ethnographers choose our field sites to respond to our own broad questions. Having focused my academic training on the fields of environmental and urban/community sociology, I chose farmers markets because they seemed to be an urban site in which the themes of environment and community would be apparent. Moreover, having become interested in environmental justice, I was particularly curious about how environment and community would be differently understood among racially privileged and marginalized groups.

In both my research approach and analysis, I combined grounded theory with Burawoy's extended case method (Burawoy et al. 1991). Grounded theory emphasizes gathering as much data as possible, coding that data in order to find patterns, and then building an ethnographic account. Analysis, in this sense, consists of the rigorous examination of field data and the search for a productive and relevant story. The extended case method, on the other hand, emphasizes an ongoing dialogue between theory and observation, guiding a researcher toward questions relevant to her discipline. Moreover, it challenges ethnographers to build theory beyond the specificity of our cases by bringing in the larger political and economic structures that shape our research sites. In my account, these include relevant aspects of local history; trajectories of the environmental, food, and environmental justice movements; and the growing emphasis on market responses to environmental and social problems.

My fieldwork in general began with the broadest possible research questions, such as "(How) is environmentalism happening at these farmers markets?" This question oriented me to pay particular attention when those I studied mentioned environmentally relevant themes such as pesticides, land use, and access to resources. After approximately half my time in the field, I began coding and developed a file of environmentally relevant themes. During this time, I also read (and reread) accounts of how the environment is defined in environmental versus environmental justice organizations. I had already recognized from my coded data that access to resources was the most common environmental discourse in West Oakland, but in light of this literature I began to recognize their framings as similar to the EJ movement. I then constructed chapter 4 to examine how the themes of environment and social justice are embodied and practiced by participants in each farmers market. I followed a similar process for my other empirical chapters.

Before I wrote individual empirical chapters, however, I had written both a prospectus and an outline. My writing process was a back-and-forth between the microlevel work of the chapters and attempts to focus my overall framework. I initially wrote parts of chapters 3 and 5 as journal articles and chapter 4 as a conference paper. Only after I had constructed each empirical chapter did I begin to understand the larger argument.

Overall, my research process can be understood as a series of compromises between what I believed would best serve those I studied and what would best drive the academic literature (and my own career). With regard to my career, the latter was most important, and I was often advised not to pursue nontraditional approaches. This factor did not preclude me from taking a more community-based approach to related, applied questions, however. Those I studied were most concerned with the creation of a successful market. They had little interest in building academic theory but were certainly not opposed to it. Their lack of interest in my academic work left me with the ever-problematic position of representing their lives to an academic audience. I have, however, written popular accounts that are accessible to those I studied.

WHEN THEY READ (SOME OF) WHAT WE WRITE

When I began my fieldwork, I was naively certain that because I genuinely enjoy farmers markets and genuinely believe they are capable of doing larger social change work, my interpretations would be largely positive and unproblematic. This was especially true in West Oakland, where I viewed their environmental justice approach as both groundbreaking and heroic and agreed when market managers said they could serve as a model for other marginalized communities. Even in North Berkeley, I was convinced that because I sympathized with the goal of creating an ecologically sustainable and socially just alternative to corporate agribusiness, and because the Ecology Center is explicitly dedicated to social justice as well as to environmental issues, my research would be perceived as helpful.

However, when West Oakland's management disputes ensued, I quickly understood that I could not merely use this farmers market as a standpoint from which to engage in a wider critique of food movements. I would need to critically analyze the discourses and practices its managers, vendors, and customers had developed in order to attempt to explain their social and financial struggles. On the other hand, my own activism had taught me that even bitter disputes among those attempting to run a struggling organization were quite common. Julie Sze's 2006 *Noxious New York* provided a model for how to use such disagreements to produce fruitful data rather than dwelling on the details of the dispute. I have described the overall argument of chapter 5, in which I chronicle these tensions, to both Xan and Jason. Both agreed that it was a fair treatment of the situation, and I later heard Xan incorporate my argument into her own explanation of the management disputes. Other vendors and managers, however, have seen only a short article that appeared in *Gastronomica* (Guthman 2007), which presents the farmers market in a positive light and merely alludes to challenges the market faces.

On the other hand, I am still struggling with how to share my insights concerning race and class with participants in North Berkeley. Ethnographic studies of whiteness, as Delia Kenny writes in her autoethnographic work, involve "naming the unnamable [and] marking the unmarked." Writing about whiteness requires the ethnographer "to articulate that which cannot and should not be said" (2000, 114). My challenge in North Berkeley has been when, how, and with whom to discuss racial and economic privilege. I see doing so as an ethical imperative not only to share my findings with those I study but to empower them to better direct their alternative food systems work toward the promotion of racial and economic equality.

Throughout my fieldwork, I have had casual conversations with market managers and farm employees about these issues but have avoided engaging farm and business owners, who are the most invested in the market's affluence. Recently, I have coauthored a paper on whiteness in farmers markets, which compares my North Berkeley case to a predominantly white farmers market in Davis. I have sent this paper to market managers, who have been enthusiastic and complimentary. A recent e-mail from a market manager read, "I'm glad you're examining the topic. The sustainable ag movement too often fails to acknowledge its privileged nature." I am sincerely grateful for this response but also wonder whether he is merely giving lip service to issues of privilege rather than really trying to engage with them. My hope is that market managers will want to continue a dialogue about how my research can inform their work. Both community-based research and feminist ethnography emphasize the importance of ongoing relationships between the researcher and those she studies. This process, I hope, will continue beyond the completion of this book.

In sum, I want to emphasize that my ethnographic research has been a process of building relationships and allowing those relationships to inform empirical and theoretical insights. In this piece, I have focused on the way those relationships were mediated by my own body, which is raced, classed, and stylized in particular ways. Like all social relationships, ethnographic work involves a high degree of unpredictability, and I suspect that all fieldworkers survive and adapt to tensions during the course of our work. Additionally, I hope to have provided some insights for ethnographers interested in the field of community-based research, which has been largely dominated by public health scholars. I believe it is possible to do work that is in some ways community based while maintaining an intellectually rigorous process, contributing to both those we study and our academic disciplines.

FOUR YEARS LATER

It's been nearly four years since I finished school and began a job as an assistant professor at the University of the Pacific. I felt fortunate to find a position so close to home, and given what's happened to the job market since, fortunate to have found a position at all. In addition to personal reasons, I was glad to stay local because I thought it would help me stay active and connected to those who gave of their time, lives, and insights so that this book could exist.

As I read over the first part of this epilogue and think back to the research experience, I'm conflicted in a way that the book itself does not represent, in a way that I did not feel at the time. Indeed, I remember Kimberly Nettles, an advisor with expertise in feminist ethnography, reading the above and saying it seemed too neat. There wasn't enough internal struggle. Though I respected her feedback, I knew that there was no internal struggle in the epilogue because I hadn't felt one. As a graduate student, I was focused on the task ahead — completing my research, finishing school, getting a job. My relationships with those I studied were rooted in my lived experience at the time, which was middle-class and educated but without much income. I contributed what I could — I bought food, applied for grant money in a way that would put some in their pockets, attended various events put on by the involved nonprofits. Even after I finished collecting data, I continued to purchase goods from market vendors. I helped some of the involved nonprofits write grant applications. I even served as a board member for the Oakland Food Connection, an organization Jason Harvey founded after he left the West Oakland market. At the time, it felt like enough.

It doesn't anymore. When I wandered off track during graduate school, my advisor, Tom Beamish, used to say that this project was the key to a job. Mine got me a position, a salary, and all that goes with it. By 2009, the West Oakland Farmers Market was struggling even more than it had been when I was collecting data. It closed for the winter that year, and when summertime came, the only regulars were the Scott Family Farm and Ms. Charlotte. A few additional vendors (though not people depicted in this study) rotated through. It closed again the following winter and never reopened.

About a year before I graduated I met my partner. I moved from the house I shared with housemates on the border of North and West Oakland to his one-bedroom home in North Berkeley. I continued to frequent the North Berkeley market, which was now within walking distance. Needless to say, it's doing very well. But each time I shop there, I recognize that the literal and social distance between myself and those I knew in West Oakland keeps growing. Moving made it harder to continue supporting the West Oakland Farmers Market. This difficulty only increased as I began working as an assistant professor and struggled to manage my teaching load and service requirements and to find time to revise this book. I still run into people from time to time, and our interactions are warm. I have no doubts that they care about and are happy to see me, and I feel the same way about them. But I'm equally certain that my project hasn't made any difference in their lives, despite the large difference it has made in mine.

And I'm less sure than ever how that difference might be made. Despite my initial desires to use the West Oakland and North Berkeley Farmers Markets as standpoints from which to critique systems of industrial agriculture and institutional racism, my study revealed dilemmas intrinsic to the goals and strategies these activists have chosen. How do I contribute to a movement while recognizing its faults? Yes, many social movements have a place for sympathetic critique, and this book, I hope it's clear, is very sympathetic to the needs and desires of those I studied. And yet I don't see this book as having done anything for them. Indeed, I recognize that my very desire to "help" people in West Oakland represents the kind of white, liberal privilege that activists there are working against.

My only consolation is that the predominantly white food movement increasingly recognizes the need to understand the influence of racial and economic inequality on the food system. These issues are not yet central but are moving in that direction. In some small way, I can see my writing as contributing to this effort. This book, by focusing on the inability of green economic strategies to deal with economic inequalities, adds an additional layer to the antiracist critique of the food movement. Perhaps it can inspire the creation of new discourses and practices that work toward healthy food and environmental protection as intrinsic goods rather than commodities, and thus help create a more just and sustainable world for all.

NOTES

CHAPTER ONE. *Going Green, Growing Green*

1. I have chosen not to use the apostrophe that commonly connotes farmers' owner-ship of farmers markets. Patricia Allen (2004) has convincingly argued that alternative foods movements place too much emphasis on farmers' economic success and that this is one reason social justice issues become marginalized. To subtly question that aspect of the movement's strategy, I choose to think of farmers markets as consisting of, rather than belonging to, farmers.

2. The exception is a southern California date farmer, who delivers his dried prod-ucts in bulk to a San Francisco–based employee. It is this employee who brings the fruit to the farmers market each week.

3. It is customary for ethnographers to change the names of both the places we study and the individuals involved in our research. However, participants in both farmers markets preferred to be identified by name. Managers and vendors, as well as those cus-tomers who were aware of my study, are identified accordingly. Others, who I knew or suspected did not know research was taking place, are identified only by demographic markers.

4. Ecologically, food movement activists point out industrial agriculture's depen-dence on mechanization and monoculture, arguing that this dependence creates in-creased reliance on fossil-fuel-based inputs, decreases soil fertility, and pollutes rivers and streams (Altieri 2000). Advocates also push for local food in order to lessen the environmental costs of food transport (Halweil 2004). Economically, defenders of fam-ily farms argue that reliance on fossil-fuel-based inputs creates economic advantages for those with ready supplies of capital, encouraging the consolidation of small farms into agribusiness corporations (Clapp and Fuchs 2009; Bell 2004). Such consolidation is aided by the U.S. Farm Bills, for which industrial agriculture lobbies heavily (Liebman 1983). Scholars and activists alike have noted consolidation's devastating economic and social effects on farmers and rural communities (Bell 2004, Goldschmidt 1978[1947]) and argue that industrial agriculture contributes to the impersonal nature of urban life (Lyson 2004; Berry 1990).

5. It is not uncommon for activists of color who are doing work seemingly aligned with a movement's goals to be left out of their narrative histories. For attempts to correct for this trend among feminists, see Roth 2003, and among environmentalists, see Taylor 2009.

6. This desire has been echoed by many food movement activists responding, in part, to critiques of exclusivity. Indeed, food movement calls for food justice have been so resounding as to obscure the movement's roots in marginalized communities. In con-trast to other work on food justice (Gottlieb and Joshi 2010), I believe it is important to

honor the roots of struggles for food justice in communities of color and responses to institutionalized racism.

CHAPTER TWO. *Understanding the Green Economy*

1. Although they share the same general framework, debates within these groups are often fierce. Some advocate a stronger socialism, claiming that goods should be produced and distributed by the state, while others embody an anarchist approach that seeks to abolish the state and distribute goods through civil society.

2. In this way, natural capitalism is very much aligned with the theory of ecological modernizations popular among European environmental sociologists. Eco-modernists attempt to understand how industrialized nations integrate environmental concerns into their economies. They tend to be more optimistic about the abilities of capitalist societies to address environmental problems than are Marxists (see, for example, Mol and Sonnenfeld 2000; Spaargaren 2000).

CHAPTER THREE. *The Taste of Place*

1. Just a month earlier, a strike initiated by students protesting for a Third World College, and supported by the American Federation of Teachers and Local 1570 (teaching assistants) and the student government, ended violently when then-governor Ronald Reagan called in the National Guard (Wang 1997).

2. The Black Panthers were the primary target of COINTELPRO, a program through which the FBI sought to neutralize what it called "black nationalist hate groups," regarded by FBI director J. Edgar Hoover as "the greatest threat to the internal security of the country." Agents infiltrated the groups, harassed members, and even assassinated party leaders. They also penned forged letters aimed to create violent rivalries between the BPP and other black organizations. Although the program was officially ended in 1971, federal government surveillance of left-wing organizations, particularly in communities of color, is ongoing (Lazerow and Williams 2006).

3. For an overview of race and urban renewal see Massey and Denton's *American Apartheid* (1993).

4. The Cypress Freeway was destroyed during the 1989 earthquake and was rebuilt further to the west. The original freeway is now Mandela Parkway. The West Oakland Farmers Market currently stands at the intersection of Seventh and Mandela.

5. Her assessment is a bit exaggerated. There are several freeway entrances in West Oakland, though there is a greater number of exits. Still, this vendor's sentiment reflects her interpretation of the freeways' designs.

6. Antihierarchical forms, however, often privilege the goals of those participants with the most social and cultural capital, which often correspond to privileges of race, class, and gender (Kleinman 1996).

CHAPTER 4. *Creating a Just Sustainability*

1. Dana is not related to Jason Harvey, the market manager.

2. For more information on the connection between organic farming, seed saving, and biodiversity, see Shiva 2000.

3. Because GM corn is widely used and corn is largely pollinated by wind, many alternative food activists are skeptical of any corn that is not certified organic.

4. Although her last name is common to Latinas, Deborah Koontz Garcia is a white woman. Her name refers to her late husband Jerry.

5. Farmed salmon, according to the "Fish List," should be avoided in part because the fish can genetically corrupt wild salmon stocks. They should also be avoided because high levels of pesticides and antibiotics are used to control disease among densely contained stocks, and because their concentrated feces represents a risk to the streams in which their cages are kept. The "Fish List" is a guide to healthy and sustainable seafood, produced by a partnership between the Blue Ocean Institute, Environmental Defense, and the Monterrey Bay Aquarium.

6. Market managers tended to answer my questions in terms of all three of the Berkeley Farmers Markets rather than just North Berkeley. The farm that is unionized and the farm that financed land for their former employees do not sell on Thursdays, but they are present at the larger Tuesday and Saturday markets that are held at the other locations.

7. "Food Not Bombs" is a name taken by various independent groups collecting, cooking, and serving food to homeless and low-income people as well as disaster survivors. According to their website, "For over 25 years [Food Not Bombs] has worked to end hunger and has supported actions to stop the globalization of the economy, restrictions to the movements of people, [and] exploitation and the destruction of the earth" (www.foodnotbombs.net).

8. By the time my fieldwork ended, the collaborative had disbanded and the market was managed by Mo' Better Food.

9. While most vendors and managers called one another by their first names, several preferred to be called by their honorific (Mr., Ms., Señor, Señora). Generally, this practice is reserved for elders. I have kept my writing consistent with how market participants tend to refer to one another.

10. This conversation took place in Spanish. This is a rough translation from my field notes.

11. It is possible to view this racial performance as essentialist, as has been done of Afrocentrism more generally. The dominant notion of blackness evidenced at the farmers market certainly invokes unstated class and gender identities, which are explored in chapter 5.

12. Other options included location, good-quality food, good prices, fun atmosphere, and other.

CHAPTER FIVE. *Who Participates in the Green Economy?*

1. Tönnies (1988) describes a binary between *gemeinschaft* and *gesellschaft*, or community and society, in which strong social ties reside only in the former. Similar notions can be found in Durkheim's (1997[1893]) mechanical and organic solidarity and Simmel's (1950) conception of the stranger. Contemporary notions of community as the exclusive province of rural small towns were espoused by the residents depicted in Michael Bell's (1994) *Childerly* and the rural respondents featured in David Hummon's (1990) *Commonplaces.*

2. While my survey results describe the market clientele as 40 percent white, 35 percent black, 9 percent Latino/a, and 5 percent Asian/Pacific Islander, my field notes reflect my general, though not quantified, impression that blacks were most likely to refuse to complete the survey. This may reflect, in part, my own positionality as a white, middle-class woman. Although the research assistant I hired to aid in survey distribution is an African American woman raised in West Oakland, my presence may have marked her as untrustworthy. More likely, however, is what one African American farmer identified as black individuals' common mistrust of research and researchers.

3. Jason has also confided that customers who resent him for holding a management position refer to him as "the white kid." For a discussion on the relationship between class and color among African Americans, see Keith and Herring, 1991.

4. Because my assumption was that most customers were low income, I asked for income in increments of $10,000 up to $60,000. For that reason, I do not have more specific data on the market's higher-income clients.

5. See Finney's forthcoming book, *Black Faces, White Spaces*, on the associations between whiteness and the outdoors.

6. This refers to the three managers and one special events coordinator who were employed by the market during the bulk of my fieldwork.

7. Both the race and gender counts ignore the predominantly young, white farm employees who tend to have high turnover in favor of counting only long-term vendors.

CHAPTER 6. *Greening Growth*

1. In contrast to neoclassical economists, who presume that economic decisions are based only on producers' and consumers' "rational" calculations of costs and benefits, economic sociologists and geographers have long argued that economic decisions are fundamentally social (Polanyi 2001[1944]; Zelizer 2007). In this theory, markets are not merely creators of economic conditions but also constructed social worlds (DiMaggio 1994; Fligstein 1996; Zelizer 2007). Moral systems of exchange depart strongly from neoclassical assumptions because morals and values explicitly guide economic exchange. However, economic considerations such as marketness and instrumentalism continue to influence economic behavior (Block 1990; Hinrichs 2000).

2. Washington has been widely criticized, both during his own time and since, for his focus on economic rather than political empowerment and for de-emphasizing the myriad structural constraints faced by black Americans in the decades following slavery. Interestingly, after hearing David speak at the Ecological Farming Association's annual conference, Patricia Allen remarked that David's approach was similarly flawed. Focusing on black entrepreneurship, she argues, calls for black economic development without criticizing the system that makes it so difficult.

3. This finding mirrors Kleinman's (1996) insight that regard for volunteerism among relative elites can reinforce privilege.

4. In 2009, after nearly a decade of activism, a deal was finally reached that would see the dam removed. However, it will likely be several more years before the salmon runs are restored.

EPILOGUE. *Reading, Writing, Relationship*

1. Writing in 1989, Annette Lareau claims that this has not changed, though I would argue that a wealth of ethnographic accounts have been published since that time.

2. Critics have accused ethnographers focusing on the self of navel gazing, meaning that the subject of their ethnographies becomes themselves rather than those they set out to study (for example, Behar 2003). I have sought to keep the focus on those I observed and interacted with but to intermittently refer to my own embodied presence in order to remind the reader that the understanding of these sites is filtered through my eyes.

3. Although I had no funding, I reasoned that I could do this for about a thousand dollars. I was prepared to pay out of pocket but was relieved months later when the UC Davis Small Farm Center agreed to a small grant to cover these expenses.

4. Indeed, another Davis acquaintance had become a partner in one of the North Berkeley market farms and sold regularly at the market. I remember him telling a common friend that I didn't seem that into my project. I was a bit offended but understood that what he was responding to was a lack of clear direction. I didn't always know what to do with myself during my early days at the market.

5. Ethnographers of color who have studied their own ethnic group have written that this poses a different, though not necessarily easier, set of influences (see, for example, Zavella 1991).

REFERENCES

24/7 Wall Street. 2009. "Sustainable Business Design: Top Ten Greenwashing Companies in America." http://sustainablebusinessdesign.blogspot.com/2009/04/top-ten-greenwashing-companies-in.html (accessed December 29, 2009).

Acoli, Sundiata. N.d. "A Brief History of the Black Panther Party and Its Place in the Black Liberation Movement." The Talking Drum. http://www.thetalkingdrum.com/bla2.html (accessed January 2, 2009).

Adams, Ansel. 1942. "The Tetons — Snake River." www.archives.gov (accessed July 14, 2009).

Agyeman, Julian. 2005. *Sustainable Communities and the Challenge of Environmental Justice*. New York: NYU Press.

Agyeman, Julian, Robert D. Bullard, and Bob Evans. 2003. *Just Sustainabilities: Development in an Unequal World*. Cambridge, Mass.: MIT Press.

Agyeman, Julian, and Bob Evans. 2004. "'Just Sustainability': The Emerging Discourse of Environmental Justice in Britain?" *Geographical Journal* 170(2): 155–164.

Agyeman, Julian, and Tom Evans. 2003. "Toward Just Sustainability in Urban Communities: Building Equity Rights with Sustainable Solutions." *Annals of the American Academy of Political and Social Science* 590: 35–53.

Alameda County Department of Public Health. 2005. "West Oakland Community Information Book Update." http://www.acphd.org/AXBYCZ/Admin/DataReports/2005update-westoakland.pdf (accessed December 1, 2005).

Alkon, Alison Hope. 2002. "The Hoes Down Festival." In *Putah and Cache: A Thinking Mammal's Guide to the Bioregion*, ed. Boyer, Goggans, Leroy, Robertson, and Thayer. http://bioregion.ucdavis.edu/book/Contents.html (accessed December 30, 2009).

Alkon, Alison Hope, and Christie Grace McCullen. 2010. "Whiteness and Farmers Markets: Performances, Perpetuations . . . Contestations?" *Antipode, a Radical Journal of Geography*.

Alkon, Alison Hope, and Kari Marie Norgaard. 2009. "Breaking the Food Chains: An Investigation of Food Justice Activism." *Sociological Inquiry* 79(3): 289–305.

Allen, Barbara. 2003. *Uneasy Alchemy: Citizens and Experts in Louisiana's Chemical Corridor Disputes*. Cambridge, Mass.: MIT Press.

Allen, Patricia. 2004. *Together at the Table: Sustainability and Sustenance in the American Agrifood System*. State College: Pennsylvania State University Press.

Alston, Dana. 1990. *Taking Back Our Lives: A Report to the Panos Institute on Environment, Community Development, and Race in the United States*. Washington, D.C. The Panos Institute.

Altieri, Miguel. 2000. "Ecological Impacts of Industrial Agriculture and the Possibilities for Truly Sustainable Farming." In *Hungry for Profit*, ed. Fred Magdoff, John Bellamy Foster, and Fred Buttel, 77–92. New York: Monthly Review Press.

Anders, Jentri. 1990. *Beyond Counterculture: The Community of Mateel*. Pullman: Washington State University Press.

Anderson, Elijah. 2011. *Cosmopolitan Canopy: Race and Civility in Everyday Life*. New York: W. W. Norton and Company.

Andreatta, Susan. 2005. "Urban Connections to Locally Grown Produce." In *Urban Place: Reconnecting with the Natural World*, ed. Peggy Barlett, 117–140. Cambridge, Mass.: MIT Press.

Babey, Susan H., Allison L. Diamant, Theresa A. Hastert, Stefan Harvey, Harold Goldstein, Rebecca Flournoy, Rajni Banthia, Victor Rubin, and Sarah Treudhaft. 2008. *Designed for Disease: The Link Between Local Food Environments and Obesity and Diabetes*. Los Angeles: California Center for Public Health Advocacy /PolicyLink/UCLA Center for Health Policy Research.

Bagwell, Beth. 1982. *Oakland: Story of a City*. San Francisco, Calif.: Presidio Press.

Banuri, Tariq. 2009. "Multiple Crises and Sustainable Development." United Nations Department of Economic and Social Affairs. www.un.org/esa/dsd/dsd/dsd_pdfs /MultipleCrisesandSD.pdf (accessed December 30, 2009).

Barlett, Peggy. 2005. *Urban Place: Reconnecting with the Natural World*. Cambridge, Mass.: MIT Press.

Barley, Shanta. 2009. "BP Brings 'Green Era' to a Close." *BBC*. http://news.bbc.co.uk/2 /hi/in_depth/sci_tech/green_room/8040468.stm (accessed December 31, 2009).

Bay Area Blues Society. N.d. "The Music They Played on 7th Street." http://www .bayareabluessociety.net/The_Music_They_Played_On_7th_Street_Project.html (accessed January 2, 2009).

Bay Area Regional Health Inequities Initiative. 2008. "Health Inequalities in the Bay Area." http://www.barhii.org/ (accessed January 2, 2009).

Baysden, Chris. 2008. "Clorox Buys Burt's Bees for $913 M." *Triangle Business Journal*, Feburary 15. http://triangle.bizjournals.com/triangle/stories/2008/02/18/focus4 .html (accessed July 20, 2008).

Beamish, Thomas, and Nicole W. Biggart. 2006. "Economic Worlds of Work: Uniting Economic Sociology with the Sociology of Work." In *Social Theory at Work*, ed. Marek Korczynski, Randy Hodson, and Paul K. Edwards, 233–271. New York: Oxford University Press.

Bednar, Robert. 1997. "Postmodern Vistas, Landscapes, Photography, and Tourism in the Contemporary American West." PhD dissertation, University of Texas, Austin, American Civilization Program.

Behar, Ruth. 2003. *Translated Woman: Crossing the Border with Esperanza's Story*. Boston: Beacon Press.

Belasco, Warren. 1993. *Appetite for Change: How the Counterculture Took On the Food Industry*. Ithaca, N.Y.: Cornell University Press.

Bell, Michael. 2004. *Farming for Us All: Practical Agriculture and the Cultivation of Sustainability*. State College: Penn State University Press.

———. 1994. *Childerly: Nature and Morality in a Country Village*. Chicago: University of Chicago Press.

Berry, Wendell. 1990. *What Are People For?* New York: North Point Press.

Bhagwati, Jagdish. 2004. *In Defense of Globalization*. New York: Oxford University Press.

———. 1993. "The Case for Free Trade." *Scientific American* 269(5): 18–23.

Biggart, Nicole Woolsey, and Rick Delbridge. 2004. "Systems of Exchange." *Academy of Management Review* 29: 28–49.

Biltekoff, Charlotte. Forthcoming. *Eating Right in America: Food, Health, and Citizenship from Domestic Science to Obesity*. Durham, N.C.: Duke University Press.

Bishop, Douglas L. 2008. "The Farmers Market: Think Globally, Act Locally." http://www.articlesbase.com/environment-articles (accessed July 13, 2009).

Black Farmers and Agriculturalists Association. 2004. "Statement from BFAA on the Research of the Environmental Working Group." http://www.coax.net/people/lwf/BFAA.HTM (accessed July 13, 2009).

Black Panther Party. N.d. "Rise of the Black Panther Party." http://www.blackpanther.org/legacytwo.htm (accessed January 2, 2009).

———. N.d. "Ten Point Plan." http://www.blackpanther.org/TenPoint.htm (accessed January 2, 2009).

Block, Fred. 1990. *Postindustrial Possibilities: A Critique of Economic Discourse*. Berkeley: University of California Press.

Blokland, Talja. 2003. *Urban Bonds*. Cambridge: Polity Press.

Bookchin, Murray. 2004 [1971]. *Post-Scarcity Anarchism*. Oakland: AK Press.

———. 1999. *Anarchism, Marxism, and the Future of the Left: Interviews and Essays, 1993–1998*. Oakland: AK Press.

Bourdieu, Pierre. 1984. *Distinction: A Social Critique of the Judgment of Taste*. London: Routledge.

Boyer, Amy J., Jan Goggans, Daniel Leroy, David Robertson, and Rob Thayer, eds. 2002. *Putah and Cache: A Thinking Mammal's Guide to the Watershed*. http://bioregion.ucdavis.edu/book/Contents.html (accessed December 30, 2009).

Bradley, Karen J. 1995. "Agrarian Ideology: California Grangers and the Post–World War II Farm Policy Debate." *Agriculture History* 69(2): 240–256.

Braun, Bruce, and Noel Castree, eds. 1988. *Remaking Reality: Nature at the Millennium*. New York: Routledge.

Brenneman, Richard. 2004. "The Bloody Beginnings of People's Park." *Berkeley Daily Planet.* April 20. http://www.berkeleydailyplanet.com/issue/2004-04-20/article /18700?status=301 (accessed January 2, 2009).

Bretell, Caroline. 1993. *When They Read What We Write: The Politics of Ethnography.* Westport, Conn.: Bergin and Garvey.

Brockington, Dan, Jim Igoe, and Kai Schmidt-Soltau. 2006. "Conservation, Human Rights, and Poverty Reduction." *Conservation Biology* 20(1): 250–252.

Brown, Phil, and F. I. T. Ferguson. 1995. "Making a Big Stink: Women's Work, Women's Relationships, and Toxic Waste Activism." *Gender and Society* 9(2): 145–172.

Brown, Phil, and Edwin J. Mikkelsen. 1997. *No Safe Place: Toxic Waste, Leukemia, and Community Action.* Berkeley: University of California Press.

Brown, Sandy, and Christy Getz. 2008. "Privatizing Farm Worker Justice: Regulating Labor Through Voluntary Certification and Labeling." *Geoforum* 39: 1184–1196.

Brulle, Robert. 2000. *Agency, Democracy, and Nature: The U.S. Environmental Movement from a Critical Theory Perspective.* Cambridge, Mass.: MIT Press.

Brundtland Commission. 1987. *Our Common Future.* Oxford: Oxford University Press.

Bryant, Bunyard, and Paul Mohai. 1992. *Race and the Incidence of Environmental Hazards: A Time for Discourse.* Boulder, Colo.: Westview.

Bryant, Raymond L., and Sinead Bailey. 1997. *Third World Political Ecology.* New York: Routledge.

Bullard, Robert. 1990. *Dumping in Dixie.* Boulder, Colo.: Westview.

Burawoy, Michael, Alice Burton, Ann Arnett Ferguson, and Kathryn J. Fox. 1991. *Ethnography Unbound: Power and Resistance in the Modern Metropolis.* Berkeley: University of California Press.

Butler, Richard, and Tom Hinch. 2007. *Tourism and Indigenous Peoples: Issues and Implications.* Oxford and Burlington, Mass.: Elsevier.

Butler, Tom. 2002. *Wild Earth: Wild Ideas for a World out of Balance.* Minneapolis, Minn.: Milkweed Press.

Buttel, Fred, Olaf F. Larson, and Gilbert W. Gillespie Jr. 1990. *The Sociology of Agriculture.* New York: Greenwood Press.

California Alcoholic Beverage Control. 2006. "Fact Sheet: Oakland Alcohol Retailers." Z;\Community Safety and Justice/Alcohol outlets\Website\Factsheet_1.24.6.doc (accessed April 3, 2006).

Campbell, Scott. 1996. "Green Cities, Growing Cities, Just Cities: Urban Planning and the Contradictions of Sustainable Development." *Journal of the American Planning Association* 62(3): 296–312.

Capek, Stella. 1993. "The 'Environmental Justice' Frame: A Conceptual Discussion and an Application." *Social Problems* 40(1): 5–24.

Carney, Judith. 2010. *In the Shadow of Slavery: Africa's Botanical Legacy in the Atlantic World.* Berkeley: University of California Press.

Castree, Noel. 2008. "Neoliberalising Nature: Processes, Effects, and Evaluations." *Environment and Planning A* 40(1): 153–173.

Catton, William. 1980. *Overshoot: The Ecological Basis of Revolutionary Change.* Urbana: University of Illinois Press.

Center for Urban Education about Sustainable Agriculture. N.d. "Lucero Organic Farms." http://cuesa.org/markets/farmers/farm_58.php (accessed July 13, 2009).

Chu, Jeff. 2009. "Are Fair Trade Goods Recession Proof? Wal-mart, Starbucks, and Cadbury Hope So." http://www.fastcompany.com/blog/jeff-chu/inquisition/fair-trade-recession-proof (accessed July 13, 2009).

Clapp, Jennifer, and Doris Fuchs. 2009. *Corporate Power in Global Agrifood Governance.* Cambridge, Mass.: MIT Press.

Clark, Anna. 2010. "The Foodie Indictment of Feminism." *Salon Magazine.* http://www.salon.com/life/broadsheet/2010/05/26/foodies_and_feminism/index.html (accessed June 8, 2010).

Cleaver, Eldridge. 1969. *Soul on Ice.* New York: Delta.

Cole, Luke, and Sheila Foster. 2001. *From the Ground Up: The Rise of the Environmental Justice Movement.* New York: NYU Press.

Collins, Patricia Hill. 2000 [1990]. *Black Feminist Thought: Knowledge, Consciousness, and the Politics of Empowerment.* New York: Routledge.

Coontz, Stephanie. 2000. *The Way We Never Were: The American Family and the Nostalgia Trap.* New York: Basic Books.

Copeland, Alan. 1969. *People's Park.* New York: Ballantine Books.

Corburn, Jason. 2005. *Street Science: Community Knowledge and Environmental Health Justice.* Cambridge, Mass.: MIT Press.

Covey, Herbert C. 2007. *African American Slave Medicine: Herbal and Non-Herbal Treatments.* New York: Lexington Books.

Creed, Gerald W. 2006. *The Seductions of Community: Emancipations, Oppressions, Questions.* Santa Fe: School of American Research Press.

Cronon, William. 1995. "The Trouble with Wilderness, or, Getting Back to the Wrong Nature." In *Uncommon Ground: Exploring New Pathways for Change,* ed. William Cronon, 23–68. New York: Norton.

Curtis, Karen, and Stephanie McClellan. 1995. "Falling through the Safety Net: Poverty, Food Assistance, and Shopping Constraints in an American City." *Urban Anthropology* 24: 93–130.

Daly, Herman. 1996. *Beyond Growth: The Economics of Sustainable Development.* Boston, Mass.: Beacon Press.

Daly, Herman, and Kenneth Townsend. 1993. *Valuing the Earth: Economics, Ecology, Ethics.* Cambridge, Mass.: MIT Press.

Danaher, Kevin, Shannon Biggs, and Jason Mark. 2007. *Building the Green Economy: Success Stories from the Grassroots.* New York: Paradigm.

Daniel, Cletus E. 1981. *Bitter Harvest: A History of California Farmworkers.* Ithaca, N.Y.: Cornell University Press.

DeLuca, Kevin. 2007. "A Wilderness Environmentalism Manifesto: Contesting the Infinite Self-absorption of Humans." In *Environmental Justice and*

Environmentalism: The Environmental Justice Challenge to the Environmental Justice Movement, ed. Ronald Sandler and Phaedra Pezzullo, 27–56. Cambridge, Mass.: MIT Press.

DiChiro, Giovanna. 1995. "Nature as Community: The Convergence of Environment and Social Justice." In *Uncommon Ground: Rethinking the Human Place in Nature*, ed. William Cronon, 298–320. New York: Norton.

Digger Archives. N.d. "Digger Bread (Made with Love)." http://www.diggers.org /diggers/digbread.html (accessed January 2, 2009).

DiMaggio, Paul. 1994. "Culture and the Economy." In *Handbook of Economic Sociology*, ed. Neil J. Smelser and Richard Swedberg, 27–57. Princeton, N.J.: Princeton University Press.

di Prima, Diane. 1969. *Revolutionary Letters*. San Francisco, Calif.: Last Gasp.

Dobson, Andrew. 2007. *Green Political Thought*. New York: Routledge.

———. 2003. "Social Justice and Environmental Sustainability: Ne'er the Twain Shall Meet?" In *Just Sustainabilities: Development in an Unequal World*, ed. Julian Agyeman, Robert Bullard, and Bob Evans, 83–96. Cambridge, Mass.: MIT Press.

Drew, Jesse. 1998. "Call Any Vegetable: The Politics of Food in San Francisco." In *Reclaiming San Francisco: History, Politics, Culture*, ed. James Brook, Chris Carlsson, and Nancy J. Peters, 317–331. San Francisco, Calif.: City Lights Books.

Dryzek, John S., and James P. Lester. 1995. "Alternative Views of the Environmental Problematic." In *Environmental Politics and Policy: Theories and Evidence*, ed. James P. Lester, 328–346. Durham, N.C.: Duke University Press.

Duneier, Mitchell. 1999. *Sidewalk*. New York: Farrar, Strauss and Giroux.

DuPuis, E. Melanie, and David Goodman. 2005. "Should We Go 'Home' to Eat?: Toward a Reflexive Politics of Localism." *Journal of Rural Studies* 21: 359–371.

Durkheim, Emile. 1997[1893]. *Suicide: A Study in Sociology*. Ed. George Simpson; trans. John A. Spaulding. Washington, D.C.: Free Press. The Ecology Center. ecologycenter.org (accessed 2005–2009).

Echols, Alice. 1994. "Nothing Distant about It: Women's Liberation and 60s Radicalism." In *The Sixties: From Memory to History*, ed. David Faber, 149–174. Chapel Hill: UNC Press.

Economist. 2011. "If You Build it, They May Not Come: A Shortage of Healthy Food Is Not the Only Problem." http://www.economist.com/node/18929190 (accessed January 26, 2012).

Eisen, Mark. 2008. "Michael Pollan: Eating Is a Political Act." *The Progressive*. http:// www.alternet.org/health/105667 (accessed January 16, 2010).

Ekins, Paul. 2000. *Economic Growth and Environmental Sustainability: The Prospects for Green Growth*. New York: Routledge.

Emerson, Robert, Rachel Fretz, and Linda Shaw. 1995. *Writing Ethnographic Fieldnotes*. Chicago: University of Chicago Press.

Estabrook, Barry. 2011. *Tomatoland: How Modern Industrial Agriculture Destroyed Our Most Alluring Fruit*. New York: Andrew McMeel.

Finney, Carolyn. Forthcoming. *Black Faces, White Spaces: African Americans and the Great Outdoors*. Chapel Hill: UNC Press.

Fischer, Frank. 2000. *Citizens, Experts, and the Environment: The Politics of Local Knowledge*. Durham: Duke University Press.

Fischer, Klaus. 2006. *America in Black, White, and Gray: The Stormy 60s*. London: Continuum International Publishing Group.

Fischman, Charles. 2007. "How Green Is Wal-Mart?" http://www.fastcompany.com /magazine/118/how-green-is-wal-mart.html (accessed July 25, 2008).

Fletcher, Thomas. 2003. *From Love Canal to Environmental Justice: The Politics of Hazardous Waste on the Canada-U.S. Border*. Ontario, Canada: Broadview Press.

Fligstein, Neil. 1996. "The Economic Sociology of the Transition from Socialism." *American Journal of Sociology* 101(4): 1074–1081.

Food Not Bombs. "The Story of Food Not Bombs." http://www.foodnotbombs.net /story.html (accessed July 14, 2009)

Foster, John Bellamy. 1995. "Global Ecology and the Common Good." *Monthly Review*, February. http://findarticles.com/p/articles/mi_m1132/is_n9_v46/ai_16687113/ (accessed February 16, 2010).

Frank, David John, Ann Hironaka, and Evan Schofer. 2000. "The Nation-State and the Natural Environment Over the Twentieth Century." *American Sociological Review* 65: 96–116.

Frankenberg, Ruth. 1993. *White Women, Race Matters: The Social Construction of Whiteness*. Minneapolis: University of Minnesota Press.

Freudenburg, William R., Scott Frickel, and Robert Gramling. 1995. "Beyond the Nature/Society Divide: Learning to Think about a Mountain." *Sociological Forum* 10(3): 361–392.

Frog Hollow Farm. N.d. http://www.froghollow.com/store/site/index.cfm (accessed July 13, 2009).

Fuller, Andrea. 2004. "A History of Food Insecurity in West Oakland, Calif.: Supermarket Location." peoplesgrocery.org (accessed January 2, 2009).

Garvey, Marcus, and Bob Blaisdell. 2005. *Selected Writings and Speeches of Marcus Garvey*. New York: Dover Publications.

Gaytan, Sarita Marie. 2004. "Globalizing Resistance: Slow Food and New Local Imaginaries." *Food, Culture and Society* 7(1): 97–116.

Gilbert, Jess, Gwen Sharp, and Sydney Felin. 2002. "The Loss and Persistence of Black-Owned Farms and Farmland: A Review of the Research Literature and Its Implications." *Southern Rural Sociology* 18: 1–30.

Gilmore, Ruth Wilson. 2007. *Golden Gulag: Surplus, Crisis, and Opposition in Globalizing California*. Berkeley: University of California Press.

Glaser, Barney, and Anselm Strauss. 1967. *The Discovery of Grounded Theory: Strategy for Qualitative Research*. Hawthorne, N.Y.: Aldine.

Goldman, Benjamin. 1996. "What Is the Future of Environmental Justice?" *Antipode* 28(2): 122–141.

Goldschmidt, Walter. 1978 [1947]. *As You Sow*. New York: Harcourt, Brace. Reprinted: Montclair, N.J.: Allanheld, Osmun.

Gottlieb, Robert. 2001. *Environmentalism Unbound: Exploring New Pathways for Change*. Cambridge, Mass.: MIT Press.

———. 1993. *Forcing the Spring: The Transformation of the American Environmental Movement*. Washington, D.C.: Island Press.

Gottlieb, Robert, and Andrew Fisher. 1996. "'First Feed the Face': Environmental Justice and Community Food Security." *Antipode* 29(2): 193–203.

Gottlieb, Robert, and Anupama Joshi. 2010. *Food Justice*. Cambridge, Mass.: MIT Press.

Gould, Kenneth, David N. Pellow, and Allan Schnaiberg. 2004. "Interrogating the Treadmill of Production: Everything You Wanted to Know about the Treadmill But Were Afraid to Ask." *Organization and Environment* 17(3): 296–316.

Green America. http://www.coopamerica.org/greengetaway/ (accessed July 13, 2009).

Grindstaff, Laura. 2002. *The Money Shot: Trash, Class, and the Making of TV Talk Shows*. Chicago: University of Chicago Press.

Gusfield, Joseph R. 1975. *Community: A Critical Response*. Oxford: Basil Blackwell.

Guthman, Julie. 2008a. "If They Only Knew: Colorblindness and Universalism in Alternative Food Institutions." *The Professional Geographer* 60(3): 387–397.

———. 2008b. "Neoliberalism and the Making of Food Politics in California." *Geoforum* 39(3): 1171–1183.

———. 2008c. "Bringing Good Food to Others: Investigating the Subjects of Alternative Food Practices." *Cultural Geographies* 15(4): 431–447.

———. 2007. "Can't Stomach It: How Michael Pollan et al. Made Me Want to Eat Cheetos." *Gastronomica: The Journal of Food and Culture* 7(3): 75–79.

———. 2004. *Agrarian Dreams: The Paradox of Organic Farming in California*. Berkeley: University of California Press.

———. 2003. "Fast Food/Organic Food: Reflexive Taste and the Making of Yuppie Chow." *Social and Cultural Geography* 4(1): 45–58.

Halweil, Brian. 2004. *Eat Here: Homegrown Pleasures in a Global Supermarket*. New York: W. W. Norton and Company.

Hamm, Michael, and Ann Bellows. 2003. "Community Food Security and Nutrition Educators." *Journal of Nutrition Education and Behavior* 35(1): 37–43.

Harrison, Jill. 2008. "Lessons Learned from Pesticide Drift: A Call to Bring Production Agriculture, Farm Labor, and Social Justice back into Agrifood Research and Activism." *Agriculture and Human Values* 25(3): 163–167.

Harvey, David. 2005. *A Brief History of Neoliberalism*. New York: Oxford University Press.

———. 1996. *Justice, Nature, and the Geography of Difference*. San Francisco, Calif.: Wiley-Blackwell.

Hatanaka, Maki, Carmen Bain, and Lawrence Busch. 2005. "Third Party Certification in the Global Agrifood System." *Food Policy* 30(3): 354–369.

Hawken, Paul. 1997. "Natural Capitalism." *Mother Jones Magazine*. March/April, 40.

Hawken, Paul, Amory Lovins, and Hunter Lovins. 2008. *Natural Capitalism: Creating the Next Industrial Revolution*. Boston, Mass.: Back Bay Books.

Hayes, Floyd, III, and Frances Kiene III. 2000. "All Power to All People: The Revolutionary Thought of Huey P. Newton and the Black Panther Party." In *Turbulent Voyage: Readings in African American Studies*, ed. Floyd Hayes III, 546–561. New York: Rowan and Littlefield.

Haynes, Bruce. 2001. *Red Lines, Black Spaces: The Politics of Race and Space in a Black Middle-Class Suburb*. New Haven, Conn.: Yale University Press.

Heany, Judy, and Tamara Hayes. N.d. "Redlining Food: How to Ensure Community Food Security." http://www.foodfirst.org/progs/humanrts/redlining.html (accessed January 15, 2008).

Heath, G. Louis. 1976. *Off the Pigs: The History and Literature of the Black Panther Party*. Metuchen, N.J.: Scarecrow Press.

Heeter, C. 2006. "The Oil in Your Oatmeal: A Lot of Fossil Fuel Goes into Producing, Packaging, and Shipping Our Breakfast." *San Francisco Chronicle* March 26, p. F-1.

Heiman, Michael. 1996. "Race, Waste, and Class: New Perspectives on Environmental Justice." *Antipode* 28(2): 111–121.

Hess, David J. 2009. *Localist Movements in a Global Economy: Sustainability, Justice, and Urban Development in the United States*. Cambridge, Mass.: MIT Press.

Heynen, Nik. 2009. "Bending the Bars of Empire from Every Ghetto for Survival: The Black Panther Party's Radical Anti-hunger Politics of Social Reproduction and Scale." *Annals of the Association of American Geographers* 99(2): 406–422.

Heynen, Nik, Maria Kaika, and Erik Swyngedouw. 2006. *In the Nature of Cities: Urban Political Ecology and the Politics of Urban Metabolism*. New York: Routledge.

Hilliard, David, and Lewis Cole. 1993. *This Side of Glory: The Autobiography of David Hilliard*. Chicago: Lawrence Hill Books.

Hinrichs, Clare. 2003. "The Practice and Politics of Food System Localization." *Journal of Rural Studies* 19(1): 33–45.

———. 2000. "Embeddedness and Local Food Systems: Notes on Two Types of Direct Agricultural Market." *Journal of Rural Studies* 16(3): 295–303.

Hochschild, Arlie, and Anne Machung. 2003. *The Second Shift*. New York: Penguin.

Holland, Brian. 2004. "Livin' la Vida LOHAS." *Southface Journal*. http://www.southface .org/web/resources&services/publications/journal/sfjv304/sfjv304-lohas.htm (accessed July 15, 2008).

Hollis, Dixon. 2007. Feeding the Revolutionary Soul: The Rhetorical Nature of the Free Breakfast for Children Program, 1968–1969." Paper presented at the NCA 93rd Annual Convention, TBA, Chicago, Ill. Online PDF. 2009-02-03 from http://www .allacademic.com/meta/p192283_index.html (accessed January 2, 2009).

Horton, David. 2003. "Green Distinctions: The Performance of Identity among Environmental Activists." *Sociological Review* 52(2): 63–77.

Hull, Gloria, Patricia Bell Scott, and Barbara Smith. 1982. *But Some of Us Are Brave: All the Women Are White, All the Blacks Are Men: Black Women's Studies*. New York: The Feminist Press at CUNY.

Hummon, David Mark. 1990. *Commonplaces: Community, Ideology, and Identity in American Culture*. Albany: State University of New York Press.

Hunnicutt, Angela. 2006. "Full Moon Rising: Jessica Prentice Shows It's Possible to Eat like a King without Leaving the Kingdom." *East Bay Monthly*. July.

Hunter, Albert. 1974. *Symbolic Communities: The Persistence and Change in Chicago's Local Communities*. Chicago: University of Chicago Press.

INCITE! Women of Color Against Violence. 2007. *The Revolution Will not Be Funded: Beyond the NGO-Industrial Complex*. Cambridge: South End Press.

International Institute for Sustainable Development. N.d. "Business and Sustainable Development." http://www.iisd.org/business (accessed December 30, 2009).

Israel, Barbara A., Amy J. Schultz, Edith A. Parker, and Adam B. Becker. 1998. "Review of Community-Based Research: Assessing Partnership Approaches to Improve Public Health." *Annual Review of Public Health* 19: 173–202.

Jackson, Bruce. 1987. *Fieldwork*. Urbana: University of Illinois Press.

Jacobs, Jane. 1961. *The Death and Life of Great American Cities*. New York: Vintage Books.

Jennings, Peter, and Todd Brewster. 1998. *The Century*. New York: Doubleday.

Johnson, Marilynn S. 1993. *The Second Gold Rush: Oakland and the East Bay in World War II*. Berkeley: University of California Press.

Jones, Brenda Payton. 2007. "The Black Panthers Still Making a Difference: The 40th Anniversary of the Party Brings It Back to the Forefront." *Ebony*. http://findarticles.com/p/articles/mi_m1077/is_4_62/ai_n27115702/ (accessed August 27, 2009).

Jones, Van. 2008. *The Green Collar Economy: How One Solution Can Fix Our Two Biggest Problems*. New York: Harper One.

Kaika, Maria. 2005. *City of Flows: Nature, Modernity, and the City*. New York: Routledge.

Katz, Michael. 1990. *The Undeserving Poor: From the War on Poverty to the War on Welfare*. New York: Pantheon.

Keith, Verna M., and Cedric Herring. 1991. "Skin Tone and Stratification in the Black Community." *American Journal of Sociology* 97(3): 760–778.

Kenny, Lorraine Delia. 2000. "Doing My Homework: The Autoethnography of a White Teenage Girl." In *Racing Research, Researching Race: Methodological Dilemmas in Critical Race Studies*, ed. France Winddance Twine and Jonathan W. Warren, 111–134. New York: New York University Press.

Kimbrell, Andrew. 2002. *Fatal Harvest: The Tragedy of Industrial Agriculture*. Sausalito, Calif.: Foundation for Deep Ecology.

Kingsolver, Barbara. 2007. *Animal, Vegetable, Miracle*. New York: Harper Collins.

Kinte Center. N.d. "Essay on Black-Owned Commerce and Community That Was in West Oakland." http://www.kintecenter.org/PAGES/seventhst.html. (accessed January 2, 2009).

Kitchell, Mark. 1990. *Berkeley in the 60s*. Kitchell Films.

Klein, Naomi. 2000. *No Logo: No Space, No Choice, No Jobs*. New York: Picador.

Kleinman, Sheryl. 1996. *Opposing Ambitions: Gender and Identity in an Alternative Organization*. Chicago: University of Chicago Press.

Kloppenburg, Jack, Jr., Jon Hendrickson, and G. W. Stevenson. 1996. "Coming into the Foodshed." *Agriculture and Human Values* 13: 33–42.

Knighton, Jose. 2002. "Ecoporn and the Manipulation of Desire." In *Wild Earth: Wild Ideas for a World out of Balance*, ed. Tom Butler, 165–171. Minneapolis, Minn.: Milkweed.

Kobayashi, Audrey, and Linda Peake. 2000. "Racism out of Place: Thoughts on Whiteness and an Anti-racist Geography in the New Millennium." *Annals of the Association of American Geographers* 90: 392–403.

Lander, Christian. 2008. *Stuff White People Like: A Definitive Guide to the Unique Taste of Millions*. New York: Random House.

Larner, Wendy, and David Craig. 2005. "After Neoliberalism? Community Activism and Local Partnerships in Aotearoa New Zealand." *Antipode* 37(3): 402–424.

Lavie, Smadar. 1990. *The Poetics of Military Occupation*. Berkeley: University of California Press.

Lazerow, Jama, and Yohuru Williams. 2006. *In Search of the Black Panther Party: New Perspectives on a Revolutionary Movement*. Durham, N.C.: Duke University Press.

Lee, Charles. 2005. "Collaborative Models to Achieve Environmental Justice and Healthy Communities." In *Power, Justice, and the Environment: A Critical Appraisal of the Environmental Justice Movement*, ed. Robert Brulle and David N. Pellow, 219–252. Cambridge, Mass.: MIT Press.

Lee, Roger. 2000. "Shelter from the Storm? Geographies of Regard in the World of Horticultural Consumption and Production." *Geoforum* 31: 137–157.

Lefebvre, Henri. 1992. *The Production of Space*. New York: Wiley-Blackwell.

LePla, F. Joseph, Susan V. Davis, and Lynne M. Parker. 2003. *Brand Driven: The Route to Integrated Branding through Great Leadership*. London: Kogan Page.

Liebman, Eliot. 1983. *California Farmland: A History of Large Agricultural Landholdings*. New York: Rowman and Allanheld.

Light, Andrew, and Aurora Wallace. 2005. "Not out of the Woods: Preserving the Human in Environmental Architecture." *Environmental Values* 14: 3–20

Liverman, Diana. 2004. "Who Governs, at What Scale and at What Price? Geography, Environmental Governance, and the Commodification of Nature." *Annals of the Association of American Geographers* 94(4): 734–738.

Lofland, John, and Lyn H. Lofland. 1984. *Analyzing Social Settings*. Belmont, Calif.: Wadsworth.

Lofland, Lyn H. 1998. *The Public Realm: Exploring the City's Quintessential Social Territory*. Hawthorne, N.Y.: Aldine de Gruyter.

Lyon, Sarah. 2007. "Rethinking Free Trade/Fair Trade." *Culture and Agriculture* 29(2): 58–62.

Lyson, Thomas A. 2004. *Civic Agriculture: Reconnecting Farm, Food, and Community*. Boston, Mass.: Tufts University Press.

Lyson, Thomas A., and Judy Green. 1999. "The Agricultural Marketscape: A Framework for Sustaining Agriculture and Communities in the Northeast U.S." *Journal of Sustainable Agriculture* 15(2): 133–150.

MacKinnon, Dan. 2000. "Managerialism, Governmentality and the State: A Neo-Foucauldian Approach to Local Economic Governance." *Political Geography* 19(3): 293–314.

Madison, Mike. 2006. *Blithe Tomato*. Berkeley, Calif.: Great Valley Books.

Magdoff, Fred, John Bellamy Foster, and Fred Buttel, eds. 2000. *Hungry for Profit: The Agribusiness Threat to Farmers, Food, and the Environment*. New York: Monthly Review Press.

Malinowski, Bronislaw. 1922. *Argonauts of the Western Pacific*. London: Routledge and Kegan Paul.

Mannle, Andy. 2010. "Why the Green Economy Is Unstoppable — and 10 Ways It's Making Life Better." http://www.huffingtonpost.com/andy-mannle/why-the-green -economy-is-_b_735220.html (accessed January 26, 2012).

Mansfield, Becky. 2004. "Neoliberalism in the Oceans: 'Rationalization,' Property Rights, and the Commons Question." *Geoforum* 35(3): 313–326.

MapMuse. "Locate Farmers Markets: Fresh Organic Food Close to Home near You." http://find.mapmuse.com/interest/farmer_markets (accessed July 13, 2009).

Mares, Teresa, and Devon Peña. 2010. "Urban Agriculture in the Making of Insurgent Spaces in Los Angeles and Seattle." In *Insurgent Public Space: Guerrilla Urbanism and the Remaking of Contemporary Cities*, ed. Jeffrey Hou, 241–254. New York: Routledge.

Marx, Karl. 1992[1867]. *Capital: A Critique of Political Economy*. New York: Penguin.

Massey, Douglass, and Nancy Denton. 1993. *American Apartheid: Segregation and the Making of the Underclass*. Cambridge, Mass.: Harvard University Press.

Masumoto, David Mas. 2007. "The Day without Farm Workers." *Wildflower Stew*. http://goodwordswan.wildflowerstew.com/peaches/ (accessed December 30, 2009).

McAfee, Kathleen. 1999. "Selling Nature to Save It? Biodiversity and Green Developmentalism." *Environment and Planning D — Society and Space* 17(2): 133–154.

McCarthy, James, and Scott Prudham. 2004. "Neoliberal Nature and the Nature of Neoliberalism." *Geoforum* 35(3): 275–283.

McClintock, Nathan. 2011. "From Industrial Garden to Food Desert: Demarcated Devaluation in the Flatlands of Oakland, California." In *Cultivating Food Justice:*

Race, Class, and Sustainability, ed. Alison Hope Alkon and Julian Agyeman, 90–120. Cambridge, Mass.: MIT Press.

McGrath, Maria. 2004. "'That's Capitalism, Not a Co-op': Countercultural Idealism and Business Realism in 1970s U.S. Food Co-ops." www.thebhc.org/publications /BEHonline/2004/McGrath.pdf (accessed January 26, 2012).

McKibben, Bill. 2007. *Deep Economy: The Wealth of Communities and the Durable Future.* New York: Times Books.

McLean, Stephanie. 2006. "Electoral Legitimacy in the United States: Effects on Political Efficacy, Trust, and Participation." PhD dissertation, University of Pittsburgh.

McNamee, Thomas. 2007. *Alice Waters and Chez Panisse.* New York: Penguin.

McWilliams, Carey. 2000[1939]. *Factories in the Field: The Story of Migratory Farm Labor.* Berkeley: University of California Press.

Meadows, Donella, Jorgen Randers, and Dennis Meadows. 2004[1973]. *The Limits to Growth: The Thirty-Year Update.* New York: Chelsea Green.

Merchant, Carolyn. 2003. "Shades of Darkness: Race and Environmental History. *Environmental History* 8(3): 380–394.

Metevsky, George. 1966. "Delving the Diggers." *Berkeley Barb.* Oct 21. http://www .diggers.org/diggers/digart2.html (accessed January 2, 2009).

Meyers, Norman, and Jennifer Kent. 2001. *Perverse Subsidies: How Tax Dollars Undercut the Environment and the Economy.* Washington, D.C.: Island Press.

Minkoff-Zern, Laura-Anne. 2010. "Migrations of Hunger and Knowledge: Food Insecurity and California's Indigenous Farm Workers." Paper presented at the Association of American Geographers National Conference; Washington, D.C.

Mo' Better Foods. mobetterfood.com (accessed 2005–2008).

Mohanty, Chandra T. 1991. Under Western Eyes: Feminist Scholarship and Colonial Discourses. In *Third World Women and the Politics of Feminism,* ed. Chandra T. Mohanty, Ann Russo, and Lourdes Torres, 1–47. Bloomington: Indiana University Press.

Mol, Arthur P. J., and David A. Sonnenfeld. 2000. *Ecological Modernisation around the World: Perspectives and Critical Debates.* New York: Routledge.

Montague, Peter. 2002. "Rebuilding the Movement to Win." *Rachel's Environment and Health News* 744, February 14.

Moraga, Cherríe, and Gloria E. Anzaldúa. 2001. *This Bridge Called My Back: Writings by Radical Women of Color.* New York: Kitchen Table Women of Color Press.

Morgan, Edward. 1991. *The '60s Experience: Hard Lessons about Modern America.* Philadelphia: Temple University Press.

Morland, Kimberly, Steve Wing, Ana Diez Roux, and Charles Poole. 2002. "Neighborhood Characteristics Associated with the Location of Food Stores and Food Service Places." *American Journal of Preventive Medicine* 22: 23–29.

Mueller, Tim. 2006. "Why CHOOSE Organic Food?" http://riverdogfarm.com /organicfood.html (accessed July 14, 2009).

Muir, John. 1912. *The Yosemite.* New York: The Century Company.

Muir, John, and William Cronon. 1997. *John Muir: Nature Writings: The Story of My Boyhood and Youth; My First Summer in the Sierra; The Mountains of California; Stickeen; Essays.* New York: Library of America.

Murdoch, Jonathan, and Mara Miele. 1999. "Back to Nature: Changing Worlds of Production in the Food Sector." *Sociologia Ruralis* 39: 465–483.

Murphy, David, and Jem Bendell. 1997. *In the Company of Partners: Business, Environmental Groups, and Sustainable Development Post-Rio.* Washington, D.C.: Policy Press.

Musgrave, Leroy. 2005. "Watermelons." *Then I See Horses Running.* 19. Livingston, Calif.: Goodfoot Farm.

Nabhan, Gary Paul. 2002. *Coming Home to Eat: The Pleasures and Politics of Local Food.* New York: W. W. Norton and Co.

Nadar, Laura. 1982. "Up the Anthropologist — Perspectives Gained from Studying Up." In *Anthropology for the Eighties,* ed. Jonetta Cole. 456–470. New York: The Free Press.

Naess, Arne. 1973. "The Shallow and the Deep, Long-Range Ecology Movement." *Inquiry* 16: 95–100.

Natural Marketing Institute. 2005. "The LOHAS Market Report." http://www.nmisolutions.com/reports.html (accessed July 12, 2008).

Natural Resources Defense Council. N.d. "Recovering from Katrina." http://www.nrdc.org/ej/ (accessed March 8, 2008).

Neil, Earl. N.d. "Black Panther Party and Father Neil." *It's About Time: Black Panther Party Legacy and Alumni.* http://www.itsabouttimebpp.com/Our_Stories/Chapter1/BPP_and_Father_Neil.html (accessed January 2, 2009).

Ness, Carol. 2008. "California's Prop. 2 Spurs Big-Bucks Battle over Farm-Animal Treatment." *Grist.* http://www.grist.org/member/1716.

Nestle, Marion. 2002. *Food Politics: How the Food Industry Influences Nutrition and Health.* Berkeley: University of California Press.

Newton, Huey. 1973. *Revolutionary Suicide.* New York: Harcourt Brace Jovanovich.

Newton, Huey, and Toni Morrison. 1999. *To Die for the People: The Writings of Huey P. Newton.* New York: Writers and Readers Publishing.

Novotny, Patrick. 2000. *Where We Live, Work, and Play: The Environmental Justice Movement and the Struggle for a new Environmentalism.* Westport, Conn.: Praeger.

Obach, Brian. 2004. *Labor and the Environmental Movement: The Quest for Common Ground.* Cambridge, Mass.: MIT Press.

O'Connor, James. 1994. "Is Sustainable Capitalism Possible?" In *Is Capitalism Sustainable?* ed. Martin O'Connor, 152–175. New York: The Guilford Press.

Offer, Avner. 1997. "Between the Gift and the Market: The Economy of Regard." *Economic History Review* 3: 450–476.

Olmstead, Nancy, and Roger W. Olmstead. 1994. "History of West Oakland." In *West*

Oakland, A Place to Start From, ed. Mary Praetzellis 9–223. Rohnert Park, Calif.: Sonoma State University.

Omi, Michael, and Howard Winant. 1986. *Racial Formation in the United States: From the 1960s to the 1990s*. New York: Routledge.

Organic Consumers Association. 2007. "US Organic Food Sales up 22%, Hit $17 Billion in 2006." http://www.organicconsumers.org/articles/article_5109.cfm (accessed January 26, 2012).

Ovetz, Robert. 2008. "Ships Contribute 15–21% of Cancer Cases in West Oakland." http://www.vesselwatchproject.org/node/42 (accessed January 2, 2009).

Pape, Janet L. "Archeology Outreach: It Takes a Community." In *Past Meets Present: Archaeologists Partnering with Museum Curators, Teachers, and Community Groups*, ed. John H. Jameson and Sherene Bauher, 379–392. New York: Springer.

Park, Lisa Sun-Hee, and David Naguib Pellow. 2011. *The Slums of Aspen: Immigrants vs. the Environment in America's Eden*. New York: NYU Press.

Park, Robert E. 1925. "The City: Suggestions for the Investigation of Human Behavior in the Urban Environment." In *The City*, ed. Robert E. Park, Ernest W. Burgess, and Roderick D. McKenzie, 1–46. Chicago: University of Chicago Press.

Parr, Adrian. 2009. *Hijacking Sustainability*. Cambridge, Mass.: MIT Press.

Patel, Raj. 2011. "Survival Pending Revolution: What the Black Panthers Can Teach the US Food Movement." In *Food Movements Unite*, ed. Eric Holt-Gimenez. Oakland, Calif.: Food First Books.

Patillo-McCoy, Mary. 2002. *Black Picket Fences: Privilege and Peril among the Black Middle Class*. Chicago: University of Chicago Press.

Peck, Jamie, and Adam Tickell. 2002. "Neoliberalizing Space." *Antipode* 34(3): 380–404.

Pellow, David N., and Robert J. Brulle. 2005. *Power, Justice, and the Environment: A Critical Appraisal of the Environmental Justice Movement*. Cambridge, Mass.: MIT Press.

Pellow, David N., Allan Schnaiberg, and Adam S. Weinberg. 2000. "Putting Ecological Modernization to the Test: Accounting for Recycling's Promises and Performances." In *Ecological Modernization Around the World*, ed. Arthur P. J. Mol and David A. Sonnenfeld. Portland: Frank Cass.

Peña, Devon. 2005. "Autonomy, Equity, and Environmental Justice." In *Power, Justice, and the Environment: A Critical Appraisal of the Environmental Justice Movement*, ed. David N. Pellow and Robert Brulle. Cambridge, Mass.: MIT Press.

———. 1999. *Chicano Culture, Ecology, Politics: Subversive Kin*. Tucson: University of Arizona Press.

Perry, Charles. 2005[1964]. *The Haight-Ashbury: A History*. Berkeley, Calif.: Wenner.

Philpott, Tom. 2008. "Schlosser: Food industry abuses workers as matter of course." *Grist*. http://www.grist.org/article/slow-food-nation-farmworkers-at-the-table/ (accessed October 30, 2009).

Pinderhughes, Raquel Rivera. 2006. "Green Collar Jobs: Work Force Opportunities in the Growing Green Economy." *Journal of Race, Poverty, and the Environment* 13(1).

Poe, Tracy 1999. "Origins of Black Southern Urban Identity: 1915–1947." *American Studies International* 37(1): 4–33.

Polanyi, Karl. 2001[1944]. *The Great Transformation: The Political and Economic Origins of Our Time*. Boston, Mass.: Beacon Press.

Pollan, Michael. 2010. "The Food Movement, Rising." *New York Times Review of Books*. http://www.nybooks.com/articles/archives/2010/jun/10/food-movement -rising/ (accessed February 7, 2012).

——. 2008. *In Defense of Food: An Eater's Manifesto*. New York: Penguin.

——. 2006. *The Omnivore's Dilemma: A Natural History of Four Meals*. New York: Penguin Press.

Polletta, Francesca. 2006. *It Was Like a Fever: Storytelling in Protest and Politics*. Chicago: University of Chicago Press.

Polyface Farms. N.d. "Speaking Protocol." http://www.polyfacefarms.com/speaking -protocol (accessed DATE, 2012).

Prentice, Jessica. 2007. "The Birth of Locavore." Oxford University Press. http://blog .oup.com/2007/11/prentice (accessed July 13, 2009).

——. 2006. *Full Moon Feast: Food and the Hunger for Connection*. New York: Chelsea Green.

Princen, Thomas, Michael Manites, and Kenneth Conca. 2002. *Confronting Consumption*. Cambridge, Mass.: MIT Press.

Pudup, Mary Beth. 2008. "It Takes a Garden: Cultivating Citizen-Subjects in Organized Garden Projects." *Geoforum* 39: 1228–1240.

Pulido, Laura. 1998. "Ecological Legitimacy and Cultural Essentialism: Hispano Grazing in Northern New Mexico." In *Chicano Culture, Ecology, Politics: Subversive Kin*, ed. Devon G. Peña. Tucson: University of Arizona Press.

——. 1996. *Environmentalism and Economic Justice: Two Chicano Cases from the Southwest*. Tucson: University of Arizona Press.

Pulido, Laura, and Devon Peña. 1998. "Environmentalism and Positionality: The Early Pesticide Campaign of the United Farmworkers' Organizing Committee, 1965–1971." *Race, Gender, and Class* 6 (1):33.

Quimby, Roxanne. N.d. "The Burt's Bees Story." http://www.burtsbees.com/c/story /history/burt-s-story.html (accessed December 30, 2009).

Rausser, Gordon C. 1992. "Predatory versus Productive Government: The Case of U.S. Agricultural Policies." *The Journal of Economic Perspectives* 6(3): 133–157.

Redclift, Michael. 2006. "Sustainable Development (1987–2005) — an Oxymoron Comes of Age." *Horizontes Antropológicos* 12(25): 65–84.

Rhomberg, Chris. 2004. *No There There: Race, Class, and Political Community in Oakland*. Berkeley: University of California Press.

Robnett, Belinda. 1997. *How Long? How Long?: African American Women in the Struggle for Civil Rights*. Oxford: Oxford University Press.

Rose, Nikolas. 1999. *Powers of Freedom: Reframing Political Thought*. Cambridge, U.K.: Cambridge University Press.

Rosenbaum, Michael S. 2007. "The Jeep People: Identity, Consumption, and Culture in a Lifestyle Community." PhD dissertation, Indiana University.

Rosenwald, Michael S. 2006. "Showcasing the Growth of the Green Economy." *Washington Post* October 16. http://www.washingtonpost.com/wp-dyn/content/article/2006/10/15/AR2006101500685.html (accessed August 27, 2009).

Roth, Benita. 2003. *Separate Roads to Feminism: Black, Chicana, and White Feminist Movements in America's Second Wave*. Cambridge, U.K.: Cambridge University Press.

Sandler, Ronald, and Phaedra C. Pezzullo. 2007. *Environmental Justice and Environmentalism: The Social Justice Challenge to the Environmental Movement*. Cambridge: MIT Press.

Schlossberg, David. 1999. *Environmental Justice and the New Pluralism: The Challenge of Difference for Environmentalism*. Oxford: Oxford University Press.

Schlosser, Eric. 2002. *Fast Food Nation: The Dark Side of the All-American Meal*. New York: Harper Perennial.

Schmidheiny, Stephan. 1992. *Changing Course*. Cambridge, Mass.: MIT Press.

Schnaiberg, Allan. 1980. *The Environment: From Surplus to Scarcity*. New York: Oxford University Press.

Schnaiberg, Alan, and Kenneth N. Gould. 1994. *Environment and Society: The Enduring Conflict*. New York: St. Martin's Press.

Schumacher, E. F. 1989[1973]. *Small Is Beautiful: Economics as if People Mattered*. New York: Harper Perennial.

Seale, Bobby 1991. *Seize the Time: The Story of the Black Panther Party and Huey P. Newton*. Baltimore, Md.: Black Classic Press.

Self, Robert O. 2003. *American Babylon: Race and the Struggle for Postwar Oakland*. Princeton, N.J.: Princeton University Press.

Shekar, Preti Mangala, and Tram Nguyen. 2008. "Who Gains from the Green Economy?" *Colorlines: News for Action*. http://colorlines.com/archives/2008/03/who_gains_from_the_green_economy.html (accessed January 26, 2012).

Shiva, Vandana. 2000. *Stolen Harvest: The Hijacking of the Global Food System*. Boston, Mass.: South End Press.

Shrader-Frechette, Kristin. 2002. *Environmental Justice: Creating Equality, Reclaiming Democracy*. New York: Oxford University Press.

Shreck, Aimee, Christy Getz, and Gail Feenstra. 2006. "Social Sustainability, Farm Labor, and Organic Agriculture: Findings from an Exploratory Analysis." *Agriculture and Human Values* 23(4): 439–449.

Sierra Club. N.d. "Guidelines for the Sierra Club's National Environmental Justice Grassroots Organizing Program." www.sierraclub.org/environmental_justice/principles2.asp (accessed March 9, 2008).

Simmel, Georg. 1950. "The Metropolis and Mental Life." In *The Sociology of Georg Simmel*, ed. Kurt H. Wolff, 409–423. Mankato, Minn.: The Free Press.

Slocum, Rachel. 2006. "Anti-racist Practice and the Work of Community Food Organizations." *Antipode* 38(2): 327–349.

Smith, Neil. 1984. *Uneven Development: Nature, Capital and the Production of Space.* Oxford: Blackwell.

Spaargaren, Gert. 2000. "Ecological Modernization Theory and Domestic Consumption." *Journal of Environmental Policy and Planning* 2(4): 323–335.

Strauss, Anselm. 2007[1968]. *The American City: A Sourcebook of Urban Imagery.* New York: Aldine de Gruyter.

SustainLane. 2006. "Most Sustainable Cities." sustainlane.com (accessed July 15, 2008).

Suttles, Gerald. 1972. *The Social Construction of Communities.* Chicago: University of Chicago Press.

Swyngedouw, Eric, and Maria Kaika. 2000. "The Environment of the City or . . . The Urbanization of Nature." In *Reader in Urban Studies*, ed. Gary Bridge and Sophie Watson. Oxford: Blackwell.

Szasz, Andrew. 2007. *Shopping Our Way to Safety: How We Changed from Protecting the Environment to Protecting Ourselves.* Minneapolis: University of Minnesota Press.

Sze, Julie. 2006. *Noxious New York: The Racial Politics of Urban Health and Environmental Justice.* Cambridge, Mass.: MIT Press.

Sze, Julie, and Jonathan London. 2008. "Environmental justice at the crossroads." *Sociology Compass* 2(4): 1331–1354

Taylor, Dorcetta. 2009. *The Environment and the People in American Cities, 1600s–1900s: Disorder, Inequality, and Social Change.* Durham, N.C.: Duke University Press.

———. 2000. "The Rise of the Environmental Justice Paradigm." *American Behavioral Scientist* 43: 508–590.

———. 1997. "American Environmentalism: The Role of Race, Class, and Gender in Shaping Activism, 1820–1995." *Race, Gender, and Class* 5: 16–62.

Taylor, Edwin J., and Paul L. Martin. 1997. "The Immigrant Subsidy in U.S. Agriculture: Farm Employment, Poverty, and Welfare." *Population and Development Review* 23(4): 855–874.

Thayer, Robert. 2003. *LifePlace: Bioregional Thought and Practice.* Berkeley: University of California Press.

Tönnies, Ferdinand. 1988. *Community and Society (Gemeinschaft und Gesellschaft).* Piscataway, N.J.: Transaction.

Tovey, Hillary. 2002. "Alternative Agriculture Movements and Rural Development Cosmologies." *International Journal of Sociology of Agriculture and Food* 10(1): 1–11.

Twine, Francine Winddance. 2000. "Racial Ideologies and Racial Methodologies." In *Racing Research, Researching Race: Methodological Dilemmas in Critical Race*

Studies, ed. Francine Winddance Twine and Jonathan Warren, 1–34. New York: New York University Press.

United Church of Christ. 2007. *Toxic Waste and Race at Twenty*. New York: United Church of Christ.

———. 1987. *Toxic Wastes and Race in the United States: A National Report on the Racial and Socio-economic Characteristics with Hazardous Waste Sites*. New York: United Church of Christ, Commission for Racial Justice.

United States Department of Agriculture. 2006. "USDA Farmers Markets." http://www .ams.usda.gov/farmersmarkets (accessed December 23, 2007).

United States Department of Agriculture, National Agricultural Statistics Service. 1999. 1997 Census of Agriculture. United States: Summary and State Data. Vol. 1, Part 51. Washington, D.C.: U.S. Government Printing Office.

Van Mannen, John. 1988. *Tales of the Field: On Writing Ethnography*. Chicago: University of Chicago Press.

Walker, Richard. 2005. *The Conquest of Bread: 150 Years of Agribusiness in California*. Berkeley: University of California Press.

Walton, John. 2001. *Storied Land: Community and Memory in Monterey*. Berkeley: University of California Press.

Wang, Ling-chi. 1997. "Chronology of Ethnic Studies at UC Berkeley." *Newsletter of the Department of Ethnic Studies at UC Berkeley*, 2(2).

Warde, Alan. 1994. "Consumption, Identity Formation, and Uncertainty." *Sociology* 28(4): 877–898.

Waters, Alice. 2005. "The Delicious Revolution." www.chezpanisse.com/pdf /alicespeech0501A.pdf (accessed January 2, 2009).

———. 1993. "The Farm-Restaurant Connection." www.drs.wisc.edu/.../Waters %201993%20the%20farm-restaurant%20connection.pdf (accessed January 2, 2009).

WE ACT Environmental Justice Leadership Forum on Climate Change. 2010. "Principles of Climate Justice." weact.org/portals/7/EJ%20leadership%20forum %20principles.pdf (accessed January 26, 2012).

West Oakland Food Collaborative. www.wo-foodcollaborative.org (accessed March 1, 2008).

White, Monica Marie. 2010. "Shouldering Responsibility for the Delivery of Human Rights: A Case Study of the D-Town Farmers of Detroit." *Race/Ethnicity: Multidisciplinary Global Perspectives* 3(2): 189–211.

Whyte, William F. 1991[1943]. *Streetcorner Society: The Social Structure of an Italian Slum*. Chicago: University of Chicago Press.

Whyte, William H. 1980. *The Social Life of Small Urban Spaces*. New York: The Conservation Foundation.

Wiegand, Erin. 2007. "We Can't Shop Our Way to Safety." AlterNet. http://www .alternet.org/health/67706 (accessed January 26, 2012).

Williams, Juan. 2002. "Introduction." In *Black Farmers in America*, photographs by John Francis Ficara, essay by Juan Williams. Lexington: University Press of Kentucky.

Williams, Raymond. 1975. *The Country and the City*. New York: Oxford University Press.

Winson, Anthony. 1993. *The Intimate Commodity*. Toronto, Ontario: Garamond.

Wirth, Louis. 1938. "Urbanism as a Way of Life." *American Journal of Sociology* 44: 1–24.

Wit, Doris. 1999. *Black Hunger: Soul Food and America*. Minneapolis: University of Minnesota Press.

Wittmeyer, Alicia. 2004. "From Rubble to Refuge." *Daily Californian*. April 26. ttp:// www.dailycal.org/article/15086/from_rubble_to_refuge (accessed January 2, 2009).

Wolf, Diane. 1996. *Feminist Dilemmas in Fieldwork*. Boulder, Colo.: Westview.

Wood, Spencer D., and Jess Gilbert. 2000. "Returning African-American Farmers to the Land: Recent Trends and a Policy Rationale." *Review of Black Political Economy* 27(4): 43–64.

Worster, Donald. 1994. *The Wealth of Nature: Environmental History and the Ecological Imagination*. New York: Oxford University Press.

Wrigley, Neil, Daniel Warm, Barrie Margarett, and Amanda Whelan. 2002. "Assessing the Impact of Improved Retail Access on Diet in a 'Food Desert': A Preliminary Report." *Urban Studies* 39: 2061–2082.

Zavella, Patricia. 1991. "Reflections on Diversity among Chicanas." *Frontiers* 12: 73–85.

Zelizer, Viviana. 2007. *The Purchase of Intimacy*. Princeton, N.J.: Princeton University Press.

INDEX

GEOGRAPHIES OF JUSTICE AND SOCIAL TRANSFORMATION